"Dr. Whitney's book is an important contribution to those of us interested in the East–West dialog about the nature of consciousness. She has the rare gift of expertise in both Jung's psychology and Patañjali's metaphysics, and her text reveals the important similarities and distinctions found in the work of these two gigantic figures. Students of transformation will benefit by Dr. Whitney's clear articulation of the ways in which depth psychology and yoga philosophy complement each other."

—Lionel Corbett, *Professor, Pacifica Graduate Institute, USA*

"*Consciousness in Jung and Patañjali* is a brilliant analysis of Western and Eastern concepts of consciousness, motivated by the author's personal experience that there's something beyond a materialistic brain-based explanation of consciousness. A deep dive into personal ego, impersonal awareness, dual and nondual realities, and beyond. Highly recommended."

—Dean Radin, *PhD, Chief Scientist, Institute of Noetic Sciences, USA*

"When Carl Jung studied Yoga traditions, he dealt with an abstraction, a relic of the exotic 'other.' With wide practice of Yoga worldwide, one can no longer dismiss its insights as inappropriate for non-Asians. Leanne Whitney's book updates our thinking about Yoga and shows its benefits to contemporary psycho-therapeutic theory and practice."

—Christopher Key Chapple, *Doshi Professor of Indic and Comparative Theology and Director, Master of Arts in Yoga Studies, Loyola Marymount University, USA*

Consciousness in Jung and Patañjali

The East–West dialogue increasingly seeks to compare and clarify contrasting views on the nature of consciousness. For the Eastern liberatory models, in which a nondual view of consciousness is primary, the challenge lies in articulating how consciousness and the manifold contents of consciousness are singular. Western empirical science, on the other hand, must provide a convincing account of how consciousness arises from matter. By placing the theories of Jung and Patañjali in dialogue with one another, *Consciousness in Jung and Patañjali* illuminates significant differences between dual and nondual psychological theory and teases apart the essential discernments that theoreticians must make between epistemic states and ontic beliefs.

Patañjali's Classical Yoga, one of the six orthodox Hindu philosophies, is a classic of Eastern and world thought. Patañjali teaches that notions of a separate egoic "I" are little more than forms of mistaken identity that we experience in our attempts to take ownership of consciousness. Carl Jung's depth psychology, which remains deeply influential to psychologists, religious scholars, and artists alike, argues that ego-consciousness developed out of the unconscious over the course of evolution. By exploring the work of key theoreticians from both schools of thought, particularly those whose ideas are derived from an integration of theory and practice, Whitney explores the extent to which the seemingly irremediable split between Jung and Patañjali's ontological beliefs can in fact be reconciled.

This thorough and insightful work will be essential reading for academics, theoreticians, and postgraduate students in the fields of psychology, philosophy of science, and consciousness studies. It will also appeal to those interested in the East–West psychological and philosophical dialogue.

Leanne Whitney received her PhD in depth psychology from Pacifica Graduate Institute in Santa Barbara, California. She works as a transformational coach, Yoga teacher, and documentary filmmaker. Leanne's professional papers include *Depth psychology through the lens of Classical Yoga: a reconsideration of Jung's ontic reality* and *Jung and non-duality: some clinical and theoretical implications of the self as totality of the psyche* co-authored with Dr. Lionel Corbett.

Research in Analytical Psychology and Jungian Studies

Series Advisor: Andrew Samuels
Professor of Analytical Psychology, Essex University, UK.

For more information about this series, please visit: www.routledge.com/Research-in-Analytical-Psychology-and-Jungian-Studies/book-series/JUNGIANSTUDIES.

The *Research in Analytical Psychology and Jungian Studies* series features research-focused volumes involving qualitative and quantitative research, historical/archival research, theoretical developments, heuristic research, grounded theory, narrative approaches, collaborative research, practitioner-led research, and self-study. The series also includes focused works by clinical practitioners and provides new research informed explorations of the work of C. G. Jung that will appeal to researchers, academics, and scholars alike.

Books in this series:

Post-Jungian Psychology and the Short Stories of Ray Bradbury and Kurt Vonnegut
Golden Apples of the Monkey House
Steve Gronert Ellerhoff

Eros and Economy
Jung, Deleuze, Sexual Difference
Barbara Jenkins

Towards a Jungian Theory of the Ego
Karen Evers-Fahey

A Japanese Jungian Perspective on Mental Health and Culture Wandering Madness
Iwao Akita
Translated by Waka Shibata and Kittredge Stephenson

Jung and Kierkegaard
Researching a Kindred Spirit in the Shadows
Amy Cook

Consciousness in Jung and Patañjali
Leanne Whitney

Consciousness in Jung and Patañjali

Leanne Whitney

Routledge
Taylor & Francis Group
LONDON AND NEW YORK

First published 2018
by Routledge

2 Park Square, Milton Park, Abingdon, Oxfordshire OX14 4RN
52 Vanderbilt Avenue, New York, NY 10017

Routledge is an imprint of the Taylor & Francis Group, an informa business

First issued in paperback 2018

British Library Cataloguing-in-Publication Data
A catalogue record for this book is available from the British Library

Library of Congress Cataloging-in-Publication Data
A catalog record for this book has been requested

ISBN: 978-1-138-21352-4 (hbk)
ISBN: 978-0-367-19872-5 (pbk)

Typeset in Sabon
by Apex CoVantage, LLC

To Getachew Dagne
ልጄ እወድሃለሁ።

Contents

Acknowledgements

I would like to take this opportunity to acknowledge the following individuals without whom this project could not have been completed successfully. *Consciousness in Jung and Patañjali* originally began as my doctoral dissertation for the depth psychology degree program at Pacifica Graduate Institute in Santa Barbara, California. I am deeply grateful to Dr. Lionel Corbett, Dr. Christopher Chapple, and Dr. Maurice Stevens, who offered instrumental support and feedback over the course of the incubation, creation, and finalization of the original work. My years at Pacifica were pivotal, greatly expanding my knowledge, of both the benefits and the limitations, of the Western academic tradition.

In addition to being developed out of my doctoral dissertation, earlier versions of several passages of this research monograph originated in articles published in two editions of *Cosmos and History: The Journal of Natural and Social Philosophy*: "Beyond Conception: Ontic Reality, Pure Consciousness and Matter," Vol. 11, no.2 (2015), and "Jung in Dialogue with Freud and Patañjali: Instinct, Affective Neuroscience, and the Reconciliation of Science and Religious Experience," Vol. 13, no.2 (2017). The present manuscript is also derived in part from an article published in *International Journal of Jungian Studies* on 05 Oct 2016, available online at www.tandfonline.com/10.1080/19409052.2016.1240702.

Consciousness in Jung and Patañjali was not completed in isolation from other key areas of my professional or personal life. The experiences shared with many friends, family, and clients have been essential to the construction of this work. In particular, I would like to thank Caroline Shabbaz, Wendi Hill, Susan Voss, Homayoun Saeid, Matthew Fike, Kimberly Berg, and Oreet Rees, whose questions, insights, and kindheartedness are interwoven throughout this project. Equally, my heartfelt gratitude goes to my family, whose generosity supported me during the many years of completing my dissertation and rewriting the manuscript. I would also like to acknowledge and sincerely thank my editorial and production teams at Routledge, in particular, my editor, Heidi Lee, and editorial assistant, Chloe Barnes, for their guidance and expert support. Last, and perhaps most significantly, I would like to express my deep appreciation for the scholars who left the enduring legacies upon which this research has been built, Carl Gustav Jung and Patañjali.

Introduction

Depth psychology developed in the early part of the twentieth century as an empirical science of the unconscious. Swiss psychiatrist Carl Gustav Jung (1875–1961), most widely known today as the father of analytical psychology, and Austrian neurologist and founder of psychoanalysis Sigmund Freud (1856–1939), are two of the founding fathers of the field. Focusing on what the conscious personality is not aware of, depth psychology is a psychology of the hidden, the secret, and the repressed. The developers of the discipline thought the science of the unconscious to be utterly revolutionary in its approach to understanding the human psyche. While the focus in contemporary depth psychology remains on unconscious contents and processes, the discipline since its inception has also been equally concerned with consciousness.

Through studying the nature of the psyche and the conscious–unconscious dynamic, Jung's depth psychology aimed, in part, at reconciling science and religious experience. In Jung's view, religious structures and traditions have been failing us, giving rise to scientific materialism and religious fundamentalism. Through postulating instinctual forms of mental functioning, Jung relocated religious experience into everyday life. In turn, by following certain methods in an approach to the numinous, he observed the healing of mild mental disturbances, such as anxiety, stress and obsessive-compulsive behavior, in his patients. Although his scientific body of work remained incomplete upon his death, one of the most prominent aspects of his legacy is his belief in the religious function of the psyche.

While working to find empirical evidence of the psyche's religious function, Jung studied a variety of subjects, including Western philosophy, quantum physics, and mystical teachings. In Eastern liberatory traditions, in particular orthodox and nonorthodox Hindu philosophy, he found parallel evidence to what he termed *individuation,* the central process of human development and the spiritual development of the personality. Consequently, he found Eastern philosophy and psychology, including Patañjali's Classical Yoga, to be of tremendous value to his psychological research.

Composed around the second to fifth century of the current era, Patañjali's *Yoga Sūtra* is both a classic of Eastern and world thought, formulating one of six orthodox Hindu philosophies situated within the Upaniṣadic and Brahmanic tradition. Brahmanism adheres to the metaphysical concept of *brahman*, the Hindu term for God or the Absolute. Although often rendered as Self, *brahman* eludes a simple English translation and is also variously described as ultimate reality, pure consciousness, and being-consciousness-bliss. As a discriminatory science of knowledge, Patañjali's Yoga guides practitioners to direct experience of *puruṣa*, the localized expression of pure consciousness. Patañjali's methodology, through the re-collection of all projections and the total involution of thought forms, mobilizes a radically empirical scientific methodology, which – it could be said – succeeds in reconciling science and religious experience.

In the domains of psychology and philosophy, comparing the work of Jung and Patañjali in particular and Eastern and Western ideas in general offers a rich source of deep discussion in relation to the nature of consciousness, the reality of thought, dualistic and nondualistic worldviews, and religious experience. For many Eastern liberatory models, including Patañjali's, reality is not always the way it appears. Furthermore, in many of these Eastern liberatory models, dualism and materialistic monism are falsifiable. Notably, although the present study uses an East–West comparison – in the end, there really is no divide. Like the equator, East–West is merely a descriptive tool.

As one of the first to emphasize the importance of bridging East and West, Jung went to great lengths to research the East and understand it. He carried around *The Tibetan Book of the Dead*, gave lectures on Kundalini Yoga, and studied the *Tao Te Ching*. Jung (1929/1983) acknowledged, "The European invasion of the East was an act of violence on a grand scale, and it has left us with the duty – *noblesse oblige* – of understanding the mind of the East" (para. 84). Jung believed that a fruitful relationship between Western and Eastern concepts of mind could be realized. However, because of cultural differences, there were significant challenges in this dialogical endeavor for Jung, and those challenges by and large remain today. A portion of the challenge lies in the approach to the numinous. For instance, whereas God is directly accessible according to orthodox Hindu philosophy, for the Abrahamic religions and a multitude of Western philosophers, God is ontically inaccessible. Putting the work of Jung and Patañjali into dialogue challenges the religious fundamentalism as well as the orthodox scientific view of the West.

In the West, science and religion, each in its own way, set out to describe reality. Science does so through observing the behavior of the physical world and studying the underpinning mathematical theories, while religious descriptions most often result through revelation or the reliance upon doctrine. While any connection between science and religion may initially seem cursory at best or antagonistic at worst, today their relationship is becoming far more nuanced on account of the field of consciousness studies. The field, while fostering the ongoing dialogue between science and religion, interestingly, also addresses many of the unsolved problems in science.

Science still knows very little about how thought is produced, correlated with our neuronal hardware, or related to reality. Being highly interdisciplinary, the field of consciousness studies approaches these problems from multiple angles and points of view. Within the field, researchers from psychology, anthropology, biology, and neurology all argue for their respective views on the nature of consciousness in particular and the nature of reality in general. The crux of the consciousness debate seems to center around the arguments that present consciousness as an abiding principle of awareness underlying all transitory mental states versus the arguments for consciousness as mental activity. As of yet there is no consensus, and the discussion is sometimes heated. Furthermore, the definition of consciousness seems to be elusive, with scholars in various fields defining it differently.

Conducting research that will allow for a contemporary science of consciousness within the Western tradition has proved challenging because the subjective and qualitative nature of conscious experience resists the objectivity of orthodox scientific inquiry. Orthodox science holds tight to the primacy of physical matter, the paradigm of mind–matter dualism, and knowledge as objective and scientific – even though discoveries in quantum physics have challenged the orthodox view by revealing energy as the primary building block of the universe and the interconnected relationship between the observer and the observed.

Even though subjectivity poses a pivotal challenge to the orthodox experimental frame, several fields, including cognitive psychology and neurology, are flourishing as they unravel physical and biological mechanisms that correlate to conscious experience. Neurology undeniably provides us with information of clear value within a particular domain. Be that as it may, even if we find the neural mechanisms for perception, the neurobiological process of love, for instance, will never substitute for the direct experience of love.

Given the enormous prevalence of science and religion and their influence in contemporary society, it is obvious that as a species, we clearly seek to understand and make sense of our world. But if we truly want to understand consciousness in general and numinous experience in particular, then we must be vigilant about being aware in every moment of what we are doing and how we are drawing conclusions. Taking an in-depth look at the foundation of the beliefs and the processes of our empirical endeavors is vitally important. For instance, while neurology provides us with useful information, it should never be assumed that the neural pulse is the sole carrier of information. The spikeless neurons and gap junctions are providing us with equally valuable directives (Freeman, 2014). With too heavy a focus on the obviously visible, the subtle and invisible become neglected.

By presupposing an objective and subjective realm, empirical scientists base their research on reductionistic principles with the belief that "I" as a subject can "objectively" investigate independent objects. Interestingly, materialist science does not see the subject–object distinction as an assumption but rather wholeheartedly believes the distinction to be real. As a result, the general public more often than not assumes the subject–object distinction without question. There is an awesome power to this official narrative because it continues to self-reinforce and construct the lens through which many, if not most, Westerners view the world.

Our worldview determines what tests we want to invest in, how we construct them, what results we look for, and how we interpret the data. For instance, orthodox science views numinous experience as a function (or dysfunction) of brain process, while the world's great religious traditions tend to regard numinous experience either as a manifestation of the deities and prophets of their tradition or as Reality itself. Therefore, if orthodox science deems itself capable of regarding (or disregarding) religious experience as "simply" a brain process, then questioning the reliability of the scientific worldview is mandatory. Furthermore, there is such an abundance of research going on within different fields that often scientists from one field do not know what is happening outside the domain of their expertise. Merging disciplines, as neuropsychoanalysis and interpersonal neurobiology have done, may help to foster a much-needed vigilance.

For those working within the bounds of the empirical platform, dualistic scientific methodology is oftentimes seen not only as an adequate means of investigation but also as the only one. This belief constitutes a major block for further dialogue and development across disciplines in the area of consciousness studies. It is a massive assumption that the subject–object relation is capable of accounting for life or of understanding it. For instance, when the orthodox empirical platform is challenged by nondualists, those who do not perceive the world through a subject–object dichotomy, the disputes are most often met with scorn by the players holding the positions of power within the academic institutions. An alternative view of the world appears extremely threatening to scientific orthodoxy. Yet an understanding of science is dependent upon knowing how the mind works. If the aim is to understand, then disregarding descriptions of the world simply because they are challenging to conventional science is illogical and irrational, or in other words, contradictory to the tenets of science itself.

Neither science nor religion is an isolated system. They exist within a much greater whole. Knowledge constructed through religious or scientific systems offers a part of knowledge, not the whole of it. They are constructed languages, constrained like any other, that attempt to form relationships. Relationships formed this way are bound by the very human thought processes that isolate and choose which parts to relate. As important as these relationships may be within a specific framework, they are context dependent.

How does one describe the infinite, unlimited, and immeasurable using language that is finite, limited, and measured? The overall integrity of life is compromised when we are only focused on its parts. Yet if the subset is in alignment with the set or if the measurable in harmony with the immeasurable, language can offer us different ways to consider the undivided whole and, perhaps, help us realize deeper insight.

Researching Jungian and Patañjalian thought calls attention to the fact that, in the endeavor of consciousness research, it may be time for science that is solely based in conventional modes of thought to proceed with cautious reservation. When it comes to the human psyche in particular, we must acknowledge that progress can occur outside the scientific domain. The human psyche is a naturally occurring phenomenon in life. Science, on the other hand, is a particular lens humans have constructed to take a look into, and back at, life. Therefore, in the case of conventional science, if it is built on the foundation of falsifiability, then its very foundation should also be falsifiable.

My own reservations about the ways in which we habitually perceive through cultural construction prompted this study: reservations drawn from my life experience in general but from one all-encompassing moment in particular. At age 33, I had what is referred to in the religious studies literature as a pure consciousness event (PCE) (Forman, 1998). This unplanned incident instantaneously catapulted "me," a woman born, cultivated, and conditioned in a Western framework of duality, or subject–object consciousness, into nonduality, whereupon the distinction between subject and object – indeed all distinctions – broke down. Prior to this event, I had no knowledge of the essence of the teachings in any liberatory psychologies or nondual philosophies, although I was in a yoga asana room at the time of the event. Indeed, I had no knowledge that PCEs even existed. Yet in that fraction of a moment, an immediate incontrovertible knowledge arose, that in addition to what appears on the surface of reality, beyond what we can perceive with our five physical senses, everything is interconnected and interdependent, with an essence that seems to be an all-knowing luminosity. In other words, what I suddenly understood at the deepest level of my being, and without any prior knowledge, seeking, or research, was that the subject–object split is merely an appearance.

The PCE and enormous perceptual shift did not simultaneously eradicate the deeper patterns of my dualistic conditioning. It did, however, infuse me with the determination to do so. Knowing without a doubt that all is one and self-luminous, I wanted to understand how this could be so, given all the suffering and strife that appears and is experienced in the consensus reality we call life. I understood that the false beliefs under which "I" was conditioned would need to be extinguished.

The way we perceive everyday reality through our five physical senses leads many of us to conclude that the world is a multiplicity. Separation, independence, and plurality are powerful and ingrained ways of perceiving the world in Western culture. The PCE I experienced gave me a radically different understanding of our visible world. But it also produced deeply philosophical questions. How could the world be both a unity and a multiplicity? I have made an unceasing exploration of the world in front of our eyes, and behind it, in an effort to viscerally experience how a dualistic and nondualistic worldview could be united. I have had to learn through experience, much of it trial and error, how to bridge these two worlds.

As I began exploring, one of the first texts I was intuitively guided to read was Padmasambhava's *The Tibetan Book of the Dead*. His lucid description of Clear Light was extremely comforting. The text was evidence that the reality of radiance I had awakened into was known and documented. Not long after reading this classic text of Tibetan Buddhism, I discovered the writings of Jung and Patañjali. Patañjali's Classical Yoga and Jung's depth psychology have provided fruitful perspectives, tools, and approaches during my explorations of the world in front of, and behind, our eyes – and consequently, I have remained drawn to these two highly influential authors and their related schools of thought for over fifteen years. There are intriguing places where their works intersect, despite cultural and epochal variation, and also decisive areas of divergence.

One aspect of the debate between East and West is located around the nature of the egoic "I." Freud emphasized the ego in his structural and topographical models of the psyche and at the same time emphatically stated that it is not master of the house. In his model, the conscious and unconscious became a duality split by an ego. Throughout his career, Freud constructed and deconstructed, postulating theories of the self. As an atheist, Freud disagreed with religious practice, but he studied it. His psychology aimed to return us to ourselves, to assist us in overcoming states of alienation. Yet at the same time, he also imprinted, through psychoanalytical language and terminology, a dualistic model by treating the ego as real (Watts, 1971). Although the spiritually oriented Jung spotted what he believed to be some flaws in Freud's thinking, he never did away with Freud's model entirely. He merely modified it. The models Freud and Jung adhered to, may have been bound, or co-determined, by deeming depth psychology an empirical science. Hence, depth psychology, while considering itself an empirical science, benefits by turning its lens back on itself and finding viable ways of comparing its reductions and subject–object splits with views that are foundationally holistic. Views that see wholeness as the real, the given, and our fragmentary thought as a symptom or illusory perception.

Yoga psychology and philosophy teach us that viewing our world through our conditioned mind, which consists of fragmentary thought and illusory perception, brings about a misunderstanding of our true nature – and the obscuration of pure consciousness. In distinction to Western psychology, all Eastern liberatory psychologies maintain that our egoic consciousness has no foundation in reality: that our ideas on a separate subject, a duality between ego and world, are based in limited thinking. In Yoga, the isolated mind and egoic "I" are concepts that can be completely deconstructed. To state this slightly differently, while the West cannot yet explain the origin of thought, in Western psychology it is believed that the ego, or a personal independent subjectivity, is a determinant of consciousness. In sharp contrast, in the Yoga tradition, when we differentiate pure consciousness from thought, we are led to the realization that only consciousness truly exists.

Investigations of consciousness lead us deep into the heart of the mystery of life. Therefore, what seems vitally important for research on consciousness is an open perspective. As Jung (1938/1981) himself admitted, psychological theories "are the very devil. It is true that we need certain points of view for orienting and heuristic value; but they should always be regarded as mere auxiliary concepts that can be laid aside at any time" (p. 7). Studying consciousness psychologically means studying all the phenomena that are available to human perception, even if these phenomena are not available to all humans at once. For instance, psychic phenomena, such as remote viewing and precognition, offer us valuable insights into the nature of consciousness and indeed the nature of reality. Fundamentalist science tends to want to silence these phenomena, but at what expense? If the rigidity of the statistically empirical scientific model is hindering us from discovery, then the true scientific endeavor has been lost. If the subject–object distinction does not exist at the deeper levels of reality but is merely an appearance on the surface, dualistic models misrepresent the true nature of our *being*.

Are we meant to discover reality through test results or through the process of our own trial and error? If theorists and educators rely on test results that have already been shown to sometimes be less reliable than once thought (Economist, 2013), what kind of foundation are we creating? If our orthodox scientific methods are such that we can set up tests and quite literally create an outcome rather than observing one, science becomes a tool to obfuscate rather than understand. In other words, perhaps a radical empiricism, based on our direct experience of the world, is the foremost science needed when it comes to a science of consciousness and the reality of being. Along these lines, researching Jung and Patañjali brings the imperative necessity of discerning between the ontic and epistemic into sharp focus.

Seeking to replicate scientific results, we can approach the methodology and design of an initial experiment as closely as possible, but repeat studies will never be the same. That idea is true for our life in general when we see and experience "life" as a verb, even though the word literally is a noun. We can attempt to re-produce how life functions through scientific means, but the original creativity of life in its wholeness cannot be, and will never be, re-produced. It is one constant flow of activity that does not stand still so that one species can make a static model of it. It is a huge assumption that we can pull apart life and find biological, psychological, neurological, quantum, and other correlates and then put it back together to formulate the whole. We may be able to find the skeleton, the musculature, the neurons, for instance, or we may be able to understand cycles of change and the system(s) of life, but the cycles, the system, and the parts can ever be separated from the awareness in which they arise. It is incorrect to assume that life can be *conceptualized* in a manner that gives us answers to the nature of consciousness and to our experience of being.

Over the past several decades, many scholars have researched Jung's dialogue with Eastern thought (Ajaya, 1983; Clarke, 1994; Coward, 1985, 2002; Jordens, 1964; Stein, 2010; Watts, 1971). Much of the research has uncovered the challenges in the discourse. My aim in this study, in part, is to unearth more distinctly where Jung met his limits in relation to yogic thought. The dualistic Judeo-Christian and Cartesian confines that boxed Jung in are still prevalent in much of our thinking today. Likewise, from a depth psychological view, it is important to explore any limitations that may exist within the work of Patañjali, in particular with Classical Yoga's description of the physical world. The other more implicit aim of the present research is to question the notion of duality in its entirety: to question a basic duality in nature – or the subject–object split – and to question the idea that reality is not empty-of-other.

Consciousness in Jung and Patañjali is broken down into seven chapters. Chapter 1 is an overview of Patañjali in which the background of his thought is explored. In particular, the relationships of Classical Yoga to Upaniṣadic, Buddhistic, Sāṃkhyan, and Advaitic ideas are examined. Although Patañjali's sūtras are often read as a companion text to Sāṃkhya, due in large measure to shared terminology and the use of a dualistic metaphysics, Yoga's intersection with the nondual tradition of Advaita Vedānta is discussed. In contradistinction to certain prominent Advaita teachings, which view the world as illusory, particular emphasis is placed on Patañjali's confirmation of the reality of the world. For Patañjali, matter is real; it is the materialistic outlook that is flawed. Sanskrit terms relevant to Patañjali's text are also defined and interpreted. Further explorations in this chapter include Patañjali's approach to consciousness, mind–psyche, ego–Self, and the transformation of human consciousness.

Chapter 2 is an overview of Jung in which the background of his thought is explored. How and when depth psychology arose in the Western hemisphere are considered, as is the relationship of Jung's thought to that of the Freudian, scientific, and religious ideas of his day. In particular, the divergence between Freud's and Jung's thoughts on the nature of the unconscious is studied, and Jung's confrontations with the unconscious are explored. Jung's early experiences through dreams are considered as well as his conviction that religious belief should be backed up by direct experience. Further explorations in this chapter include Jung's approach to consciousness, mind–psyche, ego–Self, and the transformation of human consciousness.

While Chapters 1 and 2 can stand alone as individual studies, Chapter 3 puts Jung's and Patañjali's thought directly into dialogue. Jung's and Patañjali's approaches to consciousness, mind–psyche, ego–Self, and the transformation of human consciousness are considered back-to-back. Their areas of similarity and difference are introduced and examined.

Chapter 4 inquires into Jung's analysis and understanding of yogic texts and liberatory thought with an emphasis on uncovering where Jung met his limits in relation to nondual ideas. The teleological directedness of the psyche is explored as are the potential problems depth psychology faces as a result of Jung's assertion that the ego and the unconscious are ontically real.

Chapter 5 continues the dialogue between Jung and Patañjali and – while factoring in their decisive areas of divergence – explores a potential synthesis of their ideas. The efficacy of the unconscious is looked at closely. Depth psychological and yogic ideas on the mind–body unity are explored. Affect as an empirical means of entering the psyche and Jung's synchronicity hypothesis are examined as possible means of forging a bridge between depth psychology and Classical Yoga. A holograph heuristic device is mobilized to explore how pure consciousness can be Reality and yet not realized as such, at the level of human awareness. Chapter 6 concludes the research by summing up the results and by returning to the conundrum orthodox scientists face as they work toward a science of consciousness.

Consciousness in Jung and Patañjali explores how consciousness is accounted for in the work of Jung and Patañjali, with an aim towards finding a common psychological language, or synthesis, between depth psychology and Classical Yoga. Through a synthesis of the work of Jung and Patañjali can a more comprehensive view of consciousness and its relationship to matter be discovered? If so, from that union, can deeper insights around human experience be gleaned? In an age of ongoing oppressive power structures, the threat of nuclear holocaust, environmental stressors, and increasing anxiety, it seems imperative that we persevere in finding means of addressing the amelioration of human suffering and unveiling visions that offer the deeper sense of our shared humanity. I believe that our explorations in the field of consciousness studies can assist us in accomplishing this task. As we move rapidly into a global society, as we continue to unearth national and cultural limitations, and as science and religion continue to collide, exploring a synthesis of Eastern and Western psychology offers an opportunity to forge the foundation of a new, perhaps global, psychology.

References

Ajaya, S. (1983). *Psychotherapy east and west: A unifying paradigm*. Honesdale, PA: The Himalayan Institute.

Clarke, J. (1994). Jung and eastern thought: A dialogue with the orient. New York, NY: Routledge.

Coward, H. (1985). *Jung and eastern thought*. New York, NY: State University of New York Press.

Coward, H. (2002). *Yoga and psychology*. New York, NY: State University of New York Press.

Economist. (2013). *How science goes wrong: Scientific research has changed the world. Now it needs to change itself*. Retrieved from www.economist.com/news/leaders/21588069-scientific-research-has-changed-world-now-it-needs-change-itself-how-science-goes-wrong

Forman, R. K. C. (1998). What does mysticism have to teach us about consciousness? *Journal of Consciousness Studies*, *5*(2), 185–201.

Freeman, W. (2014). Book review: "Karl H. Pribram (2013) The Form Within: My Point of View." *Journal of Integrative Neuroscience*, *13*(2), 429–433.

Jordens, J. (1964). Jung and yoga. The Journal of the Indian Academy of Philosophy, 3, 1–21.

Jung, C. G. (1981). Foreword to the third edition: Psychic conflicts in a child. In H. Read, M. Fordham, G. Adler, & W. McGuire (Eds.), *The collected works of C. G. Jung* (R. F. C. Hull, Trans., 3rd ed., Vol. 17, pp. 6–7). Princeton, NJ: Princeton University Press. (Original work published 1938)

Jung, C. G. (1983). Commentary on "The secret of the golden flower." In H. Read, M. Fordham, G. Adler, & W. McGuire (Eds.), *The collected works of C. G. Jung* (R. F. C. Hull, Trans., Vol. 13, pp. 1–56). Princeton, NJ: Princeton University Press. (Original work published 1929)

Stein, R. (2010). Snapshots from the void: Reflections on Jung's relationship to Indian yoga. *Jung Journal: Culture & Psyche*, *4*(2), 62–84.

Watts, A. (1971). *Psychotherapy east and west*. New York, NY: Ballantine.

Chapter 1

Patañjali

An overview of Patañjali

Patañjali was a Yoga scholar in India and the reputed author of the *Yoga Sūtra*. He was a pivotal theoretician whose work was derived from an integration of theory and practice. There is much argument in the scholarly literature regarding several aspects of Patañjali Yoga, including whether the *Yoga Sūtra* was written by one man or many and whether the Patañjali who authored the *Yoga Sūtra* is the same Patañjali who authored other ancient texts. The manner in which Patañjali's *Sūtras* were composed is also questionable. For example, it is thought that the first three chapters may have been composed around the second century, but the fourth seems to be highly influenced by late-Buddhistic thought and was perhaps composed centuries later. Although no exact date is known, scholars have deduced the text would have been written no later than the fifth century of the current era (Bryant, 2009; Zimmer, 1969). While the majority of scholars believe Patañjali lived around the second to fifth century of the current era, still others have surmised a date a few centuries earlier. Given that written records were not of concern in India centuries ago, the country's philosophical history is not always well documented (Radhakrishnan & Moore, 1957).

With its roots in a long lineage of tradition in India, the science of Patañjali's Classical Yoga is an integral part of Hindu philosophy. Like any system of thought, Classical Yoga undoubtedly developed over a length of time and was then compiled by Patañjali in the *Yoga Sūtra*. There is much scholarship, old and new, around this very concise text, the oldest book of the Classical Yoga school. Both a classic of Eastern and world thought, few other written works on the planet, with fewer than 200 lines, provide such an enduring focus of international scholarship. According to renowned Indologist Henrich Zimmer (1969), the *Yoga Sūtra*, "must be reckoned among the most astounding works of philosophical prose in the literature of the world" (p. 283).

Yoga is a term etymologically derived from the root *yuj* meaning yoke, bind together, or harness. As both the method that joins and the harnessed state, this Sanskrit term has a variety of meanings. Most often the connotation of yoga is to unite or connect. The union referred to in Patañjali Yoga can be envisioned from multiple perspectives. It is both the union of the transcendent pole representing the possessor of power and the dynamic pole of creative power and energy and the union of the individual psyche with the transcendent Self (Whicher, 1998a). The individual psyche and the transcendent Self in Hindu philosophy are in essence the same and indivisible; however, the individual self, through misperception, becomes subjectively separated from the transcendent Self.

There are several paths of Indian yoga, including jñāna, the yoga of pure knowledge; hatha, the yoga of physical technique; and bhakti, the yoga of devotion and love. Many of these techniques are detectable in Patañjali's text, but his main approach is Self-realization through the transformation of the mind, which is often referred to as Rāja Yoga, meaning royal union. While the approaches of the many historical yoga paths are distinct, the experience of Self-realization and the transcendence of suffering is the aim of all.

Indian thought centers around the problem of human conditioning, or suffering. Our conditioned mind stems from the confines of time and culture, binding us into a conceptual reality and limiting our ability to rest in our true nature. Pragmatic in approach, Hindu thought provides viable means towards the process of deconditioning and therefore viable means for releasing the bondage. Because of the holistic nature and integrative process of Classical Yoga methodology, Patañjali's text has been noted to stand on its own: it "does not require the support of any science or philosophical system to uphold its claim" (Taimni, 1961, p. vii). So although little background information is known about Patañjali and although what is known is replete with contradictions, symbolically perhaps, the text can be studied apart from its author. Of course, the personal history of Patañjali may be interesting, but when considering the ultimate vision of the *Sūtras*, his personal history is ultimately not necessary. The *Sūtras* can therefore be amplified through situating the text within a rough time period in the canon of Hindu thought and classical Indian philosophy.

Indian philosophy is ancient and diverse, with six orthodox and three heterodox schools subsequently evolving into different streams and doctrines, each providing differing images and explanations for ultimate Reality and the manifest world. It is notable that there are significant foundational differences among the various traditions, specifically, in regards to consciousness as eternal being, theories of mind, and reliance upon the authority of scripture. For the purposes of this study, a general background of some of the influential systems that pre- and postdate Patañjali will be given to acknowledge the roots of the tradition and its ongoing development. Most specifically, Patañjali's work will be positioned between the particular philosophical schools of Sāṃkhya and Advaita.

General background

There are four major periods in Indian philosophy: Vedic, Epic, Sūtra, and Scholastic. Most often the Vedic Period is situated between 2500 and 600 BCE, the Epic Period is between 500 BCE and 200 CE, the Sūtra Period is dated from the early centuries of the current era, and the Scholastic Period is from the Sūtra Period up until 1700 CE (Radhakrishnan & Moore, 1957).

The Vedic Period produced the *Ṛg Veda* (ca. 1200 BCE), the first known Indo-European text. Composed of Sanskrit hymns focusing on ritualism and sacrificial rites, this ancient text documents meditation on divine light (Radhakrishnan, 1996), indicating that the basic ideas and practices of Yoga arose during the time of the *Ṛg Veda*, if not before. The Yoga doctrine itself is believed to be as old as Brahmā, otherwise known as *brahman*,[1] the supreme Reality in Hindu thought (Radhakrishnan, 1996).

The Vedas were purportedly authored by seers (*ṛṣis*), people believed able to hear and see directly into the cosmos; hence, the Vedas are categorized as *śruti*, revealed and authoritative scripture. "Veda" signifies wisdom, a term that implies the scholarly search for understanding (Radhakrishnan & Moore, 1957). Through their search, the Supreme reality, *brahman*, was revealed to these *ṛṣis* as imperishable, unchanging, and partless, even though it appears in a multiplicity of transient images and forms. This realization "has been decisive" both for the history of Indian civilization and the course of Indian philosophy (Zimmer, 1969, p. 3). With the understanding that what is not permanent is not worth striving for, the directive of Indian philosophy is to know *brahman*, the Self.

Whereas the early Vedas often focused on ritualism and sacrificial rites, the later Vedas, the *Upaniṣads* (ca. 800–500 BCE), focused on philosophical discourse in connection to *brahman* and *ātman*, its localized expression. In this sacred scripture, gaining knowledge of *ātman* "is the most significant clue" to both personal and universal reality (Radhakrishnan & Moore, 1957, p. xxv). The Upaniṣadic or Vedāntic doctrines of spiritual monism, in which *ātman* and *brahman* are singular, have established "the tone if not the precise pattern" of Indian philosophical development to the present day (Radhakrishnan & Moore, 1957, p. xviii).

In the *Kaṭha*, *Taittirīya*, and *Maitrāyaṇīya Upaniṣads,* yoga as a technical term can be found, although the yoga mentioned is not identical with Patañjali Yoga (Radhakrishnan, 1996, p. 339). Complete uniformity notwithstanding, the echoes between the *Upaniṣads* and Patañjali's sūtras, in regards to concentration and the conscious inward search for true nature, are audible. The *Upaniṣads* alongside the *Brahma Sūtras* and the *Bhagavad Gītā* comprise the three basic texts of Hindu philosophy.

The *Bhagavad Gītā* (ca. 150 BCE–250 CE), perhaps the Epic Period's most famous text, is part of the heroic Hindu tale the *Mahābhārata*. The

Bhagavad Gītā is not formally a part of primary, revealed scripture, or the canonical *śruti*. The epic texts are classed as noncanonical sacred literature known as "tradition" or *smṛti* (lit. "remembering" past wisdom) (Whicher, 1998a, p. 22). *Smṛti* texts are accepted by the Vedānta tradition if they are not incongruent with *śruti*. Within the *Mahābhārata*, "The terms *yoga* and *yogī* occur about nine hundred times" according to Bryant (2009), referencing "practices that are clearly relatable to the system of *yoga* as taught by Patañjali" (p. xxiv). An epic poem, the *Mahābhārata* is Indian epistemology in narrative form.

In addition to the Vedānta tradition, another significant system predating Patañjali's Yoga is Buddhism, which developed in Northeast India around the fifth century BCE. Buddhism and Vedānta share many essential ideas, for example, karma, rebirth, and the universal cycles of arising, existing, and vanishing. Buddhism, however, is considered a heterodox philosophical system because it broke with Brahmanic tradition and does not prescribe to the authority of the Vedas. Specifically, Buddhism questions the Vedic authority, which claims *śruti*, or revealed truths, are not knowable by other means and posits *anātmavāda*, a refutation of *ātman* (*puruṣa*) as eternal, conscious being. Although Buddhism was a revolt against historical tradition, it could be said that it owes its inspiration to the *Upaniṣads*, hence the critical point of view that Buddhism presents does not uproot its system completely from the Indian canon (Radhakrishnan, 1996).

Although there is significant foundational difference between heterodox and orthodox thought in India, the yoga mentioned and developed in the early *Upaniṣads* would have been known to Siddhartha Gautama, the Buddha of the fifth century BCE and would have influenced his thought. For instance, early Buddhist scripture, the Pāli Canon, revealed Siddhartha Gautama as a devotee of meditation, while the later Sanskrit scriptures referred to him as a yogin (Whicher, 1998a). Buddhism and Yoga share similarities. For instance, both systems view external reality as a never-ending flow of interdependent, interconnected phenomena. Yet Buddhism and Yoga are markedly different in that they appear to hold opposing views on basic foundational hypotheses regarding mind and consciousness. In distinction to Yoga, in mainstream Buddhism, all reality is considered momentary; neither consciousness nor mind has eternal, essential existence. Consciousness in mainstream Buddhism is typically understood as arising with conditions: absolutism is consistently rejected. However, quite notably, a few passages of the Pāli Canon refer to consciousness as "infinite and shining everywhere" (Loy, 1997, p. 193). Although beyond the scope of the present project, it is important to note that the true intent of the Buddha's message remains under debate in modern scholarship, exemplified by the absolutist and non-absolutist strands in Mahāyāna Buddhism (King, 1995, p. 230). It is within Mahāyāna Buddhism that infinite consciousness gains greater distinction from conditioned consciousness in the Buddhist movement. For example, the *tathāgatagarbha* texts of Mahāyāna Buddhism (ca. 4–5 CE) teach of "a 'buddha-seed' inherent within (or perhaps even identical with) all sentient beings" (King, 1995, p. 206). Although present in all at all times, Buddha-nature is obscured by the mental phenomena that limit and distort our pristine awareness. Because what is conditioned is impermanent and subject to dissolution, we cannot take refuge in it. In postulating an unconditioned, unchanging, and eternal reality, the *dharmakāya*, the *tathāgatagarbha* texts bring absolutism into Buddhism (King, 1995) and therefore into alignment with the absolutism of Vedāntic tradition. Because the *Yoga Sūtra* at times uses terminology very similar to that of Mahāyāna Buddhism, this could indicate important connections between the two systems (Whicher, 1998a).

Arising a few centuries after Buddhism, around the beginning of the current era, there were six Brahmanical systems of thought written in sūtra style: Nyāya, Vaiśeṣika, Sāṃkhyan, Yoga, Pūrva Mīmāṃsā, and Vedānta. As opposed to the prose and poetry of the early scriptures, the six Brahmanical systems use *sūtras*, or threads, which are extremely concise aphorisms. It was through these systems of thought that "Strenuous attempts were made to justify by reason what faith implicitly accepts" (Radhakrishnan, 1996, p. 19). Being that the Vedas "were neither definite nor detailed," it encouraged philosophers in later ages to work with the core truths of the scriptures while fashioning new ways of looking at and accessing these truths (Radhakrishnan, 1996, p. 21). Hence, in the sūtra systems, succinct texts that appeal to reason are used to build upon, or relate to, that which had already been revealed. No one system "openly stands in violation of the accepted intuitive insights of the ancient seers," though they may vary in how they relate to them (Radhakrishnan & Moore, 1957, p. xxvi). All of the systems are interconnected through their honoring of Indian tradition and through the common enduring desire to "solve the mystery of existence" (Radhakrishnan, 1996, p. 20). None of the systems stand independently.

Patañjali's *Yoga Sūtra* is considered part of the Sūtra Period of texts, and therefore developed out of the older Upaniṣadic/Buddhistic systems of thought and builds upon them. Patañjali's opus is laid out in either 195 or 196 sūtras, depending upon the translation. The text is composed of very incisive statements on the practice and process of Yoga. Written back to back without commentary, and double spaced, they comprise about 11 pages of text. As much information as possible is packed into the smallest amount of words.[2]

The *Yoga Sūtra* is not an introductory text to the process of Yoga. As yoga scholar Dr. Taimni (1961) has noted, "these *Sūtras* are meant to provide in a very condensed form all the essential knowledge for the advanced student of *Yoga*" (p. 32). Extraordinarily succinct, sūtras were designed to aid easy memorization but not necessarily understanding. Commentaries arose in subsequent centuries to amplify the meaning of the text for readers of the current day. The first commentary to elaborate on Patañjali's thought, and to facilitate comprehension, was written by Vyāsa in the fifth century CE.

Whereas for foreign readers, understanding Patañjali's text is dependent upon accurate translation from Sanskrit, for many readers of the text, if not all, there is dependence on the commentaries. The commentaries and text have become embedded. Bryant (2009) has explained, "It cannot be overstated that Yoga philosophy is Patañjali's philosophy as understood and articulated by Vyāsa" (p. xl). While Vyāsa and the subsequent commentators have been relatively consistent in their rendering of Patañjali's metaphysics, whether these metaphysics are meant to be literalized or used for pedagogical purposes can be argued (Whicher, 1998a). Christopher Key Chapple (1994) has recently proposed that the standard interpretation given by Vyāsa be reconsidered, given that later commentators, apparently without exception, rely heavily upon Vyāsa for their own interpretations of the text. In the present study, Patañjali's text is used as much as possible without reference to any commentary. As a result, sometimes multiple translations of one line or word are referenced.

The *Yoga Sūtra* is divided into four chapters. Chapter 1, *Samādhi Pāda*, containing 51 sūtras, pertains to the nature of concentration and communion. Chapter 2, *Sādhana Pāda*, with 55 sūtras, focuses on the practices with an underlying theme of the suffering that prompts us to use them. Chapter 3, *Vibhūti Pāda*, containing 55 or 56 sūtras depending on the translation, emphasizes the powers and perfections attained through Yoga. The fourth and final chapter, *Kaivalya Pāda*, with 34 sūtras, describes the central theme of one's-own-ness.

Situating the *Yoga Sūtra* within the canon of Hindu thought there are many points of alignment, including the primacy of pure consciousness, the healing power of silence, and the inward search for true nature. There are points of divergence also. In contrast to Vedic traditions in which there were caste and familial restrictions in regards to the accessibility of the teachings, Yoga is not exclusive, although surrender to the authority of the teachings is required (Zimmer, 1969, pp. 59–60).

In addition to Rāja Yoga, Classical Yoga is also referred to as Yoga *Darśana*. When referring to the text as *Yoga Darśana*, the core idea of the text immediately reveals itself. *Darśana* is a Sanskrit term derived from the root √*dṛś* meaning, "see, perceive, understand" (Chapple, 2008, p. 143). The underlying thrust of the text pertains to seeing, or the process of seeing. *Darśana* – direct vision, instrument of vision, or a view through which reality is perceived – is often identified with the term *philosophy* (Timalsina, 2009b; Rambachan, 1991). However, philosophy in the Indian tradition should in no way be confused with the concepts of speculation and intellectualization used in Western thought. Where Western philosophy is an intellectual quest for truth, Indian philosophy emphasizes direct, immediate experience and the realization of truth (Rambachan, 1991). Realization of truth as intuitive direct experience produces knowledge that is undoubtable and distinct from the discursive reasoning functions of the mind. Yoga, as psychology, philosophy, and a means to realization of truth, is a discriminatory science of knowledge.

The science of Patañjali Yoga, in summary, is the ability to still the fluctuations of the mind. Through a process of integration and involution – in which one focuses on the process of reversing manifestation and the modifications of the mind – all objects are removed from the horizon of awareness. With the mind stabilized and free of conditions, pure consciousness has no alternative but to be revealed and directly experienced. To state this slightly differently, revolving around practical, disciplined activity, Patañjali created a step-by-step instruction book that teaches us that we can free the conditioned mind from suffering by discriminating pure consciousness from the modifications of the mind and physical senses, often referred to as the vehicles of activity.

A large portion of Patañjali's text focuses on the methods that assist one in cultivating the ability to perceive pure consciousness. He explains possible paths we can take, pitfalls to watch out for, and indicators that we are focused in the right direction as we head toward an embodied knowing of pure consciousness. Patañjali's text is therefore not a treatise on metaphysics, but his metaphysics can be abstracted from the text. It is notable that philosophical disputes about the process of Yoga exist throughout the literature.

Yoga and Sāṃkhya

Sāṃkhya, like Yoga, is part of the Sūtra Period. Because of the lack of documentation of historic Hindu literature, there remains scholarly debate around the evolution of Yoga in relation to Sāṃkhya philosophy and how they impacted each other. Gerald James Larson (1969/2011), Sāṃkhya scholar and author of the authoritative text *Classical Sāṃkhya: An Interpretation of Its History and Meaning*, noted that Yoga evolved from Sāṃkhya. Conversely, Yoga scholar Edwin Bryant (2009) argued the opposite, suggesting that Sāṃkhya evolved out of primordial Yoga origins (p. xxxvii). In alignment with Bryant, yoga scholar and Indic researcher Ian Whicher (1998a) has contended that the *Yoga-Sūtra* text predates the classical Sāṃkhya text and if any borrowing occurred, it was most likely by the Sāṃkhyan philosophers.

The sage Kapila is often credited as the founder of Sāṃkhya, although *Īśvarakṛṣṇa's Sāṃkhya Kārikā* (SK) of the third century CE is the earliest available text on this philosophical system. The *Sāṃkhya Kārikā* is also a very brief work, consisting of only 73 verses of text. Like Yoga, there are references to Sāṃkhyan concepts in the *Upaniṣads* as well as the *Bhagavad Gītā*. In this system of thought, realization is gained through the use of reason, theoretical investigation, and discrimination.

Sāṃkhya and Yoga use much of the same conceptual vocabulary and have many theoretical points in common. Two of the key metaphysical terms common to both, and crucial to understanding the meaning of Patañjali's opus, are *puruṣa*,[3] pure consciousness, and *prakṛti*,[4] nature or material reality. As such, the philosophy of Sāṃkhya is often considered the other side of the practice and religion of Yoga whereby they combine to form complementary aspects of one whole. They are often understood to be allied or sister schools of orthodox Hindu philosophy (Schweizer, 1993; Bryant, 2009; Eliade, 2009). Both systems are aligned, for example, in their emphasis on nonattachment and the cultivation of knowledge or discernment, as well as in the metaphysical view of *satkārya*, seeing the effect as present in the cause. Whether Patañjali Yoga subscribes to the doctrine of the plurality of *puruṣas*, as does the SK, this cannot be definitively proven and "remains an open question" (Whicher, 1998a, p. 295).

While agreement between Sāṃkhya and Yoga on the doctrine of the plurality of *puruṣas* remains open, there are some important definitive differences between the systems. For example, whereas Sāṃkhya refers to *prakṛti*, nature or material reality, as *acetana*, nonconscious, Patañjali does not use this term. Rather, Patañjali refers to *prakṛti* throughout his text as the seen, or the seeable. Also, whereas Sāṃkhyan theory holds to 25 principles of *prakṛti*, Yoga admits a 26th principle of God. The fundamental difference between the schools, however, is one of focus (Bryant, 2009). Whereas Sāṃkhya emphasizes through intellectual reasoning the metaphysics of *prakṛti* and *puruṣa*, Yoga emphasizes concentration and meditation, or the means to liberation. So although Yoga and Sāṃkhya are both soteriological, aiming to guide the practitioner to the realization of *puruṣa*, *Yoga Sūtra* seems to be based on Patañjali's direct experience, but the SK may be based on metaphysical speculation (Whicher, 1998a).

Whicher (1998a) has noted that in connection with the Epic Periods *Mahābhārata*, somewhere between 200 BCE and 200 CE, the Sāṃkhya and Classical Yoga schools were seen as distinct, having assumed separate identities from their common Vedāntic–Upaniṣadic base. Within the six orthodox schools of Hindu philosophy, they are classed separately. It follows, then, that the similarities between Sāṃkhya and Yoga do not confirm that the systems are the same, or even similar, epistemologically or ontologically.

Whicher (1998a) has noted that, "Early references to Sāṃkhya seem to indicate that pre-*Kārikā* Sāṃkhya . . . acknowledged *brahman* as the universal Self and regarded it to be the goal of life" (p. 51), lending the earlier iterations of this philosophy a close kinship to the monism of the *Upaniṣads*. However, classical Sāṃkhya is "extensively critiqued for jettisoning *Brahman* as the original source of reality (that is, as the source of both *prakṛti* and *puruṣa*)" (Bryant, 2009, p. lxiv). Because Patañjali's text does not expound upon a metaphysical theory, or refer to *brahman* directly, we do not know Patañjali's understanding of the relationship between *puruṣa* (*ātman*) and *brahman,* but there exists no evidence from which to surmise that Patañjali diverged from the shared presuppositions of the Vedāntic tradition on these matters (Bryant, 2009, p. lxiv).

Sāṃkhya is based upon the absolute transcendence of *puruṣa*. According to this philosophical school "*Puruṣa* does not descend into *prakṛti* but is merely associated with *prakṛti* in an undefined manner" (Taimni, 1961, p. 338). Gerald Larson (1969/2011) describes *puruṣa* ontologically within the Sāṃkhyan philosophical system as "a reality of a completely different order" existing "distinct from the manifest and unmanifest world" (p. 168). However, discerning the possible distinctions between Classical Sāṃkhya and Classical Yoga, Taimni (1961) has perceived the *puruṣa* of *Yoga Sūtra* as having "the dual role of *Draṣṭā* and *Kartā* (Spectator and Actor)" (p. 363), fundamentally differentiating Yoga from orthodox Sāṃkhya. The more refined distinctions between the schools become all important when attempting to understand how Patañjali and *Īśvarakṛṣṇa* see and understand the metaphysics of the world: are *puruṣa* and *prakṛti* separate and unrelatable; are they two aspects of one whole; or are they, ultimately, the same and indistinguishable? While *Īśvarakṛṣṇa's* SK ends in a radical dualism in which *puruṣa* and *prakṛti* have no relationship, there is open debate about Patañjali's vision and metaphysical understanding of them (Carrera, 2006; Whicher, 1998a).

Whicher (2001) has theorized that despite the Sāṃkhyan metaphysical orientation, in Yoga, the distinction between *puruṣa* and *prakṛti* may not have been intended by Patañjali as a metaphysical theory of truth. In Whicher's (1998a, 1998b) vision, instead of rendering pure consciousness and material reality as separate, Patañjali's Yoga endeavors to unite these two principles by correcting a misalignment between them. Other scholars argue that this interpretation is risky, coming about by "imposing meaning upon a text that was absent in its original formulation" (Burley, 2004, p. 232). One thing is for certain, even today, how consciousness becomes the physical universe is a problem still debated by philosophers of these traditions.

All speculating and philosophizing aside, as Whicher (1998a) has noted, "For one to grasp how Yoga philosophy can be lived on a practical level, one must understand how *puruṣa* and *prakṛti* relate to one in practical, experiential, and personal terms" (p. 57). Yoga is not a strictly psychological technique; it is physiological. Analysis, reasoning, and conceptual formulation alone do not bring about the embodied experience that Whicher, and a nondual reading of Patañjali, point to.

Other scholars try to clarify this conundrum of alliance between Sāṃkhya and Yoga by emphasizing Yoga's wide range of influences and inheritance. "Although the *Yoga-sūtras* are considered generally to be based entirely on *Sāṃkhya* they are best understood on the basis of both *Sāṃkhya* and *Vedāntic* doctrines," Taimni (1961) has explained: "there is really no justification for the arbitrary exclusion of *Vedāntic* doctrines in discussing the problems of higher *Yoga*" (p. 337).

Patañjali's Yoga soteriology aims, as does Sāṃkhya, to lead one to *kaivalya*. Like many other Sanskrit terms, in modern scholarship, there is a lack of consensus in understanding *kaivalya* in large measure because there is no English equivalent (Burley, 2004; Chapple, 2008). *Kaivalya* has been translated as "the state of *kevala*, or aloneness, onlyness, one's-ownness, not-connected-with-anything-else-ness" (Bryant, 2009, p. 457) and as "isolation-integration" (Zimmer, 1969, p. 280). While *kaivalya* is most often understood as liberation, Timalsina (2006) clarified that, "This term does not convey the same semantic resonance as *mokṣa*, which literally means liberation. The term *kevala*, having the suffic *valac* in the meaning *svārtha* (itself or oneself) from the base *ka*, is basically 'to rest upon oneself' " (p. 141n). In Sāṃkhya, upon *kaivalya*, the phenomenal world, having been seen, ceases, because there is no longer a reason for it to act. However, Swami Satyananda Saraswati (2008) emphasized the crucial significance of understanding this term in relation to Vedāntic doctrines – because *kaivalya* cannot, ultimately, be understood through explanation. "It can be had only by losing or giving up everything else. It is a state of absoluteness, of onlyness, or *advaita*. (p. 297). It is through the notion of *kaivalya* "that Vedanta comes into yoga" (p. 297). After Patañjali leads his readers to *kaivalya,* his text ends. He never elaborates on what *kaivalya* is or what qualities are subsequently manifest. It is perhaps in large measure because of Patañjali's silence that "there appears to be a great deal of confusion over the implications of *kaivalya* for the existence of the empirical world" (Burley, 2004, p. 223).

In summary, whereas Sāṃkhya ultimately holds pure consciousness and the phenomenal realm, *puruṣa* and *prakṛti*, as two ontologically distinct categories, this cannot be definitively stated about Classical Yoga. Patañjali's metaphysical ideas are not directly explained in the text. In Whicher's (1998a, 1998b, 2001) understanding, as well as in Chapple's (2002) and Saraswati's (2008), there is no evidence that Patañjali's opus ends in a radical dualism in which the phenomenal realm ceases upon *kaivalya*.

Yoga and Advaita

Both before and after Patañjali, there is argument in Hindu philosophy between dualistic (*dvaita*) and nondualistic (*advaita*) ways of perceiving the world. Although all philosophical systems that are grounded upon Upaniṣadic tradition agree that consciousness is the sole reality, what constitutes that reality is debated between these dualistic and nondualistic systems. Sāṃkhya is an example of a dualistic model, in which *puruṣa* and *prakṛti* are ultimately seen as unrelatable. As noted earlier, the shared dualistic metaphysics between Yoga and Sāṃkhya often cause readers to assume Patañjali's text resolves to a duality. One notable nondualistic tradition post-Patañjali that is worth considering to illuminate the possibility of the *Yoga Sūtra* being a nondualistic text is Advaita Vedānta (Carrera, 2006; Saraswati, 2008; Timalsina, 2009b). There is immense breadth and depth of thought in the various streams of the Advaita system; hence, a full discussion of Advaita is beyond the scope of this project. I only introduce Advaita here, as well as one major consideration that threads throughout the dualist–nondualist argument: the notion of *avidyā*, most commonly translated as ignorance.

The school of Advaita Vedānta was developed by Adi Śaṅkara a few centuries after Patañjali wove together the sūtras. The majority of scholars believe him to have existed around the eighth century of the current era; however, like Patañjali and many other historical figures in Indian philosophy, the date is often debated and can vary widely (Radhakrishnan, 1996). Considered one of the greatest thinkers of Indian philosophy, Śaṅkara was well versed in orthodox Brahmanical traditions and wrote commentaries on leading Hindu texts, including the principle *Upaniṣads*, the *Brahma Sūtras* and the *Bhagavad Gītā*. His works also reveal familiarity with Mahāyāna Buddhism (Mayeda, 1992). Most of the noncommentarial works attributed to him are debatable; however, the *Upadesasāhasrī*, or *A Thousand Teachings,* is considered his most prominent independent writing (Mayeda, 1992). A text dedicated to explaining the identity of *ātman* and *brahman*, the *Upadesasāhasrī* emphasizes that we obtain final release only through realization of this identity. To state this slightly differently, with the understanding that consciousness is the sole reality, the goal of the Advaita school is the realization of the self as *brahman.*

Adi Śaṅkara leads seekers mired in, and tired of, confused ideas of the intellect, to release from change and bondage. Release is awareness of discriminating knowledge, lucid perception, and realization of *brahman.* Notably, the sources and means of attaining valid knowledge are emphasized by Śaṅkara. Perhaps most significantly, he stresses *anubhava*, "direct insight," "direct access;" "not a movement around the object of knowledge but a vision from the inside" (Rambachan, 1991, p. 11). Like any of the Upaniṣadic masters, Śaṅkara directs the mind of the student. There are scholars who acknowledge the relationship between Vedanta and Yoga (Aruna, 2012; Saraswati, 2008), including Larson, who has suggested "that the core of Sankara's teaching is really a Vedāntinization of Sāṃkhya-Yoga" (Coward, 2002, p. 12).

Just as Yoga did not develop in a cultural vacuum, Advaita also developed like other philosophical schools through the dialogue between numerous advocates of a particular position and their opponents. One particular Advaitin doctrine notable in relation to the present study, in that it identifies "creation" (*sṛṣṭi*) with "seeing" (*dṛṣṭi*), is *dṛṣṭisṛṣṭi*. Because reality itself is identified as "seeing" (*dṛṣṭi*), the analysis of perception is significant to the *dṛṣṭisṛṣṭi* philosophy (Timalsina, 2009b). Given that Patañjali uses the terms *draṣṭṛ* (perceiver) and *dṛś* (seeing) interchangeably with *puruṣa* throughout his work, his influence, I believe, is notable in the *dṛṣṭisṛṣṭi* doctrine.

Although all advocates of Advaita confirm the nonduality of the self and *brahman*, as well as of subject and object, and do not admit a second entity, different Advaita models express varying ideas on phenomenal experience, or the world of appearances. There is no agreement between the different streams of Advaita on what constitutes the world. Some schools posit the world as the transformation of consciousness, others as false appearance, and some as the experience of only *brahman* in all modes of consciousness (Timalsina, 2006).

A popular question that often arises in relation to nondual thought is; if *brahman* is pure consciousness, changeless, and undivided, why does *brahman* appear as change, multiplicity, and fleeting consciousness? The Advaita philosophical system uses the concept of *avidyā* to account for the apparent difference between the self and *brahman* at the phenomenal level. Although all Advaitin derivations accept *avidyā* as a category, its nature is interpreted in multiple ways (Timalsina, 2009a). This is common in Indic philosophy. Between various philosophical models and schools, it is not unusual to have subtle and nuanced variations, although the terminology is shared (Radhakrishnan & Moore, 1957). For instance, there are multiple arguments between the various Advaitin models around where *avidyā* is located and what function it serves. Does it belong to the individual self or *brahman*? Who is really suffering if only *brahman* exists? How is it removed? How ignorance arises is a topic considered unresolvable by the human intellect. It is deemed futile in all Indic knowledge systems to speculate on its genesis (Bryant, 2009).

"*Avidyā* is the fundamental existential problem and the fundamental philosophical/theological problem within Advaita Vedānta," Kaplan has noted (2007, p. 178). A doctrine riddled with contradictions, it "is the most crucial problem which Śaṅkara left for his followers" (Mayeda, 1992, p. 82). As a result, questions in reference to *avidyā* – in particular, to its substrate – persist.

Through the doctrine of *avidyā,* an important connection between Classical Yoga and Advaita can be observed. As Timalsina (2009b) has noted, "Arguably, the application of *avidyā* in Advaita as a cosmic principle and a major defilement comes from *Yoga Sūtra* (p. 65). While most often translated as ignorance, *avidyā* at heart means a fundamental misunderstanding in the nature of reality. Chapple (2008) has given a comprehensive analysis of the term in which he notes *avidyā* as feminine, denoting "ignorance, nonwisdom, delusion; *a* (not) + *vidyā*, wisdom; from √*vid* (known)" (p. 163). Acknowledging wisdom as a form of pure vision, *avidyā* can therefore also be understood as misperception. By extension, because we are speaking about Patañjali's *darśana*, *avidyā* can also be understood to indicate an absence of vision. Absence of vision and misunderstanding are the most suitable translations of *avidyā* for the purposes of the present study.

Falling under the category of *avidyā*, Śaṅkara believed the spatiotemporal world to be an illusion; it is "mental constructions produced by ignorance, superimpositions on the only real existent, Brahman" (Bryant, 2009, p. 221). Advaita scholar Andrew Fort (1996) has explained that Śaṅkara argued "that one is bodiless while embodied when one knows that the Self is not the body and that embodiedness itself is a false notion" (p. 151). In contrast, Radhakrishnan (1996) noted that the world is not an illusion for Śaṅkara: "The world of everyday events and things is not ultimate reality, to be sure, but neither is it unreality. He has defended the reality of the empirical world; it finds its basis in the Absolute" (p. 610). Given that it is the mind that is transcended in the realization of *brahman*, notions such as nonduality and body are rendered as conceptual attributes upon transcendence. To state this slightly differently, direct knowledge of *brahman* transcends duality and nonduality, bodiless and embodied. Therefore, although in agreement that only the Self exists, the various attempts at expression beyond empirical terms present a tangled web of philosophical commentary. It is thus crucial to understand the core of the nondual teaching, that although study can guide us, it can also produce unnecessary agitation in the mind. Therefore, entering into the arguments should not be about intellectual interest per se. The direct experience of Self-realization is the aim.

In regard to the reality of the physical world, the Classical Yoga school may be distinguished from Śaṅkara's Adavita. As Bryant (2009) has explained, Patañjali confirmed that "the world in its essence – *prakṛti* – is real and eternal, and therefore the evolutes from this matrix, the world, are also in this sense real, albeit temporary and continually changing, mutating, and eventually dissolving back into their source" (p. 221). Therefore, on appearance, there may be a crucial distinction between Classical Yoga and Advaita. Is the material world real, or is it an illusion? Although this aspect of Śaṅkara's teachings is important, what is relevant for the present research is that continually trying to present *avidyā* in intelligible ways, the Advaitin's efforts to do so "raise at least as many questions as they answer" (Kaplan, 2007, p. 178).

As esoteric as these arguments around *avidyā* may sound, this term is a crucial concept to acknowledge because it forms the basis, or the concept, through which the appearance and experience of duality arises for many Indian philosophers. And it might be said that the consequences of the visions and the descriptions of any religion or philosophy may very well be the impediments, or release mechanisms, on our path of healing.

As mentioned, Patañjali's text is a practice, not an argument per se. Philosophy is not his main concern. Argument plays a secondary role if the text is looked at as a manifestation of Patañjali's direct experience. Therefore, as a methodology and not a metaphysical treatise, he most likely assumes that the answers to deep philosophical inquiry on topics such as duality, nonduality, and *avidyā* resolve themselves when *kaivalya* is realized.

That Patañjali's *Yoga Sūtra* can be read as nondual does not mean that Classical Yoga is compatible with Advaita Vedanta. I am not in any way implying here that Advaita and Classical Yoga are snuggled into the same bed. Advaita Vedānta is woven throughout the present research because

Patañjali's influence can be seen within the Advaita tradition. I must emphasize that although the nondual lens of Classical Yoga is the orientation in the study at hand, the lens is not an Advaitic lens per se.

Patañjali on consciousness–unconsciousness

Consciousness

Because Patañjali's *Yoga Sūtra* (YS) is a methodological treatise, not a metaphysical one, the properties and qualities of consciousness are for the most part not out rightly given. His ideas about consciousness must be inferred or understood through direct experience.

The methodology in Patañjali's text revolves around, and resolves to, a crucial discernment between two orientations of consciousness. For Patañjali, there is a discernible difference between pure consciousness, *puruṣa*, abiding in its true essential nature (YS 1.3), and consciousness when it is not dwelling there but rather assuming the modifications of the mind and its contents (YS 1.4). For the sake of simplicity, throughout this work, I will refer to consciousness in its true nature as orientation A and consciousness assuming the modifications of mind as orientation B.

In Patañjali's world, *puruṣa*, pure consciousness, is the fundamental ontological reality. Using the terms *draṣṭṛ* (perceiver) and *dṛś* (seeing) interchangeably with *puruṣa* throughout his work, an equation between the terms is implied. *Ātman*, frequently translated as the Self, is also a term used to denote *puruṣa* (Eliade, 1958/2009; Chapple, 2008).

The qualities inherent in *puruṣa*, or orientation A, are purity (YS 2.20), stillness (YS 1.2, 4.22), self-illumination (YS 4.19, 4.22), self-knowing (YS 4.18, 4.22), immutability (YS 4.18), eternity (YS 2.5), the ability to abide in own form (YS 1.3), power (YS 2.6, 2.20, 2.23, 4.34), and singularity (YS 2.25, 4.34). Implied in the quality of singularity is *puruṣa's* nondual nature or, very loosely speaking, pure subjectivity (YS 2.22). If one is not born able to recognize true essential nature or if this knowledge and ability is not brought about spontaneously, it can be gained by following Patañjali's Classical Yoga methodology (YS 1.19, 1.20, 2.26).

According to Patañjali, the subtlest movements of matter and mind can lead to pure consciousness, at the level of human awareness, being lost or thrown out if its true nature and into orientation B (YS 1.4, 3.35, 4.13). In other words, when the perceiving, seeing, and abiding of pure consciousness in its true essential nature do not occur, pure consciousness is being modified, often invisibly, by the mind and the senses (YS 1.4). The invisible modifications give rise to object awareness or to the Seen, in contradistinction to the pure subjectivity and Seeing of orientation A. To look at this from another angle, if the Seen is the focus, pure Seeing is concealed. Orientation A can therefore also be thought of as Seeing, and orientation B as the Seen.

The modified consciousness in orientation B results in quite different qualities of experience from those of orientation A, including change and transience (YS 1.4, 2.5, 2.13, 4.22), impurity (YS 2.5), *avidyā* (YS 2.3), egoic I-sense (YS 2.3), attraction (YS 2.3, 2.7), aversion (YS 2.3, 2.8), fear of death (YS 2.3, 2.9), suffering (YS 2.5, 2.15), confusion (YS 2.6), and conflation (YS 2.17, 3.35).

In addition to the aforementioned qualities of orientation B, there is also the quality of clear, uninterrupted discriminative knowledge (YS 2.26). Given that B is an orientation that changes, it can be deduced that at a certain change or position, in particular when clear, uninterrupted discriminative knowledge is present, orientation B is in direct alignment with orientation A (YS 3.44, 3.49). As already noted, Patañjali's text is a methodology that serves to guide one toward the ability to discriminate between orientation A and B. From this discrimination, the pairs of opposites cease to have any impact (YS 2.48), and one is then able to transition from experiencing the world through the modifications of consciousness and object awareness, or orientation B, into experience of pure consciousness and nonduality, or orientation A.

With precision, the essence of Patañjali's methodology is summed up early on in his text in the four words of its second line, where he stated, *yogaś citta vṛttis nirodhaḥ*, "*Yoga* is the stilling of the changing states of mind" (Bryant, 2009, p. 10). Where Bryant (2009) has translated *nirodha* as stilling, Swami Bharati (n.d.) has given multiple interpretive translations of this term: "control, regulation, channeling, mastery, integration, coordination, understanding, stilling, quieting, and setting aside of" (p. 4), indicating all that *nirodha* may entail. With a still mind, orientation A can be known and experienced. Without a still mind, orientation B prevails. To put it another way, pure consciousness has a tendency to disappear when mental impressions arise: The awareness of objects obscures pure consciousness. When there is no knowledge of the discernment between orientations A and B, and when we have contracted so completely around the mental impressions, *puruṣa* disappears completely from our awareness. To experience orientation A, the "control, regulation, channeling, mastery, integration, coordination, understanding, stilling, quieting, and setting aside of" (Bharati, n.d., p. 4), the mind is required. There is no alternative.

Although the Seer is pure consciousness, or the absolute knower, confusion arises in human experience when we assume that we can see clearly through the mind, when in fact, what we most often see is distortion brought about by mind patterns. A moving mind is not clear: it is engaged in activity brought about by deep-seated, and often invisible, patterns of energy. Clear seeing through the mind is a possibility according to Patañjali but only after the highest levels of *samādhi* (absorption) have been attained. Without the highest levels of *samādhi*, our everyday consciousness is perception through the gross and subtle contents of mind. This is to say that, although pure consciousness already knows and sees when abiding in its own true nature, through the thinking function, pure consciousness also cognizes and sees, but through this orientation, it does so through contents. Mind itself being one of the contents of pure consciousness. Patañjali stated this clearly in sūtra 2.20, *draṣṭā dṛśimātraḥ śuddho 'pi pratyayānupaśyaḥ*, "The Seer is pure consciousness but though pure, appears to see through the mind" (Taimni, 1961, p. 185).

Taimni (1961) has explained that "the Seer is pure consciousness, and not consciousness as modified by the vehicles." However, when manifested through a vehicle, such as the mind, pure consciousness "*seems* to be lost" in the content (*pratyaya*) that is present in the mind (p. 187). Taimni (1961) used a metaphor here to further explain Patañjali's thoughts: "Just as a mirror reflects or assumes the form of anything placed before it and seems to be that thing, in the same way the pure consciousness assumes, as it were, the form of the *Pratyaya* and appears indistinguishable" from the contents (p. 187).

Regardless of *puruṣa's* disappearance from the contracted perception of our awareness, orientation A has mastership over orientation B. In sūtra 4.18, Patañjali explained, *sadā jñātāś citta vṛttayas tat prabhoḥ puruṣasyāpariṇāmitvāt*, "The fluctuations of the mind are always known due to the changelessness of their master, *puruṣa*" (Chapple, 2008, p. 136). In addition to this knowing, the mind, and the mind's objects, exist for *puruṣa's* experience (YS 2.18, 2.23, 3.35, 4.24) and benefit (YS 2.23, 4.24).

Understanding that the mind and the mind's objects exist for *puruṣa's* experience and benefit, it can be inferred that because *puruṣa* knows itself, *puruṣa* knows what it is doing through the function of the mind and its countless impressions. In Patañjali's world, for pure consciousness, which is fully aware, knowing is (YS 4.31). So although the mind may be moving about to grasp onto objects of knowledge, pure consciousness already knows and doesn't need to move or grasp. One of the implications here is that the mind doesn't illuminate consciousness, but rather consciousness illuminates the mind (YS 4.19). That is to say, *puruṣa* perceives by its own "over-all and all-inclusive power of perception" (Taimni, 1961, p. 362). It does not need the intellect in order to perceive or to know.

From orientation B, it looks as if consciousness is evolving or that there are stages to the unfolding of consciousness, which is why Patañjali has stressed in sutra 1.4 that the Seer appears to take on the modifications of the mind. From orientation A, this notion of stages of consciousness is false because pure consciousness does not change or move. The mind moves. Matter moves. When the mind moves, it makes it appear to the indiscriminate as if consciousness is moving. In other words, because of its eternal essence, all along, through hours, days, years, or even lifetimes of mental movement, pure consciousness has simultaneously existed without changes or stages, knowing exactly what the mind was doing as it moved, grasped, and oftentimes suffered as a result.

Prior to discerning between orientation A and B and when experiencing the world through orientation B, the union of mental modifications and pure consciousness is founded on *avidyā*, absence of vision or misunderstanding (YS 2.24). It is a sort of mistaken identity. We are unaware that there are actually two orientations that are enmeshed. To say this another way, when there is enmeshment, there is no discernment between ontic reality and psychological experience. Patañjali did not explain what throws us out of true nature or how absence of vision arises.

As mentioned earlier, right at the beginning of the text in sūtra 1.2, Patañjali explained that when we stabilize awareness and still the states of mind, knowledge of yoga – and therefore pure consciousness – is realized. Towards the end of his text, in sūtra 4.22, he stated this in a slightly different way, *citer apratisaṁkramāyās tad ākārāpattau svabuddhi saṃvedanam*, "Knowledge of its own nature through self-cognition (is obtained) when consciousness assumes that form in which it does not pass from place to place" (Taimni, 1961, p. 420). Therefore, when the mind's reflected consciousness is stabilized, no longer passing between states, knowledge of the nature of pure consciousness arises.

Although orientations A and B are discernible, they are not independent because objects exist for *puruṣa's* experience. Furthermore, Patañjali stated that the conflation of pure consciousness with its objects is indicative of an alliance that serves the purpose of birthing the powers of both *puruṣa*, pure consciousness, and *prakṛti*, nature, including mind (YS 2.23, 4.24). Here Patañjali has implied that pure consciousness correlates to phenomenology, as well as to ontology and that orientation B is infused with coherence. Therefore, although no-thing exists from the perspective of true nature, that does not necessarily signify that nothing matters. Again, Classical Yoga affirms the reality of the world.

After the conflation between pure consciousness and the objects of its awareness is cleared and the relinquishment of all objects of awareness has been accomplished, pure consciousness is confirmed in itself and is able to rest in its pure power (YS 2.6, 4.34). No longer appearing as two, pure consciousness, its power, and its ability to see and perceive, established in itself, resolves as singular (YS 2.25, 4.34).

Unconsciousness

There is no term or reference to the unconscious in Patañjali's work. In Appendix I to his book *Yoga as Depth-Psychology and Para-Psychology*, Dr. Kenghe (1976) listed five references to *acitti*, the unconscious, from the *Rgveda Saṃhitā* (ca. 1200 BCE). "Surprisingly enough, we get a clear word connoting the concept of the unconscious in early Vedic literature," Kenghe (1976) noted; however, this word "became obsolete in subsequent periods" (p. 255).

What does surface throughout Vedic literature and throughout Patañjali's text is the notion of *avidyā*. It is possible that Patañjali, and other Vedic philosophers use this term instead of *unconscious* to be clear and consistent. In Upaniṣadic thought, consciousness is all there is. It is the contents of consciousness that can, however, be invisible, or unknown, to us in our human awareness. Because pure consciousness can never go unconscious but can only be obscured at the level of our human awareness, the term *unconscious* is not consistent with the ontological reality of *puruṣa*. This use of terminology may be highly significant in that the discrimination between orientations A and B can never take place until one fully understands that pure consciousness can never go unconscious.

Various schools take many contrasting positions around the concept of *avidyā*. Patañjali does not speak directly to the metaphysical nature of *avidyā*, only to its role in the process of Yoga. Because Patañjali defined *puruṣa* as pure and unchanging, the concept of *avidyā* will be reviewed in more detail in the following section on mind, a vehicle for pure consciousness.

Patañjali on mind–psyche

Citta (mind), which for Patañjali is a part *of prakṛti* (nature), plays a crucial role in Classical Yoga. Although Patañjali never explained what *citta* fundamentally is (Taimni, 1961), general indications regarding his thoughts on the mind's nature can be extracted from the text. His work describes how the mind functions and the methods one can follow to still it. Indeed, the major thrust of Patañjali's text is to teach yogis how to clear the distortions from the perceptual instrument of the mind. Through his vision, when we experience the world through orientation A, the mind is nondualizing, clear, and still (YS 1.3, 4.34), and when we have experience through orientation B, the mind fluctuates. These fluctuations can be understood as grasping and appropriating the world of objects, leading to distorted perception and suffering (YS 1.4, 1.30). To reiterate: the mind creates a dualistic worldly experience, or the appearance of that experience. However, the mind also facilitates its own liberation (YS 2.18, 3.09, 3.10, 4.34). It contains the seed of its own transcendence.

In this system of thought, all of nature, including mind, manifests through the interplay of three primary elements (*guṇas*) – activity (*rajas*), inertia (*tamas*), and illumination (*sattva*) (YS 2.18, 4.13). In combining, the *guṇas* can fluctuate in opposition, causing turmoil and suffering (YS 2.15), but exist for the purpose of experiencing the world (YS 2.18, 4.14).

As Vyāsa explained,

> Though distinct, these *guṇa-s* mutually affect each other. They change, they have the properties of conjunction, and disjunction, they assume forms created by their mutual co-operation. Distinct from each other,

> they are identifiable even when their powers are conjoined. They deploy their respective powers, whether of similar or dissimilar kind. When one is prominent, the presence (of the others) is inferred as existing within the predominant one from the very fact of its operation as a *guṇa*. They are effective as engaged in carrying out the purpose of the *puruṣa*.
>
> (as cited in Whicher, 2001, p. 22)

Patañjali described the functioning and activity of the mind through the concepts of *vrtti* and *saṃskāra*. *Vrttis*, or fluctuations, "refer to any sensual impression, thought, idea, cognition, psychic activity, or mental state whatsoever" (Bryant, 2009, p. 28), while *saṃskāras* are mental imprints or impressions "left by action done in the past, which conditions future action" (Chapple, 2008, p. 149). *Vrttis* and *saṃskāras* are both linked to *karma*, the laws of cause and effect, and *dharma*, characteristics and forms (YS 2.12, 3.22, 4.6, 4.12). For Patañjali, *dharma* corresponds to an irreducible substratum (YS 3.14) that "underpins past, present, and future" (Bryant, 2009, p. 324).

In Patañjali's world, the mental fluctuations, or *citta-vritti*, are the seat of the obstacles wherein the true nature of pure consciousness becomes obscured. The obscuration happens because the *vrttis* of the mind have a tendency to absorb, or appropriate, pure consciousness. Five types of *vrttis* exist, of which some are painful (*kliṣṭa*) and the others not painful (*aklistā*) (YS 1.5). The five, as listed in sūtra 1.6, are correct knowledge, error, imagination, sleep, and memory. Correct cognitions are based on right perception, inference, or through honest testimony from others who have knowledge (YS 1.7). Errors, or false knowledge, arise because of the incorrect apprehension of an object (YS 1.8). Imagining is the use of words when there is no actual object in existence (YS 1.9). Sleep *vrittis* have no mental content for their support (YS 1.10), and memory is the mental modification in which previous experiences are recalled (YS 1.11). Regardless of their painful or benign nature, all *vrittis* bind consciousness to the world of matter and must be stilled (*nirodha*) and reabsorbed in order to experience yogic union and *kaivalya* (singularity) (Bryant, 2009, p. 31). As Chapple (1990) has noted in his chapter of *The Problem of Pure Consciousness: Mysticism and Philosophy*, "The radical nature" of *nirodha* "cannot be overemphasized" (p. 64).

Patañjali named nine distractions of the mind that are obstacles to *nirodha*, or to shifting from orientation B to orientation A. They are sickness, dullness, doubt, carelessness, laziness, lack of detachment, misapprehension, non-attainment of any yogic stage, and instability in maintaining a level of practice once attained (YS 1.30). In case we are unaware how to spot or name these distractions in our self, Patañjali explained that we can know whether our mind is preoccupied or not by looking for the following symptoms: sorrow, depression, anxiety, and disturbed breathing (YS 1.31).

In addition to the mind's obstacles and symptoms, for Patañjali, five afflictions (*kleśas*) are associated with the mind, which are impediments to experiencing orientation A or from transitioning from B to A. These are *avidyā*, I-am-ness, attraction, aversion, and desire for continuity (YS 2.3). *Avidyā* is the origin of the other afflictions, which can be found in one of four states: dormant, attenuated or weakened, interrupted, or active and producing thoughts or actions (YS 2.4). If *avidyā* is the source, then *avidyā* breeds our sense of an egoic self and therefore duality, multiplicity, and the subject–object relationship. Issues around agency and freedom of action are not further developed here, leaving the question of free will open to interpretation.

Expanding the notion of *avidyā* more fully in sūtra 2.5, Patañjali defined four types of misunderstanding: "1) regarding that which is transient as eternal, 2) mistaking the impure for the pure, 3) thinking that which brings misery to bring happiness, and 4) taking that which is not-self to be self" (Bharati, n.d., p. 20). *Avidyā*, therefore, has to do with confusing something for something else.

For Patañjali, orientation A is preferred to orientation B insofar as yoga is fully known, understood, and embodied from orientation A only. Regardless of the whereabouts of the mind in orientation B, *puruṣa* always knows what is transpiring because *puruṣa* is unchanging pure perception. Because *puruṣa* is the master of the fluctuating mind, *puruṣa* is in some sense superior (YS 4.18). Hence, Patañjali uses *avidyā* as a descriptive device for psychological experience in orientation B, or an epistemological concept, with no bearing on the ontological truth of pure consciousness, orientation A. This is to stress that *avidyā* does not mean the absence of knowledge, but rather its obscuration at the level of human awareness where there is a perceptual and epistemological error.

I'd like to offer an exercise to try to elucidate this point further. Imagine that you do not know shadows are cast by blocking the sun: When you see a shadow disappear, you would not understand that phenomena moved in relation to a stable, self-illuminating source. You would have no way to describe the shadow because you do not know how it relates to either the phenomena or the sun. Shadows help describe what appears when the sun and phenomena interact, but they have no bearing on the reality of the self-illuminating nature of the sun. In truth, the shadow only appears *relative* to the way phenomena and a self-illuminating source interact.

At the personal level, *avidyā* can be seen when our identity becomes uncertain – when who we thought we were does not match up to the moment or the moment has shaken who we thought we were to the core. When moments of disorientation occur, it shows us that we are identified with patterns of our mind. We used thought to construct a reality, perhaps to stabilize and feel safe, but those thoughts are not a safety net because thoughts by nature shift. Another way to say this is wounding to our sense of self is a marker that indicates where *avidyā* lies in our mind. Although Patañjali clearly identified types of *avidyā* and the afflictions that subsequently surface, what he never described, however, is how *avidyā* originates.

As mentioned previously in the present study, *avidyā* is a concept extensively used, and fueling much debate, within Hindu philosophy. If *puruṣa*, or pure consciousness, defined interchangeably with *draṣṭṛ* (perceiver) and *dṛś* (seeing), is the ontological nature of reality, how can that reality contain absence of vision? Given that *avidyā* is the origin of the mind's afflictions in Patañjali's text, it obviously holds a very important place within his metaphysical schematic. However, because of the lack of direct philosophical discourse within the text, we do not overtly receive any answers to the seemingly paradoxical notion of the world being eternally and absolutely conscious yet experienced as quite the opposite of that through our everyday awareness in orientation B. We do know from Patañjali's text that *avidyā* is a form of misunderstanding, otherwise stated as the absence of vision of the true nature of reality. From this, we can assume that *avidyā* is solely associated with orientation B – because orientation A is the eternal, pure self, residing in true nature.

Despite the fact that our wounding is the source of psychological suffering, in sūtra 2.21, Patañjali stated that the Seen exists for the purpose of pure consciousness. Patañjali also stated in YS 2.23, *sva svāmi śaktyoḥ svarūpopalabdhi hetuḥ saṁyogaḥ*, "Having an alliance, or relationship between objects and the Self is the necessary means by which there can subsequently be realization of the true nature of those objects by the very self" (Bharati, n.d., p. 25). In other words, even the conflated union of *puruṣa* and *prakṛti* has a purpose. The Seen, or manifestation, including *avidyā*, plays a vital role in relation to pure consciousness. Because orientation A is eternal and absolute, whenever the mind is moving in orientation B, A knows it (YS 4.18) and is having a particular experience because of it (YS 2.21). In sūtra 2.24, Patañjali mentions again that it is *avidyā*, or obstructed vision, that does not allow us, through our human awareness, to see and understand this. The remedy therefore is the removal of *avidyā* (YS 2.25).

The only way to remove *avidyā* is to find the place where orientation A and B are in alignment (YS 2.26). To achieve this, we must see, perceive, and witness unflinchingly until discriminative knowledge (*vivekakhyāti*) of the two orientations is fully stabilized and known. In YS 2.13, Patañjali clearly stated, *sati mūle tad vipāko jāty āyur bhogāḥ*, "As long as the root [of the *kleśas*] exists, it fructifies as type of birth, span of life, and life experience [of an individual]" (Bryant, 2009, p. 198). The afflictions must become rootless, or seedless (*nirbīja*), to shift from orientation B and remain in orientation A. Then with the afflictions purified, the mind becomes completely stilled, and the transformation (*pariṇāma*) of the *guṇas* ceases because their purpose has been accomplished (YS 4.32). The process to follow is explored more deeply in a following section on transformation, but at its root, discriminative knowledge, *vivekakhyāti*, allows the embodied understanding that there is no-thing but pure consciousness. The power of pure consciousness is thereupon settled in its own nature (YS 4.34).

Whether clear or distorted, consciousness is seeing and experiencing through instruments of perception or vehicles (*prakṛti*). When this is completely understood, the singularity of consciousness is known, and grasping for objects through the dualizing mind, associated with orientation B, becomes obsolete (YS 4.25). Consciousness and its vehicles then resolve to their nondual state, and the Seer abides in its essential nature (YS 1.3, 4.34).

Patañjali on ego–Self

Ego

Ego, or the sense of a separate I-am-ness (*asmitā*), is one of life's five great afflictions, according to Patañjali. In sūtra 2.3, he stated, *avidyāsmitā rāga dveṣābhiniveśāḥ kleśāḥ*, "The lack of awareness of Reality, the sense of egoism or 'I-am-ness,' attractions and repulsions towards objects and the strong desire for life are the great afflictions or causes of all miseries in life" (Taimni, 1961, p. 130). In sūtra 2.4, Patañjali explained that the source of *asmitā* is *avidyā*.

As has been noted, when pure consciousness is not known at the level of our human awareness, it is due to *avidyā*, a state of misperception. For Patañjali, the egoic I-sense arises through misperception, in particular, when the Seer is confused with the instrument of perception (YS 2.6). Whicher (2001) has explained,

> *Asmitā* is that process in which *mahat* or *buddhi*, being the purest and most sattvic evolute of *prakṛti*, becomes a recipient of a "reflection" of pure consciousness. This reflected state of consciousness masquerading in the garb of *asmitā*, assumes itself to be Self/*puruṣa*.
>
> (p. 31)

Another way of saying this is that the reflection in the mirror takes itself to be the fullness of what it is reflecting. In the process of ownership, the reflection concretizes and blocks out the reality, and limited nature, of its function.

For Patañjali, seeing is eternal and all knowing. It cannot be eradicated, modified, or bound by conditions. It is pure awareness, pure consciousness. For him, that is the true ontic reality. Hence, the ownership of seeing and knowing by an "I" is an apparent reality, a psychological reality, in which there is experience of existence in its modifying, conditioning, and dualizing mode. It is this psychological reality, created by the psychological vehicles, that complicates "the expression of consciousness through the physical body" (Taimni, 1961, p. 144).

The instrument of perception is ultimately unable to authentically take ownership of the Seer no matter how much it tries, however, in the same way glasses can never be taken for the origination of sight (Bryant, 2009). Its persistent effort at trying to take ownership leads to continued suffering. Whicher (2001) has noted, *asmitā* "is an afflicted state of consciousness and identity that permeates and sustains our notions or sense of authentic identity as a bound 'entity' under the sway of *prakṛtic* existence" (p. 33). This means that egohood is an "I" that binds. However, in sūtra 2.18, Patañjali stated that the Seen exists for experience and liberation, and in sūtra 2.21, he explained that this is for "the purpose" of pure consciousness (Chapple, 2008, p. 170). Hence, both *prakṛti* and *puruṣa* are necessary. Although the "I-sense" is binding and is a cause of suffering, it serves a purpose. It is not an aberration per se. Furthermore, even though egohood is a psychological experience of false, or limited, identity, it has no bearing on the ontological truth of pure consciousness. It may be that at the level of human awareness, we have to learn what we are not in order to understand what we are.

As mentioned earlier, all of nature, including mind and the I-sense, otherwise known as *prakṛti* in this system of thought, manifests through the interplay of the three primary elements (*guṇas*) (YS 2.18, 4.13). *prakṛti* is considered extrinsic, even in its most subtle and invisible manifestation. Because of its extrinsic nature, in contradistinction to the intrinsic identity of *puruṣa*, it is therefore "classified as non-self" in Patañjali's system of thought (Whicher, 2001, p. 49). Because Patañjali's sūtras resolve to singularity, discrimination of self and non-self are most likely instructions presented as skillful methodology or functional process, *upāya*. They are not necessarily a metaphysical truth. Our ability to discriminate between the intrinsic and extrinsic, or the self and non-self, is essential in terms of healing the conditioned mind and eradicating dissatisfactory experience. This process of discrimination therefore allows the aspirant to develop clear vision and assume the power inherent in true nature.

For Patañjali, it is through the process of Yoga that our misidentification with I-sense, associated with the instrument of perception, can be removed. Pure consciousness, as the perceiver, can then be seen and experienced as abiding, unafflicted and objectless, in its true nature. But it is through *asmitā* where the appearance of choice arises and is therefore "pivotal in terms of determining the choice the mind will take, in terms of whether it wishes to direct its attention to *puruṣa* or *prakṛti*" (Bryant, 2009, p. 187).

As Taimni (1961) has expressed,

> Practice of *Yoga* is the most effective means of destroying *Asmitā* completely and permanently. As the *Yogi* leaves one vehicle of consciousness after another in *Samādhi* he destroys progressively the tendency to

identify himself with those vehicles and with the destruction of *Asmitā* in this manner the veil of *Avidyā* automatically becomes thinner.

(p. 147)

Self

In Indian philosophy, *brahman* is frequently translated as Self. Realizing self as Self is the goal of Upaniṣadic tradition and orthodox Hindu philosophy. Whereas certain Hindu traditions use *ātman* for the localized Self, Patañjali prefers the term *puruṣa* (Eliade, 1958/2009, p. 13; Chapple, 2008, p. 29). As Bryant (2009) has noted, "Patañjali himself does not refer to *Brahman*, the Absolute Truth of the *Upaniṣads*" in his text; rather, it is the commentators who "correlate *Brahman* and *puruṣa* as if this is a perfectly natural thing to do" (p. 363). So for Patañjali, the Self is *puruṣa*, pure consciousness, which has already been described in the earlier section on consciousness.

The ego–Self relationship

To reiterate: According to Patañjali, the egoic I obscures the Self. This obscuration leads to an experience of subject–object consciousness, misidentification, and suffering.

Patañjali on the transformation of human consciousness

In sūtra 2.28, Patañjali stated, "From following the limbs of Yoga, which destroy impurity, the light of knowledge arises, leading to discriminatory discernment" (Chapple, 2008, p. 172). Therefore, in Patañjali's path of transformation, one is not transforming pure consciousness; rather, one is learning to discriminate between consciousness that resides at rest in its true nature, orientation A, and consciousness that conforms to fluctuations of thought patterns, orientation B. To put it another way, Patañjali's YS elicit a transformation of the psychic organism, not the transformation of consciousness per se. Perception shifts by cleaning the instrument or perceiving function. Because pure consciousness is pure, purification plays a large role in Classical Yoga. Hence, the limbs of Patañjali's Yoga emphasize ethics and moral restraints. Patañjali lists five self-restraints (nonviolence, truthfulness, nonstealing, continence, and non-possessiveness) and five observances (purity, contentment, training the senses, study, and worship of God [self-surrender]). For Patañjali, purity, psychological order, and knowledge go hand in hand.

Discernment between orientations A and B is cultivated through Yoga practice – the practice of stilling the mind. To state this slightly differently with a bit more detail, to still the mind, the gaze must be stabilized and sustained through practice. Simultaneous to sustaining the gazing, or concentrating, one must become non-attached to the gross and subtle phenomena appearing, either externally or internally, to the senses (YS 1.15, 1.16). Therefore, in addition to a sustained and sincere Yoga practice, non-attachment aids in cultivating the ability to discern. These two elements work hand in hand – practice at sustaining the gaze and becoming unattached to the phenomena that appear to the gaze. Practice at sustaining the gaze eventually leads to a steady gaze and *samādhi*. While most commonly translated as meditative absorption, Whicher (2001) has translated *samādhi* as "placing, putting together" (p. 28). *Samādhi*, most succinctly, is the psychophysical integration of the self and Self. Concentration leading to meditative absorption, or the coming together of the subject and object, is the cornerstone of Patañjali's path. The more sincere and intense the effort, the faster one will experience states of absorption (YS 1.21).

Patañjali differentiates among different types of *samādhi*, in particular between *saṃprajñāta*, *asaṃprajñāta*, and *nirbīja*. Sūtra 1.17 informs that *saṃprajñāta* is a cognitive communion associated with forms, along with "reasoning, reflection, bliss, and sense of individuality" (Saraswati, 2008, p. 68). In *asaṃprajñāta* (YS 1.18), only latent impressions remain, and in *nirbīja*, which literally translates as seedless, one has dropped all content (YS 3.8). Again, this is to say that through continued meditative practice and the intention to cease the fluctuations in orientation B, one progresses from having one's awareness entangled with gross objects, to subtle objects, to no objects at all. By designating different types of *samādhi*, Patañjali emphasizes the refinement process, and through *nirbīja*, he denotes the complete discarding of any content, including images and symbols, whereupon orientation A is steadfast.

As mentioned in the earlier section on mind–psyche, Patañjali is very clear on naming the obstacles encountered during the process of learning to discern and what the consequences, or markers, that accompany those obstacles are (YS 1.30, 1.31). Means of stabilizing the mind include concentration on the breath (YS 1.34); concentrating on, and therefore becoming aware of, how we treat others, and cultivating certain responses to people's behaviors (YS 1.33); concentrating on the process of sensory experience (YS 1.35); concentrating on a state of lucidness or luminosity free from sorrow (YS 1.36); concentrating on a mind that is unattached and free from desires (YS 1.37); concentrating on the dream state in sleep, or even dreamless sleep (YS 1.38); or, in sūtra 1.39, Patañjali suggested that one can focus on whatever object or principle that is suitable, *yathābhimata dhyānād*. When the mind has come under control through the practice of concentration, the mind has the ability to be stable (YS 1.40). The process of stabilizing the mind prepares one to see through, and transition from, orientation B to orientation A.

On the path of Patañjali Yoga, yogis awaiting the realization of the light of knowledge are guided to minimize, or transform, *kleśas*, the colored or afflicted thought patterns. Sūtra 2.2 states, *samādhi bhāvanārthaḥ kleśa tanūkaraṇārthaś ca*: "[One engages in Kriyā yoga] for the purpose of cultivating samādhi and diminishing the afflictions" (Chapple, 2008, p. 121). Again, the five afflictions are *avidyā*, I-am-ness, attraction, aversion, and desire for continuity (YS 2.3), with absence of vision being the origin of the others (YS 2.4). When these afflicted thought patterns are subtle, they can be overcome by detaching from them (YS 2.10), in contradistinction to fueling and feeding them. Alternatively, when the afflictions are more potent, causing the mind to fluctuate more forcefully, meditation will aid in overcoming them (YS 2.11).

Patañjali's practices remove, or aim to remove, the obstacles or objects that block the light of knowledge and pure consciousness. Cleaning the instrument is a matter of clearing out the objects of perception. Following Patañjali's path, we use duality to transcend duality. We have to start where we are. Patañjali emphasized the importance of starting exactly where we are by opening his work with *atha*, now. In sūtra 1.1, he stated, "Now, an exposition of Yoga (is to be made)" (Taimni, 1961, p. 3).

The belief in the transformation of consciousness, in contradistinction to the experience of cleaning the intellect and transforming the lens, may in large measure be based on how we perceive time, in addition to, or as a correlate to, how we perceive reality. Bryant (2009) quoted the Hindu scholar Hariharānanda's description of reality as "that which exists, and existence refers to that which is present (that is, has presence)" (p. 399). The past and future are conceptual reality, in contradistinction to actual reality, as they have no present existence. But time is a concept or construct that is very embedded in how we as a species experience the world.

Perception in Yoga, therefore, is based solely on what is present. However, in Hindu cosmology, the past and the future are inherent in the present (YS 3.16, 3.17, 3.54): "The entirety of reality is compressed and encapsulated in each moment" (Bryant, 2009, p. 399). This is an esoteric point for sure and hard for the everyday mind accustomed to space-time to comprehend. As a means of trying to unpack it, it helps to refer to what Patañjali calls *aliṅga*, the transcendent core of *prakṛti*, *pradhāna* (YS 1.45, 2.19, 3.48). Indestructible, just as *puruṣa* is, *aliṅga* is capable of modification, through which it births the multidimensional universe (Whicher, 2001). As the issue on time and transformation is salient, it will be addressed more fully in Chapter 6.

In sūtra 3.55 Patañjali stated *sattva puruṣayoḥ śuddhi sāmye kaivalyam*, "with the attainment of equality between the purest aspect of sattvic buddhi and the pure consciousness of purusha, there comes absolute liberation, and that is the end" (Bharati, n.d, p. 53). With the attainment of equality, the intellect has been transformed into its purest state. The lens of perception has been cleared, and no more objects arise on the horizon. Transformation of the *guṇas*/mental modifications ceases (YS 4.32). The purposes of objectification have ceased for that yogi, and nonduality is now an embodied experience. Orientation B has resolved in orientation A. Pure consciousness, alone, resides in its true nature.

Patañjali concluded his text in sūtra 4.34 stating, *puruṣārtha śūnyānāṃ guṇānāṁ pratiprasavaḥ kaivalyaṃ svarūpa pratiṣṭhā vā citi śaktir iti*, "Ultimate liberation is when the *guṇas*, devoid of any purpose for the *puruṣa*, return to their original [latent] state; in other words, when the power of consciousness is situated in its own essential nature" (Bryant, 2009, p. 457). Notably, Patañjali represented the power of pure consciousness residing in true nature with the feminine term *citi-śakti*, where *citi* is a term for consciousness and *śakti* is a term for power. From a nondual orientation, it appears Patañjali was inferring that when the power of pure consciousness is steadfast in its own form, it is in creation – because it was creation all along.

In summary, the transformation of consciousness to Patañjali is akin to the movement of mind or matter (*prakṛti*), which occurs as experience for *puruṣa* (YS 2.21, 4.34).

Notes

1 Swiss-born psychiatrist Medard Boss (1965) visited India in 1956 and subsequently wrote *A Psychiatrist Discovers India*, in which he shared, amongst other experiences, what he learned regarding the translation of Sanskrit terms. I think it is worth noting in detail how Boss described what he learned from his teachers about *brahman:*

The supreme term "brahman" is derived from the root "braha." "Braha," however, means "to grow," "to open up," and "to let emerge." This is why it is so dangerous to translate "brahman" by "spirit." "Spirit" is still used to designate what is set over against the "physical," the sensuously perceptible realm. But the decisive point about Indian thought is that the term "brahman" is not allowed to indicate any such metaphysical splitting of reality. After all, a "universal one" can only be against the background of, and in contrast to, a "nothing" or a "duality" or a "plurality." But nothing can be set off against "brahman." For this reason, probably the only proper translation of "brahman" would be "the allowing the self-unfolding to grow" or "the opening – up which lets everything arise or come-into-being." Any simplification or abbreviation of these paraphrasic translations violates and falsifies its true meaning. (p. 125)

As Whicher (1998a) has noted in regards to *brahman*, "there is no possible way to exhaustively describe or define that supreme Reality": it must be realized to be known (p. 14). Whicher (1998a), has acknowledged how *ātman* and *brahman* are recognized as one in Hindu philosophy, where "the transcendent Source of the world is identical with the transcendent core of the human being" (p. 14). *Brahman,* here noted by Whicher as the transcendent Source of the world, is at other times translated as the ultimate absolute reality (Bryant, 2009) and is often thought to be synonymous with, or composed of, pure consciousness.

Brahman is a term that is neither masculine nor feminine but of a neuter gender (Chapple, 2008). To translate *brahman* as the absolute, or the ultimate absolute reality, in my mind, may immediately conjure up images of an anthropomorphic, masculine, world-transcending, Judeo-Christian God, leaving the door wide open for a tremendous misunderstanding of these Indian ideas. With the understanding that *brahman* and *atman* are one, the translation of both terms as pure consciousness is best suited for this study.

2 The numerous translations as well as accompanying commentaries of Patañjali's *Yoga Sūtra* are unique and offer different perspectives into Patañjali Yoga. I am not a Sanskrit scholar, so by looking at multiple translations, I hope that the very nuanced way this material is understood will be brought to the forefront. Two translations that have been important in this endeavor are Christopher Key Chapple's (2008) *Yoga and the Luminous: Patañjali's Spiritual Path to Freedom* and Swami Jnaneshvara Bharati's (n.d.) *Yoga Sutras of Patañjali Interpretive Translation*. Both offer complete translations, not only of each sūtra but also of each Sanskrit word. Other translations and commentaries used in this study include Carrera (2006), Taimni (1961), and Āranya (1963/1983). Edwin Bryant's (2009) *The Yoga Sūtra of Patañjali: A New Edition, Translation, and Commentary* is especially sweeping in scope and draws material from all the major historical commentaries. Bryant's text contains 195 sūtras and eliminates the redundant sūtra that is not included in all translations. Where the YS itself, without reference to a specific translator or commentary, is referenced throughout this work, I recommend Bryant's text as a guide.

3 The origin of the term and concept of *puruṣa* can be dated as far back as the Vedas (ca. 1200 BCE), where hymns to a monistic, cosmic *Puruṣa* are found (Timalsina, 2006). The *Ṛg* and *Atharva Vedas* use the term to express mortal or cosmic man (Larson, 2011). In the *Upaniṣads*, *puruṣa* is used synonymously with the more commonly used *ātman*.

In the translations used in this study, *puruṣa* is defined as Self, (Bharati, n.d.; Carrera, 2006; Whicher, 2001); Supreme soul, absolute awareness, (Āranya, 1983); soul, (Bryant, 2009; Carrera, 2006; Chapple, 2008); the ultimate Reality hidden behind the phenomenal world in its subjective aspect, (Taimni, 1961); and pure consciousness (Bharati, n.d.; Carrera, 2006; Jha, 1934; Saraswati, 2008; Whicher, 2001).

Chapple (2008) equated the term *puruṣa* with *ātman,* as was customary in the *Upaniṣads*, calling *puruṣa/ātman,* "one's higher self" or "true nature" (p. 3). In another section of his text Chapple gave a comprehensive analysis of the words used by Patañjali, when he noted *puruṣa* as a masculine term denoting "man, human, primeval man as source of everything, highest self; sometimes translated as soul or spirit; in Sāṃkhya, defined as inactive, witness, probably from √prī (fill, make complete)" (p. 148).

It is important to consider whether soul and self are far too conceptual and phenomenal in their Western connotations to be accurate translations of *puruṣa*. Larson (1969/2011) has emphasized, "*puruṣa* is not 'self' in the sense of intelligence, ego, or mind" (p. 12). Leading Indian philosopher Sarvepalli Radhakrishnan (1957) noted that *Ātman* with a capital A, "the ultimate as discovered introspectively," and *ātman* with a lower case a, "the individual principle in man," should not be translated as soul, although he was comfortable rendering them as Self and self (p. 39). Conversely, Bryant (2009) defined *puruṣa* as the "term favored by the Yoga school to refer to the innermost conscious self, loosely equivalent to the soul in Western Graeco-Abrahamic traditions." (p. 571).

Needless to say, finding agreement amongst scholars in regards to the translations of key Sanskrit terms into English is challenging. As scholar on Indian philosophical traditions Sthaneshwar Timalsina (2006) has remarked, "Speaking about Indian philosophy in English terminology invites obfuscation. . . . However, the rejection of all English equivalents leads to the impossibility of cross-cultural and trans-cultural discourse" (p. 22n). Along these same lines Taimni (1961) stated, "The language with which the *Sūtras* are constructed is an ancient one which, though extraordinarily effective in the expression of philosophical ideas, can lend itself to an extraordinary variety of interpretations" (p. x). He also noted that "the final justification for any interpretation is its conformity with the facts of experience" (p. xi). I contemplate whether rendering *puruṣa* as self or soul may lend itself to having Eastern ideas erroneously adapted to suit Western frameworks. The functions of intelligence, ego, and mind may be too synonymous with the independent, separate, Cartesian Western self.

4 In the multiple translations sourced for this research, *prakṛti* is defined as nature (Bharati, n.d.; Chapple, 2008; Saraswati, 2008; Whicher, 2001), Primordial Nature (Carrera, 2006), the creative, active aspect of reality, primary matter (Chapple, 2008), creative cause, subtlest material cause (Bharati n.d.), and psycho-physical being and its source (Whicher, 2001). I believe all of these definitions of *prakṛti* are interchangeable.

References

Āraṇya, S. H. (1983). Yoga philosophy of Patañjali Containing his yoga aphorisms with Vyāsa's commentary in Sanskrit and a transliteration with annotations including many suggestions for the practice of yoga (3rd ed., P. N. Mukerji, Trans.). Albany, NY: State University of New York Press. (Original work published 1963)

Aruna, A. K. (2012). *Patanjali Yoga Sutras: Translation and commentary in the light of Vedanta scripture*. Palm Desert, CA: Upasana Yoga Media.

Bharati, S. J. (n.d.). *Yoga sutras of Patañjali interpretive translation*. Retrieved from www.swamij.com/pdf/yogasutrasinterpretive.pdf

Boss, M. (1965). *A psychiatrist discovers India*. London, UK: Oswold Wolff.

Bryant, E. (2009). *The yoga sūtras of Patañjali: A new edition, translation and commentary*. New York, NY: North Point Press.

Burley, M. (2004). "Aloneness" and the problem of realism in classical Sāṃkhya and yoga. *Asian Philosophy*, *14*(3), 223–238.

Carrera, J. (2006). Inside the yoga sutras: A comprehensive sourcebook for the study and practice of Patañjali's yoga sutras. Buckingham, VA: Integral Yoga.

Chapple, C. K. (1990). The unseen seer and the field: Consciousness in Sāṃkhya and Yoga. In R. K. C. Forman (Ed.), *The problem of pure consciousness: Mysticism and philosophy* (pp. 53–70). New York, NY: Oxford University Press.

Chapple, C. K. (1994). Reading Patañjali without Vyāsa: A critique of four yoga sūtra passages. *Journal of the American Academy of Religion*, 62(1), 85–105.

Chapple, C. K. (2002). Living liberation in Sāṃkhya and Yoga. In A. O. Fort & P. Y. Mumme (Eds.), *Living liberation in Hindu thought* (pp. 115–134). Delhi, India: Sri Satguru

Chapple, C. K. (2008). *Yoga and the luminous: Patañjali's spiritual path to freedom*. Albany, NY: State University of New York Press.

Coward, H. (2002). *Yoga and psychology*. New York, NY: State University of New York Press.

Eliade, M. (2009). *Yoga immortality and freedom* (2nd ed.). Princeton, NJ: Princeton University Press. (Original work published 1958)

Fort, A. O. (2002). Liberation while living in the Jivanmuktiviveka: Vidryāraṇya's "Yogic Advaita." In A. O. Fort & P. Y. Mumme (Eds.), *Living liberation in Hindu thought* (pp. 135–155). Delhi, India: Sri Satguru.

Jha, G. (1934). *Yoga-darshana: Sūtras of Patañjali's with Bhāṣya of Vyāsa*. (2nd ed.) Freemont, CA: Asian Humanities Press. (Original work published 1907/Revised 1934)

Kaplan, S. (2007). Vidyā and avidyā: Simultaneous and coterminous? A holographic model to illuminate the advaita debate. *Philosophy East & West*, *57*(2), 178–203.

Kenghe, C. T. (1976). *Yoga as depth-psychology & para-psychology*. Varanasi, India: Bharata Manisha.

King, R. (1995). *Early Advaita Vedānta and Buddism*. Albany, NY: State University of New York Press.

Larson, G. J. (2011). *Classical Sāṃkhya: An interpretation of its history and meaning*. Delhi, India: Motilal Banarsidass. (Original work published 1969, revised 1979)

Loy, D. (1997). *Nonduality: A study in comparative philosophy*. Amherst, NY: Humanity Books.

Mayeda, S. (1992). *A thousand teachings: The Upadeśasāhasrī of Śaṅkara*. New York, NY: State University of New York Press.

Radhakrishnan, S. (1996). *Indian philosophy: Volume 2*. Delhi, India: Oxford University Press.

Radhakrishnan, S., & Moore, C. (Eds.). (1957). *A sourcebook in Indian philosophy*. Princeton, NJ: Princeton University Press.

Rambachan, A. (1991). Accomplishing the accomplished: The Vedas as a source of valid knowledge in Śaṅkara. Honolulu, Hawaii: University of Hawaii Press.

Saraswati, S. S. (2008). Four chapters on freedom: Commentary on the yoga sutras of Patañjali. Bihar, India: Yoga Publications Trust.

Schweizer, P. (1993). Mind/consciousness dualism in Sāṅkhya-Yoga philosophy. *Philosophy and Phenomenological Research*, *53*(4), 845–859.

Taimni, I. K. (1961). The science of yoga: The yoga-sūtras of Patañjali in Sanskrit with transliteration in roman, translation and commentary in English. Wheaton, IL: The Theosophical Publishing House.

Timalsina, S. (2006). *Seeing and appearance*. Aachen, Germany: Shaker.

Timalsina, S. (2009a). Bhartṛhari and Maṇḍana on avidyā. *Indian*, *37*, 367–382.

Timalsina, S. (2009b). Consciousness in Indian philosophy: The Advaita doctrine of "awareness only." New York, NY: Routledge.

Whicher, I. (1998a). *The integrity of the yoga darśana: A reconsideration of classical yoga*. Albany, NY: State University of New York Press.

Whicher, I. (1998b). Yoga and freedom: A reconsideration of Patañjali's classical yoga. *Philosophy East and West*, *48*(2), 272–322.

Whicher, I. (2001). *Patañjali's metaphysical schematic: Puruṣa and prakrti in the yogasūtra*. Chennai, India: The Adyar Library and Research Center.

Zimmer, H. (1969). *Philosophies of India* (J. Campbell, Ed.). Princeton, NJ: Princeton University Press.

Chapter 2

Jung

An overview of Jung

Swiss psychiatrist Carl Gustav Jung (July 26, 1875–June 6, 1961) was one of the founding fathers of depth psychology and the founder of analytic psychology. Like Patañjali he was a pivotal theoretician whose work was derived from an integration of theory and practice. He was born in Kesswil, in the Swiss canton of Thurgau, to Johann Paul Achilles Jung (1842–1896), a poor country pastor for the Swiss Reformed Church, and Emilie Jung (Preiswerk) (1848–1923), the daughter of a wealthy family from Basel.

Because much biographical information is readily available on Jung, it is in the best interest of the present study to focus on the cultural landscape during Jung's life. As historian Sonu Shamdasani (2003) has succinctly explained, "The formation of modern psychology and psychotherapy took place at a time of great upheaval in Western thought and culture, in which they were deeply interwoven" (p. 3).

General background

Jung's birth year, 1875, was towards the end of the Victorian era and the beginning of the new Darwinian science. To recount this cultural backdrop in brief: The Victorian era (1830–1900) came on the heels of the Industrial Revolution (1760–1850), a major turning point in our collective history and a time when human beings experienced enormous changes in their relationship to agriculture, manufacturing, technology, wealth, and society. The majority of our daily labor shifted from the fields to the factory. Inside the factory, we were unable to watch the sun move through the sky. No longer immersed in, and mirrored by, nature's daily routine, many became dispirited in their new environments.

The Industrial Revolution created a crisis that reduced humans to cogs in the factory's wheel. As a response to their predicament, Victorians constructed the "haven in a heartless world," the middle-class family that located the true self in a private or familial context (Zaretsky, 2004). In a world rendered heartless by the means of industrialization, and through the move away from agricultural communities where people were close to the land and the cycles of nature, the rift was being felt, if not clearly understood.

Additionally, in the European world of the late 1800s, there was a strong emphasis on male domination – whereby ambition, aggression, and toughness were praised (Ellenberger, 1970). Males and masculine energy were shaping the world; women and feminine energy were inferior. The air was one of authoritarianism. Society had many classes, from aristocracy and high bourgeoisie to the working class and the abject poor. Internationally, the white man dominated and colonized. "When attention was drawn to the rapid disappearance of primitive populations in various parts of the world, it was often explained as a sad but necessary consequence of progress or the struggle for life" (Ellenberger, 1970, p. 256).

Psychoanalysis and, subsequently, depth psychology arose in the Western hemisphere during the latter part of the Victorian era to address mental, emotional, and physical symptoms and suffering. Sciences of the mind, psychoanalysis rem and depth psychology attempt to grasp the human experience and to inquire into, and postulate theories about, issues such as autonomy, construction of the self, desire, and relationship.

One prevalent manifestation of the contradictions that lay within the purported understanding of autonomy and self-mastery during the Victorian era was hysteria, particularly in European women. Feeling overwhelmed by their efforts at self-control, hysterics encapsulated the cultural tensions that were characteristic of the end of the 19th century. Early pioneers in depth psychology who worked with hysteria, such as French philosopher and psychologist Pierre Janet, Austrian physician and neurophysiologist Josef Breuer, Austrian neurologist and founder of psychoanalysis Sigmund Freud, and French neurologist Jean-Martin Charcot, unearthed invisible systems of life in the shape of painful memories leading a parasitic existence outside the primary field of awareness. Freud felt as if hysterics, through splitting consciousness, were defending against feeling the depth of a traumatic wound.

In working with the crisis and sickness of the 19th century, the philosophical affirmation of the unconscious played a tremendously significant role in the development of Western psychiatry and depth psychology. Jung scholar Anthony Stevens (1999) has noted that the influence on European culture of von Hartmann's *Philosophy of the Unconscious* "would be hard to overestimate" (p. 12). As one of the cornerstones of modern dynamic psychiatry, by the 20th century, the unconscious appeared as the distinctive analytic contribution to personal life (Zaretsky, 2004).

Jung completed his medical training at the Burghölzli Psychiatric Hospital in Zurich under the direction of Eugen Bleuler, a pioneer in the study of mental illness. After the conclusion of his studies in December 1900, Jung became an innovator in experimental research into the unconscious. In his memoir, Jung (1961/1995) has made it clear how significantly the concept of the unconscious impacted his world. "My life is a story of the self-realization of the unconscious" (p. 17), he revealed. Like Freud's, Jung's work conceived the unconscious to be a natural object and aimed for the possibility of understanding the unconscious as an objective psyche. There was competition, however, around who could best map the terrain (Shamdasani, 2003).

Much of Jung's early work at the Burghölzli, in particular his research into word association, was done in parallel to Freud's work on dreams and traumatic reminiscences. In these word association tests, Jung would speak a vague and ambiguous stimulus word and calculate the time that elapsed until his subjects responded with a single word they associated to the stimulus. Jung found the speed and quality of the reactions to be less important than the way the autonomous behavior of the psyche disturbed the methodology. For Jung, there was something in us more forceful than the associations themselves. Jung discovered that the word responses and reaction times were not arbitrary: we don't choose by accident but instead retrieve something from memory. Our reactions are therefore not a result of free will but are predetermined to the smallest detail. In addition, Jung saw that our everyday life events are association experiments on a major scale, where the external world is akin to the stimulus words and to which we react according to what we are and have become. For Jung, association experiments were an empirical way of establishing unconscious complexes – core patterns of emotions, memories, and wishes in the unconscious, which are organized around a common theme.

Jung credited Freud for giving the unconscious its prominence in empirical psychology, yet Freud's orientation towards the personal, which went hand in hand with the individualism of the 19th century, did not satisfy Jung. Freud's view left no room for objective impersonal facts. In his research with individuals with schizophrenia at the Burghölzli, Jung frequently found reversion to archaic forms of association, and it was this objective fact that first gave Jung the idea of an unconscious that consists not only of morally incompatible wishes and conscious contents that have gotten lost but also consists of the mythological motifs of human imagination. In the view of the spiritually oriented Jung, Freud had not penetrated the deeper layer of the unconscious that is common to all humanity.

In tandem with Jung's dissatisfaction with the personalism emphasized by Freud was Jung's frustration with the reductive causalism of Freud's view. From Jung's perspective, Freud's view was oriented backwards, only concerning itself with where things come from and not where things are going. The teleological significance to psychological disturbances began to interest Jung at least as far back as 1899 when Jung studied and experimented with his 15-year-old medium cousin, Hélène Preiswerk, and to the subsequent publication in 1902 of his doctoral dissertation, *On the Psychology and*

Pathology of So-Called Occult Phenomena. By focusing on the teleological characteristics, Jung's work emphasized the compensatory function of the unconscious processes, holding that the unconscious is mainly composed of undeveloped and unknown parts of the personality that aim for integration in the wholeness of the individual.

The idea of the independence of the unconscious distinguished Jung's views radically from those of Freud, causing a schism that would eventually lead to their parting ways. Jung expressed that his break with Freud, at the end of 1913, began a period of inner uncertainty and a state of disorientation. He felt under constant pressure. Historian Henri Ellenberger (1970) described this time in Jung's life as a period of "creative or initiatory illness," a tremendous trial similar to that of healers in shamanic cultures (p. 39). Symptoms of Jung's creative illness included withdrawal from society, intense preoccupation with the mysteries of the human soul, emotional uneasiness, and self-imposed psychic exercises (p. 672).

From 1913 to 1917, during his period of uncertainty, Jung (1961/1995) wrote down his fantasies in what he referred to as the Black Book. "The years when I was pursuing my inner images were the most important in my life," he revealed: "In them everything essential was decided" (p. 225). In later years, he transferred this material to the *Red Book* (2009), where he tried an aesthetic elaboration of his fantasies. Never finished, the *Red Book* remained incomplete because, according to Jung, he had not yet found the right language and still needed to translate it into something else.

After his split with Freud, the early years of Jung's career were focused on harnessing and grounding the material garnered through his confrontations with the unconscious. His later years were then spent clarifying this material and demonstrating it scientifically. In Jung's (1961/1995) autobiography, *Memories, Dreams, Reflections*, he ruminated that the desire to understand must have brought about his birth because it was the strongest element in his nature. No doubt he sought to understand many things throughout his 85 years of life, and most certainly, as the founder of analytical psychology, Jung sought to understand the structure and dynamics of the psyche. It was not just his own understanding that drove him, however; Jung also shared that he did everything in his power to communicate to those closest to him a new way of seeing things. Being understood by others may have held a significant place for Jung psychologically and was why it troubled him so deeply that Freud could not hear, or see, what he was trying to articulate.

Regardless of their differences, Jung, in the end, held Freud in high regard. For Jung (1939/1966), Freud's *Interpretation of Dreams* was an "epoch-making work and probably the boldest attempt ever made to master the enigma of the unconscious psyche on the apparently firm ground of empiricism" (para. 64). He thought Freud remained true to his historical task and that he had fulfilled it. Freud, Jung believed, was an answer to the sickness of the 19th century.

Although Jung's work is often referred to as analytical psychology, denoting the emphasis on methods of analysis, at times he had difficulty deciding what to call his brand of psychoanalysis. In addition to hermeneutical psychology, Jung sometimes referred to his work as complex psychology, perhaps revealing the major significance complexes and complexities played in his opus. The term never circulated into wider circles, in particular with his English-speaking followers (Shamdasani, 2003), and analytical psychology, in addition to depth psychology and Jungian psychology, came to bear the stamp of his labor. By his own account, his work can be described as a general psychology that takes notice of the empirical material of pathology (Jung, 1973). In short, Jung's psychology is concerned with the alleviation of human suffering by means of confrontation, interpretation, and adaptation between conscious and unconscious processes. This psychological approach, Jung termed the process of individuation. Succinctly, individuation aims at the reconciliation of opposites to experience wholeness.

In addition to the aforementioned pioneers of the unconscious, Jung's other influences were broad. For example, German *Naturphilosophie*, art, religion, world mythology, parapsychology, Eastern philosophy, and quantum physics all factored into his thinking and theories. Highly influential European philosophers on Jung's body of work included Nietzsche, Kant, and Schopenhauer. Major collaborators included German sinologist and theologian Richard Wilhelm, Swiss researcher and alchemy scholar Marie-Louise von Franz, and the Austrian Nobel Prize–winning theoretical physicist Wolfgang Pauli. Although Jung's autobiography and enormous body of work do not mention his relationships to patients Sabina Spielrein and Toni Wolff, it is believed both women significantly influenced his psychological ideas. No doubt his wife Emma's role is also significant, although interestingly, and glaringly, underplayed.

Jung is credited as one of the first Westerners to note the importance of the East–West dialogue and to actively pursue it. Although Jung's interpretation of Eastern ideas is not always perceived as accurate (Clarke, 1994; Coward, 1985; Meckel & Moore, 1992), Jung's interest in Eastern thought presaged the post-colonial Easternization of the West (Shamdasani, 2003). Furthermore, the translation and widespread circulation of yoga texts historically paralleled the birth of depth psychology (Shamdasani, 1996).

Jung was exposed to Hindu culture prior to his professional life. Before he began to read, his mother read aloud to him from the *Orbis Pictus*, a children's book containing magnificent drawings from various religions, including Hinduism. Of this formative time, Jung noted that the illustrations of Brahma, Vishnu, and Shiva were an inexhaustible source of interest. That early interest was to resurface. His first two books, *Symbols of Transformation* (1912) and *Psychological Types* (1920), contain elements of research on Indian philosophy, in particular the *Upaniṣads* and the *Ṛg Veda*.

In 1920 in Darmstadt, Germany, Count Hermann Keyserling founded his School of Wisdom, where Jung, along with many other notable thinkers and visionaries of his day, including Richard Wilhelm, German novelist and Nobel Prize winner Hermann Hesse, and Nobel Prize–winning poet Rabindranath Tagore, participated in forums, providing a scholarly environment for Jung's explorations of Eastern thought (Shamdasani, 1996). In 1933, Jung continued his exploration of the links between Eastern and Western thought, along with Heinrich Zimmer, Martin Buber, and others, at *Eranos*, annual meetings held at the home of Frau Olga Froebe-Kapteyn in Ascona, Switzerland (Young-Eisendrath & Dawson, 1997/2008a).

In 1928, Richard Wilhelm sent Jung a copy of his translation of an ancient Chinese Taoist text, *The Secret of the Golden Flower*. Jung wrote a psychological commentary to the book, which was to be the first of several such East–West textual collaborations for him. In later years, he wrote forewords and commentaries for *The Tibetan Book of the Dead*, *The Tibetan Book of Great Liberation*, and *Introduction to Zen Buddhism*. Jung (1935/1989d) acknowledged how deeply these Eastern liberatory texts influenced him when he shared, for example, "For years, ever since it was first published, the *Bardo Thodol* [*The Tibetan Book of the Dead*], has been my constant companion, and to it I owe not only many stimulating ideas and discoveries, but also many fundamental insights" (para. 833).

The Collected Works, a 20-volume set, contain Jung's major writings. He was a prolific writer. He wrote out loud in the sense that he may have been working out his theories through his pen. Throughout *The Collected Works,* he frequently repeated, elaborated on, or contradicted his own ideas. The multiple revisions to certain texts, it was thought by his editors, reflected "new development of thought based upon increasingly fruitful researches into the unconscious" (Read, Fordham, & Adler, 1953, p. v). In regards to his publications, Jung (1961/1995) revealed to his secretary, Aniela Jaffé, "The way I am and the way I write are a unity. All my endeavors and my ideas are myself" (p. 14). This was a very intriguing revelation from a man who considered himself an empirical scientist, maintained he was not a philosopher, and claimed to steer clear of metaphysics and work with the objective psyche.

Jung described what he observed of psychotherapeutic activity. Because he attempted to look at things from multiple angles, the circulatory and contradictory nature of his thought was perhaps inevitable. Jaffé (1961/1995) noted how Jung "was constantly defining his concepts in new and different ways, for an ultimate definition, he felt, was not possible. He thought it wise to let the inexplicable elements that always clung to psychic realities remain as riddles and mysteries" (p. 16). As Jung himself confessed, he had not found the right language. As a result, Jung never summarized his ideas and never authored a comprehensive text that condensed his body of work.

In summary, as Jung wrestled with cultural and societal ideologies, as well as with his own and his patients' confrontations with the unconscious, he considered a host of theories, theorists, and psychic phenomena. For the purposes of this research project, there are two worldviews in particular worth looking at more closely because they seem to have greatly influenced Jung, and subsequently, the fiber of his career: religion and science.

Jung and religion

Being a pastor's son, Jung grew up in the religious environment of the Swiss Reformed Church, a modern Christian reformed branch of Protestantism. As a schoolboy, Jung wrestled uncomfortably with his father's uncontested beliefs and his willingness to take Christian jargon for granted without having direct experience of the numinous.

Jung's (1961/1995) oft-recounted dreams of a phallus sitting on a golden throne and a turd destroying a cathedral were crucial experiences of his earliest years and consequently preoccupied him all his life. Jung was certain he had not invented these thoughts and images, and he noted how deeply the violent imagery upset and impacted him. Yet no one could answer his questions regarding the origin of the images. Nor could they answer his questions around the relationship between a loving God and a devil or an overpowering God with a terrifying will. Jung felt alone before God and in need of finding answers out of his own depths.

As Jung grappled with the paradoxes himself, with the people around him unable to offer answers or engage him in fulfilling dialogue, he continued to participate in church activities and to make every effort to believe without understanding, as he felt his father did. Religious concepts, for Jung, seemed to only be serving the purpose of sparing people the necessity of understanding God's will and therefore to, in some sense, block it. Jung felt strongly that neither belief nor listening to a preacher without truly understanding is enough. One has to know. In his effort to gain understanding, Jung grappled with deep questions. For instance, he asked, how can the Trinity simultaneously be a oneness and a threeness? Jung's religious skepticism grew throughout his childhood, with the church eventually becoming a place of torment.

Participation in his first Communion proved a pivotal influence in Jung's perspective of the church and his religion. His details of the incident, as he looked back on it in his final years, demonstrate clearly crucial elements of the path that was being carved out for him in his career. For Jung, the first Communion ceremony contained no trace of God. It was an empty ritual, merely filled with words. Amongst the others in attendance, Jung (1961/1995) stated that he noticed nothing of the vast despair, the overpowering elation, and the outpouring of grace that for him constituted the essence of God. He had also observed no sign of "becoming one with"

(p. 72). Consequently, Jung could not reconcile the Communion ritual with God as he experienced Him.

Deeply affected by the Communion's inability to affect change in him, this experience was a sort of final blow that served to sever both Jung's relationship to the church and his father. He felt saddened and defeated. At this tender young age, Jung didn't know how to bridge the abyss that had opened up between him and his father. Their religious understandings were too incompatible. Jung's religious point of view – which was the meaningful aspect of his relationship to the universe – disintegrated.

Feeling involved with something inexpressible, a secret he could not share, Jung set about knowing God on his own, outside traditional conceptions, to establish a relationship to Him. In particular, it was God's character and personality that Jung wanted to know. For Jung, everything depended on that because without that knowledge, Jung felt he could not establish a relationship. In his effort to discover God's personality, Jung (1961/1995) wrestled with what he saw before him and asked: "If God is the highest good, why is the world, His creation, so imperfect, so corrupt, so pitiable" (p. 75)?

As he kept his secret and began research into God's character and personality, his mother, perhaps uncannily, recommended he read Goethe's *Faust*. The text profoundly affected the teenage Jung, as he finally found someone who took seriously the devil's adversarial nature to frustrate the perfection of God. Jung (1961/1995) was confirmed in his intuitive knowing by Goethe's similar ability to see "evil and its universal power" alongside "the mysterious role it played in delivering man from darkness and suffering" (p. 78). Jung wished, however, that Goethe did not dismiss the devilish Mephistopheles by a mere trick. Jung felt the dismissal to be a theological device and a limitation on Goethe's part.

Drawing inspiration from Faust's philosophical nature, Jung was led to research philosophical discourse that tackled similar questions around the nature of God and good and evil. Immediately, he was confronted with the philosophical presentation of God through thought and theory. Whereas for Jung it was abundantly clear that God exists, he questioned how philosophers could work with God as only an assumption or an idea, which they can either arbitrarily call forth or leave aside. God was not a hypothesis to be discussed but a living, immediate experience for Jung. As he transitioned into adulthood and developed his career, Jung knew that, as a psychic factor, God is real and able to reach humanity, albeit in limited means. Fueled by the terrifying degree to which Christian civilization appeared hollow and unable to change our inner nature, Jung set out to answer his questions scientifically through psychology. For Jung, we all have immediate experience of the divine through moments of primordial communion, for example, in dreams, symptoms, and autonomous fantasy. However, Jung (1944/1953a) noted, "Too few people have experienced the divine image as the innermost possession of their own soul" (para. 12). Jung aimed his psychology to allow for direct experience of God through psychic process.

As Jung developed his psychology, he studied archetypes and world mythology rigorously to find empirical evidence of what he believed to be the unity and collective nature of the unconscious and its representations of God. He paid focused attention to how we relate to and are transformed by, our connection to intrapsychic images, which have the potential to act as a bridge between an utterly transcendent God and one capable of being experienced directly.

Jung worked throughout his career to comprehend the relationship of good and evil as well as how good and evil relate in, and to, the God-image itself. It was not only in what good and evil stand for in moral judgments that interested Jung; he also placed emphasis on our ethical conscience and the moral dilemmas we face when confronted with conflicts between incompatible duties. In perhaps one of his most controversial texts, *Answer to Job*, Jung (1954/1989a) stated, "To believe that God is the Summum Bonum is impossible for a reflecting consciousness" (para. 662). For Jung, God is asymmetrical and incomplete when seen through the doctrine of the *privatio boni*. God is lifted to impossible heights, and humans are crushed under the weight of sin. Evil, for Jung, became characterized as a mere diminution of good and thus, he felt, deprived of substance, represented only as the accidental lack of perfection. The relativization of good and evil is prominently threaded throughout Jung's work. For instance, Jung (1944/1953a) asked "whether in this very power of evil God might not have placed some special purpose which is most important for us to know" (para. 36), perhaps implying that we must move beyond judgment to take a more intimate look at evil.

Seeking after a new orientation, in the end, Jung placed evil in God. Denoting the archetype of the God-image as the Self, Jung's Self-concept designates the whole range of psychic phenomena, which is why it is able to contain both good and evil. Jung borrowed the term *Self* from Eastern philosophy because he didn't want his theories laden with the conventional ideas enclosing the Judeo-Christian God (von Franz, 1999, p. 369). Along these lines, Jung (1916/1953b) noted that his Self might equally well be called the "God within us"" (para. 399).

By transforming the God-image from the Summum Bonum to the Self, Jung moved further away from Christianity and aligned himself, not with Eastern philosophy but with alchemy. The Self symbol in alchemy is the lapis or stone, and, unlike the Christ symbol, is a combination of good and evil and matter and spirit. Because alchemy confronts the opposites, matter, and the feminine, all areas Jung believed needed more research and understanding, alchemy was seen by him as the complete myth.

Not content on moving his ideas forward through mysticism, Jung used the science of psychology as his canvas. Jung (1959/1978a) explained,

> I am well aware that this work, far from being complete, is a mere sketch showing how certain Christian ideas look when observed from the standpoint of psychological experience . . . my main concern was to

point out the parallelism or the difference between the empirical findings and the traditional views.

(para. 429)

As Shamdasani (2003) has noted, Jung's psychology is "intent on reconciling science and religion" and perhaps because of this intent is, in large measure, why "his work has met with endless controversy at every turn" (p. 2). But Jung continually claimed not to be constructing new religious truths through his work. Instead, Jung (1944/1953a) explained, his psychology "is concerned with the act of seeing" (para. 15) – seeing, in particular, psychic archetypes. Whereas the lens of religious belief would focus its sight on the imprinter, Jung (1944/1953a) aimed his scientific psychology to focus on and emphasize the *typos*, "the imprint – the only thing it can understand" (para. 20).

Jung and science

The roots of Jung's psychology can be found prior to his post at the Burghölzli Psychiatric Hospital. In medical school at Basel University, his first two student presentations, "On the Limits of the Exact Sciences" in November 1896 and "A Few Thoughts About Psychology" in summer 1897, strongly criticized materialist science and argued for a greater interest in metaphysics, especially the soul, which he conceived to be an intelligence independent from time and space (Ellenberger, 1970). Jung proposed: "The task of rational psychology is to demonstrate the existence of a soul" while invoking somnambulism "as an argument against the prejudices of materialism" (Ellenberger, 1970, p. 688). For Jung, reductionism and scientific materialism were behind the times. He believed psychology was *the* scientific discipline of note because it was not limited to a narrow understanding of objectivity: "it was the only discipline that could grasp the subjective factor that underlay other sciences" (Shamdasani, 2003, p. 15). The dance between objective facts and subjective experience can be seen throughout Jung's enormous body of work.

While Jung eschewed scientific materialism, he aimed to remain an empiricist. His metaphysical speculations largely disappeared after his university presentations and before his first publications (Shamdasani, 2003, p. 201). Because his was an objective psyche, the dualistic basis of science, whereby a subject can examine, or be in relationship to, an object, could still remain the framework within which he conducted his research – even if he did so more loosely than other scientists. In alignment with materialist science, Jung held that metaphysical claims need not be considered or disclosed. For example, Jung (1961/1995) believed that coining the term *unconscious* for scientific purposes allowed for a "dispassionate observation which makes no metaphysical claims" (p. 369).

In his efforts to grasp the subjective factor, Jung was greatly influenced by the work of theoretical physicist Wolfgang Pauli. Jung agreed with Pauli that scientists are "faced with the impossibility of eliminating the effects of the observer by determinable correctives" (as cited in von Franz, 1964, p. 382). For instance, Jung (1935/1985b) understood that there is no therapy independent of the doctor's personality. As he explained, "Surgery and obstetrics have long been aware that it is not enough simply to wash the patient – the doctor himself must have clean hands. A neurotic psychotherapist will inevitably treat his own neurosis in the patient" (para. 23). What is not clear is whether Jung applied this same outlook to theorists and the application of their worldviews to their theories, although Jung acknowledged the typology issue in the contrasting theories of Freud and Adler. In essence, Jung understood that when looking at the world through the lens of quantum physics, the objective understanding of phenomena was relinquished.

Jung (1916/1953b) revealed why moving beyond materialist science was imperative for his work when he discussed the archetype of the Self. Jung stated, "The idea of a self is itself a transcendental postulate which, although justifiable psychologically, does not allow of scientific proof" (para. 405). Jung's need to postulate the Self was derived from his desire to formulate psychic processes, which he believed occurred objectively, and by extension, were verifiable by observation. Jung claimed the hypothesis of the Self had the same value as the hypothesis scientists held about the structure of the atom.

Moving beyond materialism and intellectual formulation, it was myth, in the end, that appealed to Jung more than science. As Jung (1912/1976c) recounted in reference to his own confrontation with his personal myth:

> I was driven to ask myself in all seriousness: "What myth are you living?" I found no answer to this question, and had to admit that I was not living with a myth, or even in a myth, but rather in an uncertain cloud of theoretical possibilities which I was beginning to regard with increasing distrust. I did not know that I was living a myth, and even had I known it, I would not have known what sort of myth was ordering my life without my knowledge. So, in the most natural way, I took it upon myself to get to know "my" myth, and I regard this as the task of tasks, for – so I told myself – how could I, when treating my patients make due allowance for the personal factor, for my personal equation, which is yet so necessary for a knowledge of the other person, if I was unconscious of it? I simply had to know what unconscious or preconscious myth was forming me, from what rhizome I sprang.
>
> (p. xxiv)

Jung's psychological roots were in this way planted in the soil of a more primordial language – which he found to be a natural part of psychic process. Jung's career may, more or less, have been an attempt to bridge myth and science just as it was an attempt to link religion and science.

Jung found myth to be an indispensable intermediate stage between conscious and unconscious knowledge. He was drawn in by the deeper, collective layers of the unconscious, with their distinctly mythological character. Perhaps for this reason, Jung considered the classical mind to be wiser, as it was still saturated with mythology and less focused on materialism. In his autobiography, Jung (1961/1995) noted, "Myth is more individual and expresses life more precisely than does science. Science works with concepts of averages which are far too general to do justice to the subjective variety of an individual life" (p. 17).

Regardless of his more than rational inclinations and despite his seemingly wholehearted interest in religion and myth, Jung retained the lens of scientific empiricism throughout his career. A leap beyond objectivity and into, loosely speaking, absolute subjectivity remained both unappealing and out of reach.

Jung on consciousness–unconsciousness

Consciousness

When considering Jung's work, consciousness and the ego go hand in hand. For Jung (1920/1976a), "Consciousness is the function or activity which maintains the relation of psychic contents to the ego" (para. 700). For him, no consciousness can exist without an ego, a subject, to which the contents are related. Consciousness needs a center, to which something is conscious. He believed there can be no consciousness without someone there to say: "*I* am conscious." Jung believed it is the human capacity for consciousness alone that is the defining characteristic of our species.

For Jung, our immediate experience, conscious and known, is a reflected state. Jung (1961/1995) argued that the ego, and its capacity to consciously reflect, is of such evolutionary importance because it is only through the human capacity of conscious reflection that "the world becomes the phenomenal world" (p. 371). Without the human capacity of conscious reflection, in Jung's opinion, the world would not be.

In Jung's view, all ego-consciousness separates and is therefore isolated because ego knowledge only contains knowledge of particulars. In Jung's (1939/1980b) opinion, "Exclusion, selection, and discrimination are the root and essence of everything that lays claim to the name 'consciousness' " (para. 520).

For Jung, our conscious mind is "personal," yet in his view, consciousness does not create itself but wells up from unknown depths. Not only does consciousness awaken gradually in childhood but also each morning out of the depths of sleep. Discrimination of opposites, like the ego, is also a hallmark of consciousness for Jung. "This is the paternal principle, the Logos," Jung (1938/1980d) stated, "which eternally struggles to extricate itself from the primal warmth and primal darkness of the material womb; in a word, from unconsciousness" (para. 178).

In summary, for Jung, consciousness is a secondary phenomenon that needs the primary phenomena of psyche, in particular the human "I" sense, or ego, as well as the play of opposites, as it eternally struggles to free itself from unconsciousness.

Unconsciousness

In Jung's (1920/1976a) eyes, the concept of the unconscious is not a philosophical concept making metaphysical claims but is an *exclusively psychological* concept that covers all psychic contents or processes that are not conscious. Although he struggled with the term *unconscious* because he thought it gave the impression that the object was solely negative, the concept of the unconscious was for Jung a fact of revolutionary importance.

Comparing the unconscious to the atom, which is not indivisible, Jung believed the unconscious is not merely unconscious. He believed the unconscious must consist of earlier evolutionary stages of our conscious psyche. He believed that 'mana,' 'daimon,' and 'God' are synonyms for the unconscious in the sense that we know as little about them. In Jung's (1943/1976b) opinion, the unconscious is a highly complex phenomenon to which one single concept can never do justice – which is why Jung believed his theories differ from the other principle founders of depth psychology. Each school – Jung's, Freud's, and Adler's – focused on a different aspect of the unconscious, allowing for various conceptions.

Jung's (1939/1980b) psychology discriminates between a personal and a collective unconscious. The personal unconscious, often referred to as the shadow, includes incompatible tendencies or inferior traits of character: it personifies everything a person refuses to acknowledge about himself or herself, although it is always presenting itself upon him or her directly or indirectly. The contents of the collective unconscious are not personal in nature. These deeper images, Jung (1943/1989f) believed, "have a distinctly mythological character. That is to say, in form and content they coincide with those widespread primordial ideas which underlie the myths" (para. 944). Most succinctly, Jung's unconscious is an objective and collective psyche, which contains the sum of all psychic processes below the threshold of consciousness.

The relationship between consciousness and the unconscious

For Jung, as was noted earlier, our conscious mind is one-sided and personal. Outside of the sphere of the personal lie the natural processes of the unconscious. The unconscious maintains a counter position, which compensates the personal, one-sided nature of consciousness. Jung (1916/1953b) clarified his choice in using "the word 'compensatory' in contradistinction to the word 'opposed'" because, for him, "conscious and unconscious are not necessarily in opposition to one another, but complement one another to form a totality" (para. 274). The compensatory relationship, or partnership, that Jung envisioned between the conscious and unconscious, indicated to him that the unconscious is not simply acting contrary to the conscious mind but instead modifies it.

For Jung, the opposites clashing together in a compensatory way meant a raising of consciousness, and for him, it is in life on earth where this is to be found, seemingly, as our metaphysical task. Human destiny, in Jung's view, is to create more and more consciousness. In his view, it is through the conscious act emerging from the darkness of unconsciousness that humans take possession of nature by recognizing the existence of the world.

Not just a product of repression, the unconscious for Jung was also the creative matrix of consciousness. In addition to a matrix of consciousness, Jung also referred to the unconscious as the mother of consciousness, and consciousness, he believed, is in the pride of its youth – and unable to deny its mother. In a slightly different manner, Jung (1939/1980b) stated: "Consciousness grows out of an unconscious psyche which is older than it, and which goes on functioning together with it or even in spite of it" (para. 502). As he worked through this metaphor, Jung ruminated on the order achieved, just as, although unseen and uncontrolled by the mother, a baby grows inside the womb. Therefore, the unconscious must not be just an accumulation of chaotic instincts and images. Jung (1939/1980b) stated, "There must be something to hold it together and give expression to the whole" (para. 503). But the center would not be the ego because the ego is born out of the unconscious and into consciousness.

For Jung, the collective unconscious, with its primordial ideas and mythological character, is the Unknown as it immediately affects us. And Jung's work revolves around attempting to understand this Unknown. Jung (1934/1980a) believed, "Our concern with the unconscious has become a vital question for us – a question of spiritual being or non-being" (para. 51). Resolving this question of spiritual being or non-being is our human task and responsibility. We must become conscious of the contents that press upwards from the unconscious. And for Jung (1961/1995), the way we relate to these unconscious contents is vital. "It is by no means a matter of indifference what attitude the conscious mind takes" towards the contents of the unconscious, he explained (p. 233).

Towards the end of his 1916 essay *The Relations Between the Ego and the Unconscious*, which was revised and expanded in 1934, Jung (1916/1953b) stated, "I would not pretend to have formulated these answers with any degree of finality. I shall, therefore, be well satisfied if my essay may be counted as a tentative attempt at an answer" (para. 406). Upon Jung's passing, the crucial problem of the nature and essence of the unconscious process was still left unanswered.

Jung on mind–psyche

Jung often avoided the term *mind* because he thought it to be too restrictive and more or less identical to ego-consciousness and rational processing. He preferred the concept of *psyche* for his work. In Jung's world, psyche is a phenomenon in its own right. He described psyche as both the subject of knowledge and the object of the science of psychology. For Jung (1946/1972b), psyche was "the greatest of all cosmic wonders and the sine qua non of the world as an object" (para. 357). Jung believed psyche to be an irrational datum with innumerable facets that seeks an expression that will embrace its total nature. As part of nature, with an ancestry going back millions of years, Jung experienced psyche's enigma to be never-ending. Throughout his vast body of work, he never defined psyche or nature. Jung (1964) wrote: "We can merely state what we believe them to be and describe, as best we can, how they function" (p. 6).

Jung did not agree with the materialistic prejudice that explains psyche as a mere epiphenomenal byproduct of organic processes in the brain. For him, the connection between the psyche and the brain was undeniable. Whether psychic disturbances are of a psychic or physical nature, was, and still is, open to question. In Jung's (1928/1972a) opinion, treating the mind as an epiphenomenon is simply a brain-psychology and not a complex enough theory to bear the fruit he was after.

For Jung, psyche is not identical to consciousness because the psyche represents the totality of all psychic processes and contents, not just those related to the ego. In Jung's (1939/1989b) world, psychic entities can be conscious, or represented contents, only if they have the quality of an image. So an image, or an imagining, is interdependent with consciousness in his theory, and without it, "no consciousness could exist" (para. 889).

In Jung's world, psyche has a distinctive structure, just like any organism. Jung described the deeper structure and dynamics of psychic life through complexes and archetypes. For Jung, a complex denotes an image of a particular psychic situation that has a strong emotional accent and is incompatible with our normal egoic orientation. Jung (1934/1972c) explained, "This image has a powerful inner coherence, it has its own wholeness" (para. 201). Complexes originate with a trauma, emotional shock, or moral conflict, which splits off a bit of the psyche. For example, if we are abandoned in childhood, we may have a mother complex. Complexes surface in the present without any assistance from the conscious mind and can be controlled by the conscious mind only to a limited extent.

Where the complexes begin, the freedom of the ego ceases as the power and autonomy of a complex disrupts the ego as the center of the field of consciousness. When activated, the complex assimilates the ego, generating compulsive thinking and acting, resulting in a temporary unconscious alteration of the personality whereby one becomes identified with the complex. In Jung's view, we can suppress our complexes through effort and control, but we do not have the capacity to eliminate them. At the first suitable opportunity, the complex will reappear in all its original strength. If we try to assimilate the complex through ego-consciousness, it will eventually lead to a neurotic dissociation of the personality. This lack of ability throws doubt on the supremacy of the will and the unity of consciousness, revealing for Jung an unsettling picture.

While painful, complexes do not indicate pathology. For Jung, suffering is not an illness. Even though the deeper nature of the complexes remained unfathomable for Jung, he believed they are the royal road to the unconscious and the architect of dreams and symptoms.

Jung's (1934/1972c) word association research and the subsequent discovery of complexes unveiled, for him, the impossibility of investigating *isolated* psychic processes. Jung explained, "There are no isolated psychic processes, just as there are no isolated life-processes." And if there are, he noted, "no means have yet been found of isolating them experimentally" (para. 197). Although they are not isolated, as just mentioned, for Jung, complexes are dissociated, much like the splittings of the personality discovered by Janet and Morton Pierce – fragments of the psyche subsisting relatively independently of one another (Ellenberger, 1970).

"Complexes are very much a part of the psychic constitution," Jung (1934/1972c) said, "which is the most absolutely prejudiced thing in every individual" (para. 213). It is our human prejudice, for Jung, that does not allow for the full phenomena of psychic life to flourish. The validity of psychological observation is therefore limited to the constitution of the observer.

In Jung's view, at the heart, or affective core, of our complexes lie archetypes. As uniform autonomous elements of the unconscious psyche and *a priori* structural forms, archetypes are pre-existent to consciousness and condition it, in contradistinction to being conditioned by it. For Jung (1945/1980c), "They represent the unalterable structure of a psychic world whose 'reality' is attested by the determining effects it has upon the conscious mind" (para. 451). Etymologically, Jung (1944/1953a) explained, the word "type" is "derived from (Greek), 'blow' or 'imprint'; thus an archetype presupposes an imprinter" (para. 15).

Jung (1961/1995) stressed the importance of acknowledging that the archetypes do not in any way "represent things as they are in themselves, but rather the forms in which things can be perceived and conceived" (p. 380). They are ineradicable, unable to be grasped intellectually, and have a numinous quality that can induce fear.

Because they are in themselves irrepresentable, Jung interpreted archetypes as modes of psychic behavior, equivalent to the pattern of behavior in biology. Jung believed that archetypal forms are grounded on the instincts and are the psychic expressions or manifestations of instinct. Just as instinct is a highly significant descriptor for all other animals, Jung stressed that the fact that our conscious activity is rooted in, and derives its dynamism and ideational forms from, instinct is highly significant for human psychology. Archetypes are such an important aspect of his vision, Jung (1946/1972b) asserted, "The archetype as an image of instinct is a spiritual goal toward which the whole nature of man strives; it is the sea to which all rivers wend their way, the prize which the hero wrests from the fight with the dragon" (para. 415).

Archetypes, being of an instinctual nature, are considered to be organs of the psyche that at first have no specific content. Elucidating the irrepresentable nature of archetypes, Jung noted that, to the extent we can observe and experience them at all, archetypes – through an unconscious process that is invisible until it crosses a threshold into consciousness – manifest themselves only through their ability to organize images and ideas. They are patterns of behavior whose specific associations and memory images vary from individual to individual. Archetypes have mythological and etymological variants across epochs and cultures, but they can be found at all times, among all peoples. They are universal components of the unconscious psyche, which form a deeper stratum of a collective nature. Jung found archetypal patterns to occur in highly emotional conditions, and he thought they often seemed to be the cause of them.

Although Jung believed psyche to have a process that seeks its own goal independently of external factors, he also described a relationship of correspondence between psyche and outward images or creeds. For example, Jung thought that people who do not experience sacred images and their kinship with psychic structure encounter a spiritual loss. This relationship between sacred images and psyche is part of what Jung considers to be a "religious function" of the psyche. In his view, acknowledging the religious function carries significance. This is to say that, the emotional response we have to numinous events is a marker. Jung (1944/1953a) warned,

> So long as religion is only faith and outward form, and the religious function is not experienced in our own souls, nothing of any importance has happened. It has yet to be understood that the *mysterium magnum* is not only an actuality but is first and foremost rooted in the human psyche.
>
> (para. 13)

In Jung's world, psyche is the beginning and end of all cognition, and it needs to know the meaning of its existence. In his view, by developing the religious function, we learn the art of seeing.

Beyond his fascination with psyche, nature and matter were also important to Jung. Jung emphasized the significance of the human psyche's indissoluble union with the body. What science knows about this psychophysical relation is a problem in Jung's opinion and one that remained unsolved in his lifetime. He thought that we know infinitely more about the nature of the body than we do about the structure of the psyche. Through his research on synchronicity, Jung heavily weighed the probability that psyche and matter are two different aspects of one and the same thing because they are two main components of the same world. Jung posited the psychoid aspects of archetypes to denote when the psychic and the physical are no longer differentiated from one another.

Jung on ego–Self

Ego

For Jung, the ego is a content as much as a condition of consciousness and is also referred to as an ego-complex. It is this firmly knit ego-complex that represents our empirical personality and that constitutes the center of our individual field of consciousness. Serving a unifying function for consciousness, it appears to possess a high degree of continuity and identity, and it seeks to shut out the unconscious as much as possible. Therefore, it has an essence of limitation. In Jung's world, the ego is only one complex of the many that psyche contains; hence, it is not identical to the totality of the psyche. Jung, at times, referred to our immediate experience of this ego-complex as a reflected state. When contents cease to be reflected by the ego-complex, consciousness is modified in his view.

In Jung's (1954/1989e) vision, "The ego may be depotentiated – divested, for instance, of its awareness of the body – but so long as there is awareness of something, there must be somebody who is aware" (para. 774). In Jung's world, consciousness either without an ego or without contents is virtually unthinkable: for him, this would result in complete unconsciousness.

In Jung's world, the ego separates and discriminates phenomena. Jung (1946/1972b) believed, "The ego keeps its integrity only if it does not identify with one of the opposites, and if it understands how to hold the balance between them. This is possible only if it remains conscious of both at once" (para. 425). Because the opposites are seeking to achieve a state of balance in Jung's world, the ego is of evolutionary importance. Jung argued that when the whole and all of its opposites are considered – which includes conscious as well as unconscious occurrences – the ego becomes relativized, and at that point, the ego can no longer be the center of the field of consciousness.

Self

In Jung's work, the whole range of psychic phenomena, the unity of the personality as a whole, is represented by his concept of the archetype of the

Self, the subject of one's total psyche. The Self represents the whole human, which in addition to ego-consciousness also includes the unconscious. For Jung (1959/1978a), "The self is a *complexio oppositorium* precisely because there can be no reality without polarity" (para. 423). In his theoretical outlook, conscious and unconscious complement one another; they don't necessarily oppose each other. In Jung's view, the Self also seemed to be the point of reference for the unconscious psyche. For Jung (1916/1953b), "The beginnings of our whole psychic life seem to be inextricably rooted in this point, and all our highest and ultimate purposes seem to be driving towards it" (para. 399).

To Jung, the Self seems to be completely outside the personal sphere, yet is the God within us. For Jung, the Self is the archetype of the God-image. If it appears at all, the Self does so as a religious mythologem. Symbols for the Self appear spontaneously and range from the sacred to the profane.

Keeping what he believed to be the epistemically accessible and the ontically inaccessible apart from each other, for Jung (1916/1953b), the Self is a psychological concept and no more, "a construct that serves to express an unknowable essence which we cannot grasp" because it is transcendent, unavailable to our typical modes of comprehension (para. 399). In Jung's view, the possibility of our ever being able to reach even approximate consciousness of the Self is slim because there is an indeterminate and indeterminable amount of material in the unconscious that belongs to the Self's totality.

The ego–Self relationship

The ego as part, and the Self as whole, works theoretically for Jung because in his world, everything needs an opposite in order to exist. Without the opposites, there is nothingness. Hence, Jung (1944/1989c) explained, "The ego needs the self and vice versa" (para. 961). The Self, Jung thought, is the midpoint about which the true personality turns. But the ego must maintain some sense of autonomy in Jung's (1959/1978b) view because "It must be reckoned a psychic catastrophe when the *ego is assimilated by the self*" (para. 45). "The ego is neither opposed nor subjected, but merely attached" to the Self in Jung's (1916/1953b) vision (para. 405). He explained that the ego revolves around the Self much as the earth revolves around the sun.

Jung's discoveries about the Self and the ego–Self relationship were made during his own process of development. As Jung (1961/1995) recalled in *Memories, Dreams, Reflections*, he "had to abandon the idea of the superordinate position of the ego" because he "had been brought up short" when trying to maintain it (p. 222). Between 1918 and 1920, he began to see the goal of psychic development not as the ego but the Self.

More than just the subject of my consciousness – as the ego is – for Jung, the Self is an ideal entity that embraces the ego. In Jung's (1916/1953b) view, "The ego is the only content of the self that we do know," and without it "we can say nothing about the contents of the self" (para. 405). In the end, Jung believed that forming a clear picture of what we are as a Self was beyond our imagination. The ego, as a part, will never be able to comprehend the whole. For Jung, the Self eternally remains a superordinate quantity.

Jung on the transformation of human consciousness

For Jung, the unconscious is reality in potential: that which we don't know about ourselves today lies in potential in the unconscious, our affect a sign of the contents waiting to be illuminated by consciousness. With the effects of the unconscious heavily weighted, the foremost activity of Jung's psychology is the integration of unconscious contents into consciousness. Jung terms this process of confrontation between ego-consciousness and unconscious personal and collective contents – and the subsequent transformation of unconscious contents into conscious ones – the process of individuation. Throughout his work, individuation is referred to interchangeably by Jung as coming to selfhood, self-realization, or becoming whole.

In the transformation of consciousness according to Jung, the unknown independent collective unconscious is objectively regarded from the standpoint of the conscious "I." This is possible in Jung's view because the unconscious is not an encapsulated personal system but sheer objectivity, which is as wide as the world and open to the entire world.

"The immediate goal of the analysis of the unconscious," Jung (1916/1953b) taught, "is to reach a state where the unconscious contents no longer remain unconscious and no longer express themselves indirectly" (para. 387). This is to say that, instead of being possessed by our complexes, when we make them conscious, complexes become a function of relationship between the ego and the Self.

To get to the root of our complexes and rid ourselves of autonomous contents, in Jung's view, we become conscious of unconscious components as they appear first in the factual contents of our personal unconscious and subsequently in the fantasies of the collective unconscious. This is not necessarily easy because complexes are usually bound up with our fears and resistances. We hold them off at a distance. If we split them off, neurosis results. If we are compelled towards wholeness, however, we must make our way into the fear bound regions of the psyche and depotentiate the complexes. "The more 'complexes' a man has," Jung (1916/1953b) warned, "the more he is possessed" (para. 387). He believed complexes are overcome only when they are lived out to the full.

Jung's individuation process was influenced by the separation and synthesis of the psychic opposites in alchemy. Jung (1963/1977) recognized the *opus alchymicum* to be "symbolically understood as the process of psychic integration" (p. v). Furthermore, Jung's process of transformation rests on his belief in the teleological directedness of the psyche. "From one point of view the unconscious is a purely natural process without design," Jung (1916/1953b) stated, "but from another it has that potential directedness which is characteristic of all energy processes" (para. 386). Through active participation by the conscious mind, in Jung's experience, a purposiveness and a dialogue develop in the relationship between the conscious and unconscious. This is done through the relationship between the ego and the Self. As was noted earlier, in Jung's world, the ego is the subject and the center of the field of consciousness for an individual, and the Self is the subject of the total psyche, both conscious and unconscious contents. Through the dialogic process, the idealized ego releases its sovereignty, and the second psychic authority is no longer resisted. The contrary and objective feelings, fantasies, emotions, impulses, and dreams of the Self, although irrationally given, are no longer ignored. Through acknowledgment and engagement with the contents of the Self, the ego becomes both relativized and enhanced.

In Jung's (1912/1976c) view, we need to develop this relationship between our ego-complex and the unconscious contents of psyche because it is what we don't rationally know, the irrational factors, that "play the largest, indeed the decisive, role in all processes of psychic transformation" (p. xxvii). For example, it may seem rational to move with the masses and accept our consensus reality or the status quo, but separation from our instincts, who we truly are at our core, plunges us into conflict. In Jung's view, rather than uncritically participating in group traditions – for example, in one's family or culture of origin – individuation means giving prominence to our own peculiarity. It means "fidelity to the law of one's own being" where fidelity means "trustful loyalty" (Jung, 1934/1981a, para. 295). Individuation embraces our uniqueness, the vocation for which we are destined.

In Jung's view of the psyche, there are four functions: thinking, feeling, sensing, and intuiting. We each have a superior, two auxiliary, and one inferior function. Whereas the superior function is how we consciously approach the world, the inferior function is the least differentiated and is very much contaminated by the collective unconscious. For example, if we are predominantly a thinking type, our feeling function will be weak and undifferentiated. Hence, in the process of individuation, it is the inferior function that can open the door from the personal unconscious into the collective unconscious, offering us the opportunity to access deeper contents of the unconscious including the archetype of the Self.

As Jung (1939/1980b) described, "Conscious and unconscious do not make a whole when one of them is suppressed and injured by the other" (para. 522). Using a metaphor of warfare, Jung noted that both conscious and unconscious are aspects of life and should be listened to equally. Jung (1939/1980b) stated,

> Consciousness should defend its reason and protect itself, and the chaotic life of the unconscious should be given the chance of having its way too – as much of it as we can stand. This means open conflict and open collaboration at once.
>
> (para. 522)

The process of listening and developing a relationship is gradual in Jung's world. For him, self-knowledge frequently requires a lot of painful work over a long period.

In working with the unconscious, it is imperative that we remain open despite our fear because our fear of unconscious contents will impede our self-knowledge. Jung (1957/1970) observed, "Often the fear is so great that one dares not admit it even to oneself" (para. 530). However, Jung attempted to allay fears when he explained, "Fear that anarchic instincts will thereby be let loose is a possibility that is greatly exaggerated" (para. 534).

In the example noted earlier, for a thinking type, feelings must be accessed and integrated in order to proceed in the process of becoming whole. When thinking will so easily overtake the use of feeling, it will need to step aside and begin to collaborate with the body's feelings – even its fear. It is through this new dialogue between these opposite functions where something new begins to be born. Jung (1959/1978c) observed, "The shadow is on one side regrettable and reprehensible weakness, on the other side healthy instinctivity and the prerequisite for higher consciousness" (para. 402).

In other words, holding the tension of the opposites, for example, between our superior and inferior functions or between rational and irrational factors, is a way of mediating and transcending the opposites, or splits, which have the potential to cause conflict, in contradistinction to collaboration. Sometimes when the opposition is too tense, we need to surrender and suspend our will. Jung explained that the will does not operate when every motive has an equally strong countermotive. But the suspension is only temporary because when ego-consciousness is neutralized and inactive, the unconscious is active. This cessation of activity, or personal will, forces the energy of the opposites into a common channel. Then the standstill is overcome, and life continues in a reinvigorated fashion towards new goals.

How the balance between conscious and unconscious comes about is not predetermined like following a recipe. The process is different for each of us. We must listen and learn our own intrapsychic language. The constant for all is the process of dialogue between the conscious mind and the unconscious content through the various means of dream interpretation, active imagination, mandala drawing, and perhaps work with an analyst who has knowledge of the mythic dimensions and symbol making capacity of this process. Jung (1939/1980b) explained that knowledge of symbols is indispensable "for it is in them that the union of conscious and unconscious contents is consummated" (para. 524). Symbols that are produced spontaneously by the unconscious can be subsequently amplified by the conscious mind.

As we participate in this process of transformation, we must be careful and vigilant about how we view ourselves as conscious: Jung (1925/1981b) warned,

> We constantly overestimate the existing content of consciousness, and it is a great and surprising discovery when we find that what we had supposed to be the final peak is nothing but the first step in a very long climb.
>
> (para. 327)

Jung (1916/1953b) elsewhere cautioned, "If the ego presumes to wield power over the unconscious," the unconscious will react "with a subtle attack" (para. 391). Hence, the ego is to stay open and aware, to remain in dialogue with the Self, if the transformation is to result in wholeness. No contents can ultimately be spurned that ask for acceptance, or else they will recoil upon us the moment we want to go higher.

The task of becoming whole, in Jung's (1946/1972b) world, at times may seem herculean because "between collective consciousness and the collective unconscious there is an almost unbridgeable gulf over which the subject finds himself suspended" (para. 423). Perhaps the treachery lays in the fact that, in depth psychology, "We have no more knowledge of the various states and processes of the unconscious as such than the physicist has of the process underlying physical phenomena" (para. 437). If we follow the individuation process, we must truly trust the teleological nature of the psyche that Jung believed in. Yet he forewarned us about the potential enormity of the task. Jung (1946/1985c) stated, "The meeting with the collective unconscious is a fatality of which the natural man has no inkling until it overtakes him" (para. 470).

For Jung, the task of individuation is something imposed on us by nature and the recognition of our wholeness or completeness is a binding personal commitment to the task. If we don't recognize this natural process and if we don't willingly take it on, Jung believed the process happens to us anyway but in a negative form.

Jung's process of individuation was a vision larger than the amelioration of minor psychic ailments. Jung (1939/1980b) explained, "This rounding out of the personality into a whole may well be the goal of any psychotherapy that claims to be more than a mere cure of symptoms" (para. 524). In the end, through Jung's process of transformation, although the tensions of the psychic pairs of opposites may ease off, a painful sense of innate discord always remains with the united personality because in his view liberation from suffering, in this world, is and must remain an illusion.

References

Clarke, J. (1994). Jung and eastern thought: A dialogue with the orient. New York, NY: Routledge.

Coward, H. (1985). *Jung and eastern thought*. New York, NY: State University of New York Press.

Ellenberger, H. F. (Ed.). (1970). The discovery of the unconscious: The history and evolution of dynamic psychiatry. New York, NY: BasicBooks.

Jung, C. G. (1953a). Introduction to the religious and psychological problems of alchemy. In H. Read, M. Fordham, G. Adler, & W. McGuire (Eds.), *The collected works of C. G. Jung* (R. F. C. Hull, Trans., Vol. 12, pp. 1–37). New York, NY: Pantheon. (Original work published 1944, revised 1952)

Jung, C. G. (1953b). The relations between the ego and the unconscious. In H. Read, M. Fordham, G. Adler, & W. McGuire (Eds.), *The collected works of C. G. Jung* (R. F. C. Hull, Trans., Vol. 7, pp. 121–239). New York, NY: Pantheon. (Original work published 1916, revised 1934)

Jung, C. G. (1964). Approaching the unconscious. In C. G. Jung & M. L. von Franz (Eds.), *Man and his symbols* (pp. 3–94). New York: Dell Publishing.

Jung, C. G. (1966). In memory of Sigmund Freud. In H. Read, M. Fordham, G. Adler, & W. McGuire (Eds.), *The collected works of C. G. Jung* (R. F. C. Hull, Trans., Vol. 15, pp. 41–49). Princeton, NJ: Princeton University Press. (Original work published 1939)

Jung, C. G. (1970). The undiscovered self. In H. Read, M. Fordham, G. Adler, & W. McGuire (Eds.), *The collected works of C. G. Jung* (R. F. C. Hull, Trans., Vol. 10, pp. 245–305). Princeton, NJ: Princeton University Press. (Original work published 1957)

Jung, C. G. (1972a). On psychic energy. In H. Read, M. Fordham, G. Adler, & W. McGuire (Eds.), *The collected works of C. G. Jung* (R. F. C. Hull, Trans.) (2nd ed., Vol. 8, pp. 3–66). Princeton, NJ: Princeton University Press. (Original work published 1928)

Jung, C. G. (1972b). On the nature of the psyche. In H. Read, M. Fordham, G. Adler, & W. McGuire (Eds.), *The collected works of C. G. Jung* (R. F. C. Hull, Trans., 2nd ed., Vol. 8, pp. 159–234). Princeton, NJ: Princeton University Press. (Original work published 1946, revised 1954)

Jung, C. G. (1972c). A review of the complex theory. In H. Read, M. Fordham, G. Adler, & W. McGuire (Eds.), *The collected works of C. G. Jung* (R. F. C. Hull, Trans., 2nd ed., Vol. 8, pp. 92–104). Princeton, NJ: Princeton University Press. (Original work published 1934, revised 1948)

Jung, C. G. (1973). Foreword. In J. Jacobi (Ed.), *The psychology of C. G. Jung* (p. ix). New Haven, CT: Yale University Press.

Jung, C. G. (1976a). Definitions. In H. Read, M. Fordham, G. Adler, & W. McGuire (Eds.), *The collected works of C. G. Jung* (R. F. C. Hull, Trans., Vol. 6, pp. 408–486). Princeton, NJ: Princeton University Press. (Original work published 1920, revised 1960)

Jung, C. G. (1976b). Depth psychology and self-knowledge. In H. Read, M. Fordham, G. Adler, & W. McGuire (Eds.), *The collected works of C. G. Jung* (R. F. C. Hull, Trans., Vol. 18, pp. 811–819). Princeton, NJ: Princeton University Press. (Original work published 1943)

Jung, C. G. (1976c). *Symbols of transformation*. In H. Read, M. Fordham, G. Adler, & W. McGuire (Eds.), *The collected works of C. G. Jung* (R. F. C. Hull, Trans., Vol. 5). Princeton, NJ: Princeton University Press. (Original work published 1912/Revised 1952)

Jung, C. G. (1977). *Mysterium coniunctionis*. In H. Read, M. Fordham, G. Adler, & W. McGuire (Eds.), *The collected works of C. G. Jung* (R. F. C. Hull, Trans.) (2nd ed., Vol. 14). Princeton, NJ: Princeton University Press. (Original work published 1963)

Jung, C. G. (1978a). Conclusion. In H. Read, M. Fordham, G. Adler, & W. McGuire (Eds.), *The collected works of C. G. Jung* (R. F. C. Hull, Trans., 2nd ed., Vol. 9ii, pp. 266–269). Princeton, NJ: Princeton University Press. (Original work published 1959)

Jung, C. G. (1978b). The self. In H. Read, M. Fordham, G. Adler, & W. McGuire (Eds.), *The collected works of C. G. Jung* (R. F. C. Hull, Trans., 2nd ed., Vol. 9ii, pp. 23–35). Princeton, NJ: Princeton University Press.

Jung, C. G. (1978c). The structure and dynamics of the self. In H. Read, M. Fordham, G. Adler, & W. McGuire (Eds.), *The collected works of C. G. Jung* (R. F. C. Hull, Trans., 2nd ed., Vol. 9ii, pp. 222–265). Princeton, NJ: Princeton University Press. (Original work published 1959)

Jung, C. G. (1980a). Archetypes of the collective unconscious. In H. Read, M. Fordham, G. Adler, & W. McGuire (Eds.), *The collected works of C. G. Jung* (R. F. C. Hull, Trans., 2nd ed., Vol. 9i, pp. 3–41). Princeton, NJ: Princeton University Press. (Original work published 1934, revised 1954)

Jung, C. G. (1980b). Conscious, unconscious, and individuation In H. Read, M. Fordham, G. Adler, & W. McGuire (Eds.), *The collected works of C. G. Jung* (R. F. C. Hull, Trans., 2nd ed., Vol. 9i, pp. 275–289). Princeton, NJ: Princeton University Press. (Original work published 1939)

Jung, C. G. (1980c). The phenomenology of the spirit in fairytales. In H. Read, M. Fordham, G. Adler, & W. McGuire (Eds.), *The collected works of C. G. Jung* (R. F. C. Hull, Trans., 2nd ed., Vol. 9i, pp. 207–254). Princeton, NJ: Princeton University Press. (Original work published 1945)

Jung, C. G. (1980d). Psychological aspects of the mother archetype. In H. Read, M. Fordham, G. Adler, & W. McGuire (Eds.), *The collected works of C. G. Jung* (R. F. C. Hull, Trans., 2nd ed., Vol. 9i, pp. 75–110). Princeton, NJ: Princeton University Press. (Original work published 1938, revised)

Jung, C. G. (1981a). The development of personality. In H. Read, M. Fordham, G. Adler, & W. McGuire (Eds.), *The collected works of C. G. Jung* (R. F. C. Hull, Trans., Vol. 17, pp. 167–186). Princeton, NJ: Princeton University Press. (Original work published 1934)

Jung, C. G. (1981b). Marriage as a psychological relationship. In H. Read, M. Fordham, G. Adler, & W. McGuire (Eds.), *The collected works of C. G. Jung* (R. F. C. Hull, Trans., Vol. 17, pp. 189–201). Princeton, NJ: Princeton University Press. (Original work published 1925)

Jung, C. G. (1985b). Principles of practical psychotherapy. In H. Read, M. Fordham, G. Adler, & W. McGuire (Eds.), *The collected works of C. G. Jung* (R. F. C. Hull, Trans., Vol. 16, pp. 3–20). Princeton, NJ: Princeton University Press. (Original work published 1935)

Jung, C. G. (1985c). The psychology of the transference. In H. Read, M. Fordham, G. Adler, & W. McGuire (Eds.), *The collected works of C. G. Jung* (R. F. C. Hull, Trans., Vol. 16, pp. 164–323). Princeton, NJ: Princeton University Press. (Original work published 1946)

Jung, C. G. (1989a). Answer to Job. In H. Read, M. Fordham, G. Adler, & W. McGuire (Eds.), *The collected works of C. G. Jung* (R. F. C. Hull, Trans., 2nd ed., Vol. 11, pp. 355–470). Princeton, NJ: Princeton University Press. (Original work published 1954)

Jung, C. G. (1989b). Foreword to "Introduction to Zen Buddhism." In H. Read, M. Fordham, G. Adler, & W. McGuire (Eds.), *The collected works of C. G. Jung* (R. F. C. Hull, Trans., 2nd ed., Vol. 11, pp. 538–557). Princeton, NJ: Princeton University Press. (Original work published 1939)

Jung, C. G. (1989c). The holy men of India. In H. Read, M. Fordham, G. Adler, & W. McGuire (Eds.), *The collected works of C. G. Jung* (R. F. C. Hull, Trans., 2nd ed., Vol. 11, pp. 576–586). Princeton, NJ: Princeton University Press. (Original work published 1944)

Jung, C. G. (1989d). Psychological commentary on "the Tibetan book of the dead." In H. Read, M. Fordham, G. Adler, & W. McGuire (Eds.), *The collected works of C. G. Jung* (R. F. C. Hull, Trans., 2nd ed., Vol. 11, pp. 509–526). Princeton, NJ: Princeton University Press. (Original work published 1935

Jung, C. G. (1989e). Psychological commentary on "the Tibetan book of the great liberation." In H. Read, M. Fordham, G. Adler, & W. McGuire (Eds.), *The collected works of C. G. Jung* (R. F. C. Hull, Trans., 2nd ed., Vol. 11, pp. 475–508). Princeton, NJ: Princeton University Press. (Original work published 1954)

Jung, C. G. (1989f). The psychology of eastern meditation. In H. Read, M. Fordham, G. Adler, & W. McGuire (Eds.), *The collected works of C. G. Jung* (R. F. C. Hull, Trans., 2nd ed., Vol. 11, pp. 558–575). Princeton, NJ: Princeton University Press. (Original work published 1943)

Jung, C. G. (1995). *Memories, dreams, reflections* (R. Winston & C. Winston, Trans., A. Jaffe, Ed.). London: FontanaPress. (Original work published 1961)

Jung, C. G. (2009). *The Red Book: Liber Novus*. S. Shamdasani (Ed.). M. Kyburz, J. Peck & S. Shamdasani (Trans.). New York, NY: Philemon series & W. W. Norton.

Meckel, D. J., & Moore, R. L. (1992). Introduction: The dialogue between Jungian psychoanalysis and Buddhist spirituality. In D. J. Meckel & R. L. Moore (Eds.), *Self and liberation: The Jung/Buddhism dialogue* (pp. 1–8). Mahwah, NJ: Paulist Press.

Read, H., Fordham, M., & Adler, G. (1953). Editorial note. In H. Read, M. Fordham, G. Adler, & W. McGuire (Eds.), *The collected works of C. G. Jung* (R. F. C. Hull, Trans., Vol. 7, p. v). New York, NY: Pantheon.

Shamdasani, S. (1996). Introduction. In S. Shamdasani (Ed.), *The psychology of kundalini yoga: Notes of the seminar given in 1932 by C. G. Jung* (pp. xvii–xlvi). Princeton, NJ: Princeton University Press.

Shamdasani, S. (2003). *Jung and the making of modern psychology: The dream of a science*. New York, NY: Cambridge University Press.
Stevens, A. (1999). *On Jung*. Princeton, NJ: Princeton University Press.
von Franz, M. L. (1964). Conclusion: Science and the unconscious. In C. G. Jung & M. L. von Franz (Eds.), *Man and his symbols* (pp. 375–387). New York, NY: Dell.
von Franz, M. L. (1999). Jung's discovery of the self. In *Archetypal dimensions of the psyche* (pp. 364–387). Boston, MA: Shambala.
Zaretsky, E. (2004). Secrets of the soul: A social and cultural history of psychoanalysis. New York, NY: Vintage Books.

Chapter 3

Jung and Patañjali

Back to back

While Chapters 1 and 2 were stand-alone explorations of Patañjali and Jung, respectively, the present chapter, through comparative and critical study, introduces and explores areas of difference and similarity between their bodies of work. Jung's and Patañjali's ideas on consciousness, mind–psyche, ego–Self, and the transformation of human consciousness are examined.

Jung and Patañjali on consciousness–unconsciousness

There are essential differences between Jung's and Patañjali's approaches to consciousness. Whereas for Patañjali, pure consciousness is the ontic reality, for Jung, the collective unconscious is the basic reality from which consciousness is phylogenetically and ontogenetically a secondary phenomenon, inconceivable without an ego. To state this slightly differently, for Jung, separable and objective phenomena, in particular the psyche and the contents of the collective unconscious, emerge before consciousness. Whereas Patañjali's pure consciousness is self-illuminating, eternal, and absolute, Jung's ego-consciousness, which he also refers to as reflected consciousness, is akin to a byproduct, unintended yet seemingly inevitably produced, by the evolutionary development of psyche. Jung's consciousness is neither pure nor self-illuminating as Patañjali's is. Human consciousness is therefore given tremendous significance in Jung's view: The world becomes the phenomenal world because of the human capacity of conscious reflection. Comparing Jung and Patañjali back to back, Jung's model of consciousness appears both epistemological and epistemic, known to itself only through re-presentation.

Jung's view is both in line with and divergent from the ontology and epistemology of materialist and empirical science. While Jung (1961/1995) believed our knowledge of nature comes *only through science*, which permits an increase in consciousness, Jung cannot be described as a hard-core materialist because he believed the concept of averages with which science functions are too general and are not necessarily indicative of our individual subjectivity. Furthermore, he acknowledged that all events happen within one world and therefore possess an aspect of unity the statistical method has difficulty establishing. As a means to flesh out our individual beingness, Jung aimed to observe nature's operation without prejudice or disruption. He worked with feelings, intuitions, and sensations and noted psyche as an irrational datum. In the end, however, he put tremendous faith in the rational mind.

The post-enlightenment faith in the rational mind is on clear display when empirical science rests on the foundation that we can formulate our worldview by means of researching phenomena without any metaphysical assertions. Harold Coward (1985), author of *Jung and Eastern Thought*, has accurately observed that Jung, throughout his career, "repeatedly and obsessively denies any metaphysical claims," yet his research remains within a framework that rests on the basic assumption that the "collective unconscious constitutes an original psychic entity, on which rests the conception of man as microcosm corresponding to the macrocosm." Furthermore, "in this collective unconscious the libido strives toward the emergence of the divine self" (pp. 182–183).

It is the assumption that we can think and act without a metaphysical premise that indicates Jung's alliance, or attempts to be compliant, with the materialist science worldview. Materialist science believes we can construct accurate knowledge of our world without acknowledging any metaphysical foundation to that knowledge. Yet science to this day is still unable to locate the arising of mental phenomena in any distinct physical process. As Alan Watts (1971) noted in direct reference to Jung, "Unconscious metaphysics tend to be bad metaphysics" (p. 26).

Depth psychology is rooted in Western philosophies of the unconscious. Historically, and from the inception of the conception of the unconscious, the West has believed the everyday mind can be used to objectively comment on its own nature and subsequently cultivate a definitive understanding of reality. Again, it must be emphasized that Jung (1946/1972a) did sense this problem. As a psychologist, Jung's work undoubtedly weighed heavily in favor of subjectivity. Even so, it is important to illuminate the potential pitfalls of Jung's, albeit loose, alignment with empirical science. Jung (1946/1972a) stated, "Every other science has so to speak an outside; not so psychology, whose object is the inside subject of all science" (para. 429). With manifestation rooted in a collective unconscious, which needs human conscious reflection as much as our bodies need air, Jung can be seen to retain a dualistic bias that aligns with an epistemological way of knowing the world.

In contradistinction to Jung's objectivity and alignment with empirical science, Patañjali's work with objectivity and empiricism is temporary.

Patañjali's model uses reflective awareness and the subject–object distinction to portray dualistic worldly life as suffering and to mobilize the involution of all objects of awareness. Patañjali's model relinquishes objectivity to lay emphasis on *prajñā*, a feminine term defined as "wisdom, knowledge, insight" (Chapple, 2008, p. 150), which is gained neither through factual nor intellectual knowledge. In fact, *prajñā* is much more than factual or intellectual knowledge: *Prajñā* connotes a clear experience of the nondual instrument of pure perception. In sūtra 3.5, Patañjali stated that through the mastery of the three-part process of concentration, mediation, and absorption, *prajñā* shines forth. This thread of Patañjali's text further reinforces his point that the stilling of the fluctuations of the mind is imperative in order to experience pure perception. Instead of moving around objects of knowledge, we get a vision from the inside. The mind, when concerned with factual analysis, fabrication, and ideation, for instance, only gives us a model of reality. None of this is to say that both orientations A and B aren't necessary even if B is mobilized only temporarily or intermittently. Yet for Patañjali, subject–object knowledge – indeed, all empiric consciousness and epistemic states – must be completely assimilated and released for the ontic reality of pure consciousness to be known through direct experience.

In Indian philosophy, the example often given to elucidate the limitations of subject–object knowledge is the parable of several men and an elephant. Each man is blindfolded and asked to touch a part of the elephant. The man at the tip of the tail thinks he is touching a brush, the man at the foot a pillar, the man at the trunk a plow, and so on. Each has no idea of how to conceive of the part or the whole because they are only experiencing a part without relation to the whole.

Jung (1936/1989d) recognized yoga's ability to create a psychological disposition, which allows for *prajñā*, while acknowledging how the West finds itself in a dilemma of understanding because of its highly developed scientific and philosophical critique. Regardless of the Western dilemma and the challenges Jung consequently faced, he aimed to bring psyche's religious movements and mystical experiences within the realm of a contemporary scientific understanding. However, Jung did not accomplish these aims. Furthermore, although Jung envisioned a reality beyond scientific reduction, his work, in the end, never moved beyond the subject–object split. Whereas Patañjali enfolded mystical experience directly into science of knowledge, Jung missed this mark. This may be due in large measure to Patañjali's process of radical discernment, which results in the embodied knowledge of the union of pure consciousness and matter.

Pure consciousness and the intellect are discernible in Patañjali's model, and necessarily so. In sūtra 3.35, he stated, "Worldly experience consists of the notion that there is no distinction between the *puruṣa* self and pure intelligence, although these two are completely distinct" (Bryant, 2009, p. 364). By worldly experience, he means the experience of duality, in which consciousness is enmeshed with its contents resulting in subject–object perception and the obscuration of nonduality. To state this slightly differently, if the intellect appropriates consciousness, then pure consciousness becomes hidden and ontic reality epistemically unknown. Patañjali also explained in this sūtra, and elsewhere, that whereas the intellect exists for *puruṣa*, *puruṣa*, as the ontic reality, exists for itself. This is to say, psychological experience exists for the ontic reality. In Patañjali's world, the mind can obscure pure consciousness, causing absence of vision or a reduction in visibility, at the level of human awareness; however, as *draṣṭṛ* (perceiver) with a changeless nature, pure consciousness is aware of every move the mind makes.

For Patañjali, pure consciousness is immutable (*Yoga Sūtra* [YS], 4.18), neither evolving nor ever becoming unconscious. As Taimni (1961) has explained, "It is in some way which is incomprehensible to the intellect perfect, complete, eternal" (p. 195) – hence why there is no ontic unconscious or unconscious processing in his model. The text is not explicit on whether phenomena, including the mind, emerge secondarily, or co-arise with pure consciousness; however, looking at Patañjali through a nondual orientation, non-origination, *ajātivāda*, is implied (King, 1995). The relationship between *puruṣa* and *prakṛti* is beginningless and natural (Whicher, 1998a).

In Patañjali's world, there are no states of consciousness per se. No-thing needs to move in order to illuminate consciousness, and moving phenomena never alter the true nature of consciousness (YS 2.20). However, while acknowledging that pure consciousness is the sole reality, it can be said that states become associated with our human awareness when there is enmeshment of pure consciousness with dualistically active, and often bifurcating, psychophysical phenomena (YS 1.4).[1] Professor Lloyd W. Pflueger (2003), specialist in Classical Yoga philosophy, has described states of consciousness in Patañjali's model this way: "There are only two states of matter, manifest and unmanifest, and only two states of consciousness by default – consciousness of nothing and consciousness (through *buddhi-s*) of creation" (p. 77).

Patañjali understood pure consciousness to be eternal and absolute, with the human mind and body as instruments of perception, or vehicles for consciousness. Because pure consciousness isn't transforming in Patañjali's work, movement is acknowledged as the evolutes of *prakṛti*, the *guṇas*, in particular their smallest expression, *aṇu*. The slight movement of *aṇu* appears to take on a transformation of consciousness. This is the crucial discernment that Patañjali asked practitioners of yoga to make: there is a change in characteristics but not in "substance," so to speak. Again, with no unconscious, *acitti*, Patañjali pointed to *avidyā*, absence of vision, and *ajñana*, lack of knowledge, to explain dualistic and constrained worldly life. If one does not experience nonduality, it is not because one's being is unconscious: at the level of human awareness, our vision is blocked by phenomena, thereby inhibiting and/or distorting psychological perception. Remove the inhibition, and the view clears. Phenomenal consciousness comes to rest as pure consciousness. To state this another way entirely, Patañjali is crystal clear in regards to the differences between psychological experience and ontic reality.

It must be emphasized that Patañjali explained, explicitly, what one experiences through the subject–object worldview, and he never resorted to modeling the processing of contents in terms of conscious and unconscious. To help elucidate this point further, it may be useful to look at the nondual teachings of Advaita. In Advaita, pure consciousness simultaneously supports and transcends the three states of waking, dream, and deep sleep and is known as *turiya*. To help students understand *turiya*, Advaita teachers often point to the experience of deep sleep. When we are in deep sleep, we have no awareness of contents, but when we are awake, we know whether we are well rested or slept fitfully. There is a through line for the duration of the sleep process that keeps the bodily activity going and the subtle awareness of the quality of sleep available upon waking reflection. The subtle awareness is indicative that consciousness ensues throughout all states.

Because there is no pure consciousness for Jung, consciousness in his world does not have qualities of immutability, self-illumination, or self-knowing. His general model represents states of consciousness only, for example, ego-conscious and unconscious states, or waking and dreaming states. Notably, late in his career, in his work on synchronicity, the psychoid, and the *unus mundus*, psychophysical states of consciousness and unity were of great interest to him.

Jung and Patañjali on mind–psyche

The mind is a key component in both Jung's and Patañjali's work. Where Jung may focus on the structure and dynamics of mind, or what he prefers to call psyche, Patañjali lays particular emphasis on the mind's functional nature. In comparing their understanding of mind, similarities and differences can be seen.

With a fundamental function of cognizing objects, for Patañjali, mind is a complex phenomenon emergent from instinctual processes (Borelli, 1983). In his world, mind is all-pervading inasmuch as *puruṣa* and *prakṛti* are omnipresent, and therefore phenomenal mind is interdependent with other phenomena and pure consciousness. Patañjali established the interdependence of phenomena, or psychophysical reality, with pure consciousness in sūtras 2.23 and 4.24 when he spoke of their alliance. Specifically, he stated, "The 'contact' of the potencies of the 'owned' and the 'owner' is the cause of the apprehension of their respective characters" (Jha, 1934, p. 124), where the owner is a reference to pure consciousness, *puruṣa*, and the owned a reference to *prakṛti*, all of nature including the mind.

Because of the capacity of the mind to reflect, the nature of the mind is often referred to as reflective, or reflected consciousness, by commentators of the sūtras. "*Puruṣa* sees its reflection in the mirror of *buddhi*, say the commentators, and the mind mistakes this reflection in the mirror, which is distorted due to the transformations of the *guṇas*, to be the real self" (Bryant, 2009, p. 223). Vyāsa, the original, and perhaps to date most important commentator of the text, puts forth a reflective theory of knowledge (Borelli, 1983). However, Patañjali's text makes no direct reference to a theory of reflection.

A fair portion of the *Yoga Sūtra* elucidates the psychophysical reality, or states, that mental phenomena participate in. Most notably, the mind plays a role in creating the dualistic worldly experience of orientation B, which is binding, and associated with *avidyā* (YS 4.11). Limited and biased, or impure, are other ways to describe the dualistic worldly experience of the mind (YS 4.15). The mind in orientation B is engaged in a tripartite process of grasper, grasping, and grasped – grasping both gross (*savitarka*) and subtle (*savicāra*), internal and external objects. When the modifications of the mind and the distracting thoughts have weakened, the mind, like a crystal, clearly reflects whatever is presented to it (YS 1.41). A mind, cleared of any distortion, can reflect *puruṣa*.

Psychophysical worldly experience that is dualistic and bound, along with the means of liberation, is described in the sūtras through the concepts of *vrtti* and *saṃskāra*. To review: *vrttis* are mental fluctuations that absorb or appropriate pure consciousness; *saṃskāras* are mental impressions or imprinted programs that condition future action and obscure the true nature of mind. *Vrttis* and *saṃskāras* are both painful and nonpainful mental factors linked to *karma*, the laws of cause and effect, and *dharma*, characteristics and forms. *Vrttis* and *saṃskāras* lead to the experience of the constrained psychophysical states of orientation B. Until one begins to understand and discern psychic activity – in particular, attachment and aversion – the mind, *citta*, autonomously and compulsively engages the habitual tendencies, *vāsanās*, which are brought about through the primary imprints, *saṃskāras*. That is to say, imprints activating mental formations, resulting in repetitive motivational tendencies, are all aspects of the same psychological process.

Once discernment begins, mind can contribute to its own purification by unraveling biases and constraints through its ability to be focused, and one-pointed, on a symbol or object of knowledge. And perhaps most significantly, over and above its ability to remain one-pointed, the mind in Patañjali's world has the further capacity to loosen its grip on, and identification with, objects completely, including itself (YS 1.40–1.51). The ability to drop the bifurcating dualistic mind that uses images and symbols, or any object, in order to grip psychophysical reality, is the capacity of the mind to facilitate its own liberation (YS 3.9, 4.32).

In Patañjali's world, the heart is a way to gain access to the nature of the mind. In sūtra 3.34, he stated, *hṛdaye citta saṁvit*, "From Discipline converged on the heart, follows perception of the Mind" (Jha, 1934, p. 196). In the *Upaniṣads*, the heart is the abode of *puruṣa/ātman*. Furthermore, in Hindu thought, throughout the bodymind,[2] there are seven subtle psychophysical energy centers called *cakras*. The heart *cakra*, known as *anahata* in Sanskrit, translates as "unstruck." Using our vocal chords as reference, it is understood that no sound is made until the two chords meet. The same is true for any other sound in our world: sounds are made by striking two things together. So *anahata* stands for the sound that is made when two things are not struck. This is also referred to as the primordial sound of the universe. Bryant (2009) has noted that the heart *cakra* is "considered to be the seat of intelligence. Thus, both the *ātman* and *citta* are centered in the heart" (p. 364). Sūtra 3.34 perhaps exemplifies the importance of developing *prajñā*, in contradistinction to ordinary means of cognition, or subject–object knowledge. In Patañjali Yoga, as mentioned previously, factual knowledge, or knowledge as a mental state, is not the goal. So, although yoga's approach is psychological and epistemological, for Patañjali, in the end, ontic reality, in this case expressed as embodiment through the heart center, supersedes epistemic states.

Jung (1938/1980c) made a similar claim about the mind heart connection when he stated that "emotion is the chief source of consciousness" (para. 179). Also, in a letter of 1916 to a 42-year-old female client, Jung (1973) stated, "Your vision will become clear only when you can look into your own heart. Without, everything seems discordant; only within does it coalesce into unity. Who looks outside dreams; who looks inside awakes" (p. 33). Indeed, the value of our emotional and affective life is woven throughout the *Collected Works*. For instance, Jung researched love alongside religious factors and symbols of transformation. In reference to how love appears in Christianity Jung (1912/1976b) stated,

> Accordingly, love would seem to be no trifling thing: it is God himself. But, on the other hand, "love" is an extreme example of anthropomorphism and, together with hunger, the immemorial psychic driving-force of humanity. It is, psychologically considered, a function of relationship on the one hand and a feeling-toned psychic condition on the other, which as we have seen, practically coincides with the God-image.
> (para. 97)

Coming to terms with the feeling-value of psychic contents, in addition to their intellectual value, is an essential precondition for wholeness, according to Jung (1959/1978). In reference to alchemy, which was highly influential to his work, Jung (1946/1985b) noted, "The alchemists thought that the *opus* demanded not only laboratory work, the reading of books, meditation, and patience, but also love" (para. 490). For Jung, it is imperative that we forgo a purely intellectual attitude.

In Jung's world, psyche is primary and a phenomenon in its own right, containing all contents, both conscious and unconscious, not just those directly connected with the ego. In Jung's depth psychology, psychological structure and experience are, in the main, modeled through typological functions, complexes, and archetypes. To review: autonomous complexes are images of psychic situations that are hidden and are subject to the control of the conscious mind only to a limited extent. At the heart, or affective core, of our complexes lie archetypes, imprints. Archetypes "represent the unalterable structure of a psychic world whose 'reality' is attested by the determining effects it has upon the conscious mind" (Jung, 1945/1980b, para. 451). Jung's archetypes, or organs of the psyche, are seemingly instinctual and can create painful and nonpainful experience. Jung believed complexes to be highly notable irrational psychic factors, which lead, less like a royal road and more like a devious footpath, into the unconscious.

It is the archetype of the Self, or the archetype of wholeness, and the way in which ego-consciousness relates to it, which receives notable attention in Jung's (1959/1978) model. In his book *The Religious Function of the Psyche*, Lionel Corbett (2004) has emphasized the importance of understanding Jung's model of the Self correctly by stressing how Jung makes it clear "that the Self, or any archetype, is not the same as its intrapsychic image, which points to an otherwise inexpressible 'something' beyond the image itself" (p. 44). Jung maintained that the Self is ultimately unknowable, "paralleling Kant's claim that, in terms of epistemology, human nature is finite – it can never know 'the thing itself' – and the theological claim of Christianity that human nature is fatally flawed" (Coward, 2002, p. 83).

In his acknowledgement that ego-consciousness, complexes, archetypes, and the religious function are all aspects of the same psychological process, it is apparent why Jung (1934/1972b) thought that investigating "*isolated* psychic processes" (para. 197) was not possible. That the mind has no isolated psychic processes is one of the notable similarities between Jung's and Patañjali's work. Also, for both scholars, the mind can be orientated internally or externally, has a teleological function, and can be guided on a path of transformation. More specifically, Jung and Patañjali both emphasize the activity or fluctuations of mind in relation to psychic imprints. Jung represented imprints as archetypes, primordial forms, that have a collective nature. In contrast, Patañjali represented imprints through *saṃskāras*, which are individual in nature in the sense that they are linked to *karma*, the laws of cause and effect, and *dharma*, characteristics and forms. *Saṃskāras*, then, are a result of past and present action, which are to be engaged as particular to the individual. Furthermore, for Patañjali, these imprints must be rooted out completely. Therefore, in Patañjali's world, knowing one's past lives is imperative before reaching a clear and discriminating mind, just as it was for the Buddha.

While karma and reincarnation are explicit in Patañjali's work, Jung's (1961/1995) work only reveals his contemplation of these ideas. For Jung, the question of karma was obscure. Later in life, Jung gave more weight to reincarnation as a result of a personal dream of a deceased acquaintance, but he acknowledged that because of a lack of empirical proof, he was not "in a position to assert a definite opinion" about it (p. 351). In contradistinction to past lives, Jung (1961/1995) acknowledged and emphasized ancestral components of the psyche as inherited ideas from previous ages. "We are very far from having finished completely with the Middle Ages, classical antiquity, and primitivity, as our modern psyches pretend," he noted (p. 263). While Jung can accept ancestral influence, he only speculated about past lives and karma and therefore does not include them in his theories.

Although reincarnation is known and accepted in India, only recently has Euro-American culture begun research in this area – too recently for the results to have been noted and considered by Jung. However, because past lives are an area of distinct difference between Jung and Patañjali and because they are of such importance to Patañjali's model (YS 2.39, 3.54, 4.12), the recent research is significant to note here. In the late 1950s, Canadian-born U.S. physician and psychiatrist Ian Stevenson began researching young children who seemed to have memories of a previous life (Shroder, 2001). Over the course of the next 40 years, Stevenson provided compelling evidence for survival after bodily death (Tucker, 2008). Resolute in establishing facts, his primary goal was "getting mainstream science to seriously consider reincarnation as a possibility" (Tucker, 2008, p. 41). Despite attention to detail and corroborative reports, his work, however, has been largely ignored by mainstream science. Roughly a decade before his death in 2007, Stevenson asked award-winning journalist Tom Shroder (2001), "How can scientists, professed to hold no dogma that reasonable evidence cannot overturn, ignore the volumes of reasonable evidence" (p. 15)? This is a question deeply relevant to depth psychology. Looking at the work of Stevenson, it does not appear that we lack empirical proof, although Stevenson himself professed not to "know the answer" to the phenomena he illuminated in his long career in parapsychology (Tucker, 2008, p. 42). To date, no orthodox Western psychology includes past lives. Kenghe's (1976) research, *Yoga as Depth-Psychology and Para-Psychology*, similarly revealed, "The modern theories of the unconscious do not go beyond childhood or racial inheritance at the most" (p. 48). Contemporary non-mainstream practices such as Holotropic Breathwork™, an experiential psychotherapy pioneered by Stanlislav and Christina Grof (2010), perhaps indicate the inadequacy of our mainstream models to invoke the integrated understanding and depths of healing that Buddha and Patañjali were pointing to. Grof has noted that past life experiences have occurred with extraordinary frequency in the Holotropic Breathwork™ sessions of his clients (Grof, 1998).

In addition to karma and reincarnation, there is a further point of divergence between Jung's and Patañjali's mental imprints. As noted earlier, in Patañjali's model, "The 'contact' of the potencies of the 'owned' and the 'owner' is the cause of the apprehension of their respective characters" (Jha, 1934, p. 124). Implied in this relationship is the knowledge of reality gained by *buddhi*, phenomenal mind. Hence, as part of the "owned," *saṃskāras* do play a part in understanding the nature of psychological experience. Yet ultimately, in Patañjali's world, the *saṃskāras* are understood as obstructions that must be completely removed – in order to have a clear lens of perception able to attain the fullest realization of knowledge. Resting in our true nature depends on it. By contrast, "for Jung it is through the shaping of the materials of consciousness by the archetypal 'memories' that knowledge of reality results" (Coward, 2002, p. 60). In other words, Jung's imprints are not understood as ultimately obstructing and knowledge construction is privileged. Therefore, Jung's archetypes, or psychic imprints, do not completely align to Patañjali's *saṃskāras*.

In a 1932 lecture on Kundalini yoga, Jung (1996) compared *saṃskāras* and archetypes this way:

> Our idea of heredity would be similar to the idea of *saṃskāra*, as well as our hypothesis of the collective unconscious. For the mind in a child is by no means *tabula rasa*. The unconscious mind is full of a rich world of archetypal images. The archetypes are conditions, laws, or categories of creative fantasy, and therefore the psychological equivalent of the *saṃskāra*. But mind you, in the Eastern mind the doctrine of the *saṃskāra* is so different from that definition that perhaps a Hindu would object to my attempt at a comparison. But the archetypal images are really the nearest thing we can see.
>
> (p. 9)

Jung's archetypes, while showing some similarity to Patañjali's imprints or *saṃskāras*, may bear more resemblance with the primordial ground of *prakṛti*. Whicher (2001) has explained:

> In Patañjali's Yoga, as in classical Sāṃkhya, *prakṛti* refers to both the primordial ground (*mūla-prakṛti*) of the innumerable manifest forms and those forms themselves. Also termed *pradhāna* (or *avyakta*), which denotes the transcendent matric of *prakṛti* as apart from the consciousness-principle (*puruṣa*), *prakṛti* is defined by Vācaspati Miśra as that by which the multiplicity of evolutes (*vikāra*) is brought forth (*pradhīyate*). It is the primordial, undifferentiated continuum that contains in potential the entire cosmos in all its levels and categories of being.
>
> (pp. 12–13)

When emphasizing archetypes as organs of the psyche, in contradistinction to imprints, I find a closer resemblance between Jung's archetypes and Patañjali's transcendent matric of *prakṛti*.

Keeping in mind the reversal in Jung's and Patañjali's approaches to consciousness, Jung's (1934/1985a) Mother archetype, which "stands for life at its origin" (para. 348), can specifically be seen to bear resemblance to the primordial ground and transcendent matric of *prakṛti*. Jung (1934/1985a) stated,

> "Mother" is an archetype and refers to the place of origin, to nature, to that which passively creates, hence to substance and matter, to materiality, the womb, the vegetative functions. It also means the unconscious, our natural and instinctive life, the physiological realm, the body in which we dwell or are contained; for the "mother" is also the matrix, the hollow form, the vessel that carries and nourishes, and it thus stands psychologically for the foundations of consciousness. Being inside or contained in something also suggests darkness, something nocturnal and fearful, hemming one in. These allusions give the idea of the mother in many of its mythological and etymological variants; they also represent an important part of the yin idea in Chinese philosophy . . . it is a collective inheritance, alive and recorded in language, inherited along with the structure of the psyche and therefore to be found at all times and among all peoples.
>
> (para. 344)

Elsewhere Jung (1938/1980c) queried whether psyche and archetypes ever originated at all. Noting it as a metaphysical question, he rendered it unanswerable but stated, "The structure is something given, the precondition that is found to be present in every case. And this is the *mother*, the matrix" (para. 187). As mentioned earlier, when looking at Patañjali from a non-dual orientation, because of the absolute nature of *puruṣa*, non-origination, *ajātivāda*, is implied (King, 1995). Furthermore, the transcendent core of *prakṛti*, like *puruṣa*, is indestructible. "Yet it has the capacity to undergo modification and it does so in the process of actualization or manifestation during which it gives birth to the multidimensional universe" (Whicher, 2001, p. 17). Hence, the transcendent core of *prakṛti* is indestructible but not immutable.

Prakṛti's mutability is exemplified by the *vrittis*, which appear and disappear at the level of our human awareness. *Vritti* translates as "to whirl, turn, revolve, to go on" (Carrera, 2006, p. 12). As early as his second sutra, Patañjali emphasized that our knowledge of ultimate reality is linked to our ability to stop the whirl. A majority of his text is methodology to assist one in attaining this cessation. In stark contrast, Jung never speaks to pure stillness. The closest approximation is found in Jung's (1916/1953b) references to mastering the anima, the inner feminine side responsible for the mechanism of projection:

> That superior power, however, which caused the possession – for what I cannot shake off must in some sense be superior to me – should, logically, disappear with the anima. One should then be "complex-free," psychologically house-trained, so to speak. Nothing more should happen that is not sanctioned by the ego, and when the ego wants something, nothing should be capable of interfering. The ego would thus be assured of an impregnable position, the steadfastness of a superman or the sublimity of a perfect sage.
>
> (para. 388)

Disappearance of the anima is speculation for Jung and can be seen to be partially on point with Patañjali in respect to Yoga's emphasis on rooting out all imprints. However, in Patañjali's world, it would not be a personal consciousness or ego, which is steadfast, but a mind, or instrument of perception, that has attained the purity of pure consciousness (YS 3.49, 3.55). As mentioned previously, Jung's model relies on the subject–object split and does not accommodate pure consciousness. In keeping alignment with his dualistic model, while on the one hand this quote emphasized that dissolution of the anima meant gaining "insight into the driving forces of the unconscious," Jung (1916/1953b) also speculated that this insight did not make the forces of the unconsciousness ineffective. "They can attack us at any time in new form. And they will infallibly do so if the conscious attitude has a flaw in it" (para. 391). Again, it is clear there is no rooting out of imprints, or the binding effects of *prakṛti*, in Jung's model.

Jung and Patañjali on ego–Self

Ego

Significant differences are found in regards to Jung's and Patañjali's notions of ego or "I-sense." For Jung, consciousness without an ego is virtually unthinkable because it would result in complete unconsciousness. Hence, the ego is a prerequisite for human consciousness. Furthermore, without the ego and the consciousness it facilitates, the phenomenal world "would not be" (Jung, 1961/1995, p. 371).

For Patañjali, the egoic "I", *asmitā*, is a concept we form of ourselves that is based on misunderstanding, or the inability to see true nature (YS 2.4). We only form an egoic identity by appropriating consciousness and taking ownership of the "I AM" presence. Appropriation is akin to confusing a reflected state of consciousness with pure consciousness. Whicher (1998) has explained,

> *Asmitā* is that process in which *mahat* or *buddhi*, being the purest and most *sattvic* evolute of *prakṛti*, becomes a recipient of a "reflection" of pure consciousness. This reflected state of consciousness, masquerading in the garb of *asmitā*, assumes itself to be Self/*puruṣa*. It is, by analogy, like the union of a crystal mirror with a reflection of the sun. *Puruṣa*, like the distant sun in the sky, remains unaffected by the union of its "reflection" in the mirror, but at the interface between *puruṣa* and *prakṛti* all the processes of the composite personality begin. Consciousness and life flow through this *asmitā*, which lends to the ego-principle (*asmitā-mātra*, *ahaṃkāra*) and to the mind (*citta*) a semblance of awareness. This reflected awareness generates a deluded sense of selfhood and must be understood as arising from a mistaken identity, that is the misidentification of *prakṛti* with *puruṣa* (authentic identity), beginning with *mahat*.
>
> (pp. 68–69)

This is to say that, by appropriation and by subsequent identification of ourselves as egoicly bound entities, the subject–object dichotomy arises. Because the egoic "I" is ontically false in Patañjali's world, the ego concept can be completely deconstructed (YS 3.47). This is not to say that we do not need a functional organizing principle or instruments of perception to be in the world. The mind itself is not the issue. It is how we understand those instruments, and identify with them, that is all-important.

In Patañjali's world, our experiences of *asmitā*, *puruṣa*, and *prakṛti* are correlated. So, although pure consciousness can be completely differentiated from its reflection on, and in, the mind, the mind and the experience of *asmitā* play a role in Patañjali's *darśana*. In some sense, it may be that we have to know what we are not in order to know what we are. If this is not true across epochs, it seems applicable contemporaneously. This is also to say that both epistemic and ontic experiences are necessary in Patañjali's world for comprehensive knowledge and experience of reality.

Using the broad categories of East–West in contradistinction to a more specific Classical Yoga–depth psychology comparison, Jung (1954/1989c) summed up his view on the East–West differences in notions of ego and mind:

> It is safe to assume that what the East calls "mind" has more to do with our "unconscious" than with mind as we understand it, which is more or less identical with consciousness. . . . The Eastern mind, however, has no difficulty in conceiving of a consciousness without an

ego. Consciousness is deemed capable of transcending its ego condition; indeed, in its "higher" forms, the ego disappears altogether. Such an ego-less mental condition can only be unconscious to us, for the simple reason that there would be nobody to witness it.

(para. 774)

Looking at Jung through Patañjali's lens, it appears as if Jung has conflated *prakṛti* and her instruments of perception with *asmitā*. In other words, Patañjali differentiates the mind and its functions in ways that Jung does not.

Timalsina's (2009) summation of pure consciousness in Advaita illuminates the gulf between Jung's model of consciousness that relies on subject–object distinction, or dualism, and Upaniṣadic nondualism:

> This awareness-in-itself is the constant seeing. All the cognitive modes, including the cognition of the absence of objects, are revealed by the witnessing consciousness which is the never-interrupted "seeing." This "seeing" is not the act of some subject. If it were, it would not be constant, nor would it be non-dual awareness identical to the self. It is instead the foundation upon which the duality of subject and object is imagined. Even "seeing" that is mentally constructed is revealed by this very non-dual seeing.
>
> (p. 5)

The fact that the egoic "I" – as a permanent content of consciousness – always remains present for Jung is clearly illuminated by comparing these two quotes. Whereas for Patañjali, "the empirical I-sense is not the seer, but merely masquerades as the seer" (Whicher, 1998b, p. 281), for Jung (1954/1989c) the empirical I is the seer (para. 774).

Although Jung's model might be said to heal the radical opposition between an ego and an inaccessible God placed outside, his vision never abolishes duality. So even though the ego is relativized as we loosen our resistance to the unconscious, his belief in an egoic "I" who is perceiving remains strongly endowed.

Self

Jung's (1920/1976a) notion of the Self may be one area of East–West scholarship that has caused the greatest confusion. When comparing Jung not only with Patañjali but also with many of the nondual Eastern liberatory psychologies and philosophies he studied, it is often assumed that Jung's Self maps directly to Eastern liberatory views because this is what Jung himself asserted throughout his *Collected Works*. For example, he stated, "The goal of Eastern religious practice is the same as that of Western mysticism: the shifting of the center of gravity from the ego to the self" (Jung, 1944/1989b, para. 958). In another context, he stated, "In the West the archetype is charged with the dogmatic figure of Christ; in the East, with Purusha, the Atman" (Jung, 1944/1953a, para. 20). And perhaps most comprehensively,

> The union of the conscious mind or ego-personality with the unconscious personified as anima produces a new personality compounded of both – "ut duo qui fuerant, unum quasi corpore fiant." Not that the new personality is a third thing midway between conscious and unconscious, it is both together. Since it transcends consciousness it can no longer be called "ego" but must be given the name of the "self." Reference must be made here to the Indian idea of the atman, whose personal and cosmic modes of being form an exact parallel to the psychological idea of the self and the *filius philosophorum*. The self too is both ego and non-ego, subjective and objective, individual and collective. It is the "uniting symbol" which epitomizes the total union of opposites.
>
> (Jung, 1946/1985b, para. 474)

Jung's direct mapping between his Self and the primary ground of orthodox Hinduism is not accurate.

For Jung, the Self is an archetype, subject of the total psyche, and represented intrapsychically by an image. In Jung's (1920/1976a) world, the Self-concept "designates the whole range of psychic phenomena in man" (para. 789), including the unconscious. Hence, one can never be fully conscious of the Self because the totality of unconscious contents can never be brought to consciousness. Jung (1916/1953b) stated,

> There is little hope of our ever being able to reach even approximate consciousness of the self, since however much we make conscious there will always exist an indeterminate and indeterminable amount of unconscious material which belongs to the totality of the self.
>
> (para. 274)

Objectively, or physically, our microscopes and telescopes prove this. No matter what lens we seem to take to the world, the phenomena get smaller or larger, accordingly.

Although Jung is right in his account of the vast expanse of phenomena, as Corbett (2004) has emphasized, Jung's Self was also attempting to point to "something" beyond image. Hence, it is also important to emphasize that Jung never released objective content, or the image. He favored the epistemically accessible, perhaps because of his belief that ontic reality is inaccessible. In other words, Jung's Self is not the Seer, comprehending all modes of awareness, but more akin to what we can see, frequently referred to in Eastern liberatory traditions as objects of consciousness, or for Patañjali, as *pratyaya*, content.

For Patañjali, the Self is *brahman* or *Ātman*, another term for pure consciousness, which has, among its qualities, self-illumination (YS 4.19, 4.22) and singularity (YS 2.25, 4.34). Implied in the quality of singularity or the nondual nature of the Self is, very loosely speaking, pure subjectivity (YS 2.22). *Brahman*, as ultimate reality, is pure being, unconditioned and indestructible. It is a term that does not allow for any metaphysical splitting of reality. As Timalsina (2009) explained in the earlier quote, the Seer is really beyond all subject–object distinction. Hence, Patañjali's Self is content free – nothing can be set apart and against it. Because it is pure seeing, pure perception, in which nothing can be set apart or against, it can never make an object of itself. As our true nature, *brahman/Ātman* is ontically accessible.

The ego–Self relationship

For Patañjali, identification with an ego is part of a bifurcating psychological process that obscures the Self. His whole methodology aims at quieting the changing states of mind and releasing the limitations and bondage it produced through grasping onto concepts such as "ego." The Self can be realized by releasing the grasp of objectifying thought and by seeing through the concepts and intrapsychic images.

Jung's ego–Self relationship is starkly different. Although the ego can be understood to obscure the Self in Jung's (1916/1953b) model, too, when the ego is relativized, it is given an impregnable position as "the only content of the self that we do know" (para. 405). For Jung (1944/1989b), "The ego needs the self and vice versa" (para. 961). Jung conceives the relationship between the ego and Self as "one of continuous *dialogue* which is, by definition, a never-ending process" (Salman, 2009, p. 58). Unable to transcend polarized thinking, Jung's depth psychological model continues to reinscribe the duality of subject and object through the ego–Self dynamic.

Jung and Patañjali on the transformation of human consciousness

Both Jung and Patañjali were interested in discourses on consciousness and how we understand ourselves and the world. Self and identity, and how we perceive, are the difficulties they addressed. Alongside these interests and difficulties, both trusted in the innate capacities of the mind to heal and foster the spiritual development of the personality. Although their ideas on ethics were not identical, for both scholars, ethics and numinous experience go hand in hand. Their ideas on the teleological directedness and religious function of the psyche are also similar. However, looking closely at the notions of consciousness in Jung and Patañjali, several significant differences are revealed, which ultimately result in different paths of transformation and different goals (Coward, 1985).

For Patañjali, transformation of consciousness means the transformation of the contents of consciousness. Within the first four lines of his text, Patañjali made it very clear that the path of Classical Yoga is a process of discerning between two orientations of consciousness – orientation A, when pure consciousness abides in its own nature, and orientation B, when consciousness has assumed the modifications of the mind and its contents. To experience orientation A, *nirodha* is required. To reiterate: *Nirodha* is interpreted as the "control, regulation, channeling, mastery, integration, coordination, understanding, stilling, quieting, and setting aside of" the mind (Bharati, n.d., p. 4). In other words, upon *nirodha,* a completely empty and open mind space is realized. Yoga process is the total freeing up of the bounded and conditioned mind. This means that all *vrttis* are stilled, and all *saṃskāras* are taken out at their root. To describe the rooting out of imprints in a bit more detail: through the relinquishment of subject–object identification the mind purifies; gains discriminatory discernment; and becomes capable of ascertaining truth-bearing wisdom, *ṛtambharā* (YS 1.48). The impact brought about by the *ṛtambharā* imprint is so significant that it restricts the activation of other imprints, *saṃskāras*. Then, after *nirodha* of the *ṛtambharā* imprint, seedless meditative absorption, *nirbīja samādhi*, ensues (YS 1.51). In *nirbīja samādhi*, with every impression wiped out, *kaivalya*, or one's onlyness, is attained. With *kaivalya*, the Seer, or the power of pure consciousness, is established in its true nature.

In Jung's (1939/1980a) model, we transform by relativizing the ego and by developing a relationship with the Self, which contains both conscious and unconscious processes. Through the acknowledgment and engagement with the contents of the Self, the ego becomes both relativized and enhanced. Consciousness is transformed by establishing a dialogue between the conscious mind and the unconscious content through various means, including dream interpretation, active imagination, mandala drawing, and working with the mythic dimensions and symbol-making capacity of the individuation process. Because of the depths of the contents of the unconscious, the process is eternal. Jung (1946/1985b) stated,

> A complete "emptying" of the unconscious is out of the question, if only because its creative powers are continually producing new formations. Consciousness, no matter how extensive it may be, must always remain the smaller circle within the greater circle of the unconscious, an island surrounded by the sea; and, like the sea itself, the unconscious yields an endless self-replenishing abundance of living creatures, a wealth beyond our fathoming. We may long have known the meaning, effects, and characteristics of unconscious contents without ever having fathomed

> their depths and potentialities, for they are capable of infinite variations and can never be depotentiated. The only way to get at them in practice is to try to attain a conscious attitude which allows the unconscious to co-operate instead of being driven into opposition.
>
> (para. 366)

For Jung, our task is to relieve suffering by becoming whole through the realization of a conscious attitude that allows for, and develops, a relationship to the inexhaustible contents of the unconscious. Referring again to the microscopic and telescopic lenses of science, we know the inexhaustible contents to be true. However, in contrast to Patañjali's model of full integration, which renders duality obsolete, Jung's model – which is definitely also integrative – constructs a new subject–object relationship. Jung's religious function of the psyche shifts the human–God relationship from an internal–external dichotomy to an internal duality between an ego and the archetypal God image, or Self (Ajaya, 1983). This distinction between Patañjali's path and Jung's is all-important to acknowledge. In Patañjali's world, when we remove the impure covering obscuring the omniscience of pure consciousness and thereby acknowledge the unlimited nature of knowledge, little remains to be known by the intellect (YS 4.31). For Patañjali, knowables appear few when the infinitude of knowledge is cognized. We release, and cease, our grasp on contents (YS 4.32). The releasing and ceasing our grasp on contents never happens in Jung's world.

The transformation of consciousness in Jung's (1946/1985b) model is a form of Self-inquiry, *ātma-vicāra*, which is undoubtedly in line with Upaniṣadic thought. Through the lens of Patañjali, Jung's knowledge can be seen as an attempt to gain knowledge, or empiric consciousness, through *vrtti* activity. In the Vedāntic traditions, there is *vrtti* activity during self-inquiry. However, we can never clearly understand our instrument of perception until it is completely differentiated from pure consciousness. *Vrttis*, especially as mental images, keep consciousness bound to the body–mind complex, which is an inhibited way of knowing the world. Although Patañjali and Jung would undoubtedly agree that we need an epistemic knowledge of optics, Patañjali is adamant on the mind's epistemic limitations. It must be emphatically stated that in Patañjali's model, there can be absolutely no *vrtti* activity in order to understand, or wakefully embody, ontic reality. *Puruṣa* can never be made an object of knowledge. However, for Jung, the contents of mind and objects of knowledge remain engrossing. This is to say that for Jung (1946/1985b), the transformation of consciousness is enduring. Individuation is a permanent engagement of bifurcating psychophysical process. Transformation of the mundane mind never ceases because the duality between the conscious and unconscious never ends. This is by and large because Jung's notion of consciousness is neo-Kantian – fundamentally linguistic and conceptual in nature. In contrast, for Patañjali, perpetual transformation, without relation to the still and unchanging nature of pure consciousness, is how reality appears when consciousness and the functions of mind are enmeshed and not differentiated. Unraveling the psychophysical process completely, so its bifurcating mechanism can be stilled, is Patañjali's path. For this reason, the paths of transformation of Jung and Patañjali can be seen as fundamentally different.

Although both scholars teach paths of transformation because of their concern with the amelioration of human suffering, difference can also be found in their understandings of psychophysical affliction. In Jung's (1946/1985b) world, there is no such thing as liberation from suffering or full relief from the tension of opposites. Although Jung believed that the conscious and unconscious work in harmony through the individuation process, he did not believe that the conceptual boundary between them could be seen through. Jung (1946/1985b) stated,

> Just as alchemy has a great many very different procedures, ranging from the sevenfold to the thousandfold distillation, or from the "work of one day" to "the errant quest" lasting for decades, so the tensions between the psychic pairs of opposites ease off only gradually; and like the alchemical end-product, which always betrays its essential duality, the united personality will never quite lose the painful sense of innate discord. Complete redemption from the sufferings of this world is and must remain an illusion. Christ's earthly life likewise ended, not in complacent bliss, but on a cross. . . . The goal is important only as an idea; the essential thing is the opus which leads to the goal: that is the goal of a lifetime. In its attainment "left and right" are united, and conscious and unconscious work in harmony.
>
> (para. 400)

Looking at Jung through the lens of Patañjali, Jung's idea that redemption is an illusion is a direct consequence of the reality Jung bestows to the egoic "I" and the unconscious. In Patañjali's world, the process of Yoga allows for full discernment between the bounded conditioned mind that taints and afflicts and unbounded unconditioned pure consciousness. This discernment allows for the dissolution of the egoic "I," alternatively understood as absorption into Cosmic Mind through *samādhi*. *Samādhi* permits contentment, release from suffering, and the embodiment of a superior form of joy.

Observing Jung's and Patañjali's differences from yet another perspective: whereas Patañjali speaks in terms of pure consciousness, *puruṣa*, and nature, *prakṛti*; Jung speaks in terms of a conscious and unconscious, both which contain contents. Although Jung described the relationship between conscious and unconscious as fluid and interpenetrating, it must be emphasized that both aspects contain objectified contents.

Jung (1961/1995) thought that "if the Creator were conscious of Himself, He would not need conscious creatures" (p. 371). Therefore, the human ego is necessary to bring light to darkness. Jung (1939/1997) begins in the dark because, according to his vision, "in the beginning all was unconscious" (p. 154). God is not consulting with His own omniscience (Jung, 1954/1989a para. 658). In juxtaposition to this line in Jung's thinking, the light is not imprisoned in the Upaniṣadic tradition. In fact, the Self is the light (Easwaran, 1987, p. 43). Pure consciousness and its self-luminous nature are the ontic reality. Consequently, light and luminosity permeate the YS (Chapple, 2008, p. 71). The darkness of our suffering is brought about through our misunderstanding of reality. We misunderstand, or do not know, the reality of the self-luminous, never-collapsing, pure consciousness, when our vision is obscured.

Our task in Classical Yoga is to become transparent and thereby to clearly perceive the light. In contradistinction, in depth psychology, we, as the owner of action, seem to be either seeking light or creating it (Sparks, 2007). These ideas are obstructions on the path of yoga. As Chapple (2008) has explained, "Only through the seer can the world be known, although the seen, particularly in its mistaken assumption of ego identity, seeks to claim all experience" (p. 79).

For Patañjali, through constant practice, purification, and the cultivation of razor-sharp focus on one mental impression, orientation B can come into alignment with orientation A. Layer by layer, we see through, and thereby remove, the obstructions to vision. The subtilization and subsequent release of the chosen mental impression leads one to clear seeing and sorrowless illumination (YS 1.36).

In a 1932 lecture on Kundalini yoga, Jung (1996) acknowledged the differences in approach the following way:

> The Hindu thinks in terms of the great light. . . . Our thought starts out with the individual and goes into the general. The Hindu begins with the general and works down to the individual. . . . From this aspect we realize that everywhere we are still enclosed in the world of causality. (p. 67)

Although Jung detects the differences and spends a good amount of time interpreting Eastern liberatory psychologies, resting in an experience beyond objectivity remained elusive to him. Although Jung relativizes the ego and aims to put it into accord with the stronger forces of the unconscious, by comparing Jung and Patañjali, it appears however, that a model devoid of pure consciousness, coupled with an ego that can never completely dissolve, essentially resolves to a human species that is superior to pure consciousness and nature herself.

In summary

In Patañjali's world, there is no substantial egoic "I", and to believe that there is is a misunderstanding with weighty consequences, including mental instability and suffering. The ability to differentiate and discern consciousness from its vehicles is the prerequisite to having experience whereby the power of consciousness is positioned in its own essential nature. An embodied knowing of the nature of pure consciousness is oftentimes referred to as liberation, although Patañjali did not use the term *liberation* in the sense of a goal to achieve. In contradistinction to liberation, the aim of Patañjali Yoga is *kaivalya* – an experience that ultimately cannot be explained. It is understood only by relinquishing all reduction, objectification, and knowledge construction. It is an experience of absoluteness. Since Patañjali never elaborates on what *kaivalya* is, it can be inferred that Patañjali leads the followers of his path to an embodied understanding of ontic reality – where knowing is inherent in being. Through the process of yogic integration, epistemic states dissolve into ontic reality.

Notably, it is Jung's assertion of an unconscious that sets them apart. There is no unconscious in Patañjali's model. Through the lens of Patañjali, by adhering to the ontological reality of the collective unconscious, Jung has neglected to accurately assess the empiric consciousness, or the conceptual consciousness, that is mobilized to generate his notion of "unconscious."

Jung's unconscious might best be compared to veiled contents in the Upaniṣadic tradition. As Timalsina (2009) has explained, "The moment when nothing is cognized, 'nothing' *is cognized*. In essence, the existence of the absence of awareness cannot be confirmed" (p. 22). While consciousness can be confirmed by itself, how is one to confirm unconsciousness? Absence of consciousness is absence of consciousness. This is sometimes referred to in Hindu philosophy by stating what exists exists, eternally and absolutely, and what does not exist will never exist. With consciousness and existence eternal – and the absolute ground of being – the unconscious is no-thing but fleeting shadow, appearing and disappearing according to the shadows created by the objects of the mind. In Patañjali's view, contents of psychophysical reality may be obscured, but ontic reality can never be confirmed as unconscious.

Patañjali's methodology works by relying upon a well-thought-out – and/or intuited, fully understood and experienced – strong metaphysical schematic. For Patañjali, pure consciousness, *puruṣa*, is the fundamental ontological and ontic reality. By following his path of Yoga and stilling the fluctuations of the mind, all epistemic states, and therefore all theories of being, resolve to being. In Patañjali's world, pure consciousness, which is synonymous with pure seeing and pure perception, is primary, eternally and absolutely, and therefore, even when objectified at the level of our human awareness, has no alternative but to illuminate itself, no matter how circuitous the path. If the object is the subject, the process of objectification has no alternative but to resolve itself to being because being is not founded on representation. In the inability to wholly re-present, our epistemologies and epistemic states will eventually have to reflect on their limitations.

During his research of the East, Jung undoubtedly studied Patañjali's text. From October 1938 through June 1939, he taught a seminar on "The Process of Individuation in Eastern Texts" at the Eidgenossische Technische Hochschule, Zurich, which included his analysis of the process of individuation in Patañjali's YS. In the next chapter, we will look at where Jung met his limits in relation to Patañjali's thought.

Notes

1 I purposely use the word *awareness* as a means of differentiating consciousness with an adjective of either human, reflected, phenomenal, empiric, dualistic, or subject–object from pure consciousness.

2 Through a nondual orientation, I find it quite challenging to find the right word or combination of words that would accurately portray the nonduality of mind and body. In this instance, I am using the term *bodymind* as one total system that can never be separated ontically, although it may be mentally perceived as separate. At other times throughout this work, I use *mind–body* to denote the typically Western and Cartesian way we represent the mental and physical aspects of existence. Whereas Patañjali enfolds both the mind and body into *prakṛti*, there is yet no consensus in the literature on a way to portray the mind–body unity.

References

Ajaya, S. (1983). *Psychotherapy east and west: A unifying paradigm*. Honesdale, PA: The Himalayan Institute.

Bharati, S. J. (n.d.). *Yoga sutras of Patañjali interpretive translation*. Retrieved from www.swamij.com/pdf/yogasutrasinterpretive.pdf

Borelli, J. (1983). Impression and archetype in the cognitive theories of classical yoga and analytical psychology. In C. Chapple (Ed.), *Sāṃkhya-Yoga: Proceedings of the IASWR conference, 1981* (pp. 120–161). New York, NY: The Institute for Advanced Studies of World Religions.

Bryant, E. (2009). *The yoga sutras of Patañjali*. New York, NY: North Point Press.

Carrera, J. (2006). Inside the yoga sutras: A comprehensive sourcebook for the study and practice of Patañjali's yoga sutras. Buckingham, VA: Integral Yoga.

Chapple, C. K. (2008). *Yoga and the luminous: Patañjali's spiritual path to freedom*. Albany, NY: State University of New York Press.

Corbett, L. (2004). *The religious function of the psyche*. New York, NY: Brunner-Routledge.

Coward, H. (1985). *Jung and eastern thought*. New York, NY: State University of New York Press.

Coward, H. (2002). *Yoga and psychology*. New York, NY: State University of New York Press.

Easwaran, E. (1987). *The upaniṣads*. Tomales, CA: Nilgiri Press.

Grof, S. (1998). The cosmic game: Explorations of the frontiers of human consciousness. Albany, NY: State University of New York Press.

Grof, S., & Grof, C. (2010). *Holotropic breathwork: A new approach to self-exploration in therapy*. Albany, NY: State University of New York Press.

Jha, G. (1934). *Yoga-darshana: Sūtras of Patañjali's with Bhāsya of Vyāsa* (2nd ed.) Freemont, CA: Asian Humanities Press. (Original work published 1907/Revised 1934)

Jung, C. G. (1953a). Introduction to the religious and psychological problems of alchemy. In H. Read, M. Fordham, G. Adler, & W. McGuire (Eds.), *The collected works of C. G. Jung* (R. F. C. Hull, Trans., Vol. 12, pp. 1–37). New York, NY: Pantheon. (Original work published 1944, revised 1952)

Jung, C. G. (1953b). The relations between the ego and the unconscious. In H. Read, M. Fordham, G. Adler, & W. McGuire (Eds.), *The collected works of C. G. Jung* (R. F. C. Hull, Trans., Vol. 7, pp. 121–239) New York, NY: Pantheon. (Original work published 1916, revised 1934)

Jung, C. G. (1972a). On the nature of the psyche. In H. Read, M. Fordham, G. Adler, & W. McGuire (Eds.), *The collected works of C. G. Jung* (R. F. C. Hull, Trans., 2nd ed., Vol. 8, pp. 159–234). Princeton, NJ: Princeton University Press. (Original work published 1946, revised 1954)

Jung, C. G. (1972b). A review of the complex theory. In H. Read, M. Fordham, G. Adler, & W. McGuire (Eds.), *The collected works of C. G. Jung* (R. F. C. Hull, Trans., 2nd ed., Vol. 8, pp. 92–104). Princeton, NJ: Princeton University Press. (Original work published 1934, revised 1948)

Jung, C. G. (1973). *C. G. Jung letters: Volume 1: 1906–1950* (R. F. C. Hull, Trans., G. Adler & A. Jaffé, Eds.). Princeton, NJ: Princeton University Press.

Jung, C. G. (1976a). Definitions. In H. Read, M. Fordham, G. Adler, & W. McGuire (Eds.), *The collected works of C. G. Jung* (R. F. C. Hull, Trans., Vol. 6, pp. 408–486). Princeton, NJ: Princeton University Press. (Original work published 1920, revised 1960)

Jung, C. G. (1976b). *Symbols of transformation.* In H. Read, M. Fordham, G. Adler, & W. McGuire (Eds.), *The collected works of C. G. Jung* (R. F. C. Hull, Trans., Vol. 5). Princeton, NJ: Princeton University Press. (Original work published 1912/Revised 1952)

Jung, C. G. (1978). The self. In H. Read, M. Fordham, G. Adler, & W. McGuire (Eds.), *The collected works of C. G. Jung* (R. F. C. Hull, Trans., 2nd ed., Vol. 9ii, pp. 23–35). Princeton, NJ: Princeton University Press. (Original work published 1959)

Jung, C. G. (1980a). Conscious, unconscious, and individuation In H. Read, M. Fordham, G. Adler, & W. McGuire (Eds.), *The collected works of C. G. Jung* (R. F. C. Hull, Trans., 2nd ed., Vol. 9i, pp. 275–289). Princeton, NJ: Princeton University Press. (Original work published 1939)

Jung, C. G. (1980b). The phenomenology of the spirit in fairytales. In H. Read, M. Fordham, G. Adler, & W. McGuire (Eds.), *The collected works of C. G. Jung* (R. F. C. Hull, Trans., 2nd ed., Vol. 9i, pp. 207–254). Princeton, NJ: Princeton University Press. (Original work published 1945)

Jung, C. G. (1980c). Psychological aspects of the mother archetype. In H. Read, M. Fordham, G. Adler, & W. McGuire (Eds.), *The collected works of C. G. Jung*

(R. F. C. Hull, Trans., 2nd ed., Vol. 9i, pp. 75–110). Princeton, NJ: Princeton University Press. (Original work published 1938, revised 1954)

Jung, C. G. (1985a). The practical use of dream-analysis. In H. Read, M. Fordham, G. Adler, & W. McGuire (Eds.), *The collected works of C. G. Jung* (R. F. C. Hull, Trans., Vol. 16, pp. 139–161). Princeton, NJ: Princeton University Press. (Original work published 1934)

Jung, C. G. (1985b). The psychology of the transference. In H. Read, M. Fordham, G. Adler, & W. McGuire (Eds.), *The collected works of C. G. Jung* (R. F. C. Hull, Trans., Vol. 16, pp. 164–323). Princeton, NJ: Princeton University Press. (Original work published 1946)

Jung, C. G. (1989a). Answer to Job. In H. Read, M. Fordham, G. Adler, & W. McGuire (Eds.), *The collected works of C. G. Jung* (R. F. C. Hull, Trans., 2nd ed., Vol. 11, pp. 355–470). Princeton, NJ: Princeton University Press. (Original work published 1954)

Jung, C. G. (1989b). The holy men of India. In H. Read, M. Fordham, G. Adler, & W. McGuire (Eds.), *The collected works of C. G. Jung* (R. F. C. Hull, Trans., 2nd ed., Vol. 11, pp. 576–586). Princeton, NJ: Princeton University Press. (Original work published 1944)

Jung, C. G. (1989c). Psychological commentary on "the Tibetan book of the great liberation." In H. Read, M. Fordham, G. Adler, & W. McGuire (Eds.), *The collected works of C. G. Jung* (R. F. C. Hull, Trans., 2nd ed., Vol. 11, pp. 475–508). Princeton, NJ: Princeton University Press. (Original work published 1954)

Jung, C. G. (1989d). Yoga and the west. In H. Read, M. Fordham, G. Adler, & W. McGuire (Eds.), *The collected works of C. G. Jung* (R. F. C. Hull, Trans., 2nd ed., Vol. 11, pp. 529–537). Princeton, NJ: Princeton University Press. (Original work published 1936)

Jung, C. G. (1995). *Memories, dreams, reflections* (R. Winston & C. Winston, Trans., A. Jaffe, Ed.). London: FontanaPress. (Original work published 1961)

Jung, C. G. (1996). *The psychology of kundalini yoga: Notes of the seminar given in 1932 by C. G. Jung* (S. Shamdasani, Ed.). Princeton, NJ: Princeton University Press.

Jung, C. G. (1997). *Visions: Notes of the seminar given in 1930–1934* (Vol. 1, C. Douglas, Ed.). Princeton, NJ: Princeton University Press. (Original work published 1939)

Kenghe, C. T. (1976). *Yoga as depth-psychology & para-psychology*. Varanasi, India: Bharata Manisha.

King, R. (1995). *Early Advaita Vedānta and Buddhism*. Albany, NY: State University of New York Press.

Pflueger, L. W. (2003). Dueling with dualism: Revisioning the paradox of puruṣa and prakṛti. In I. Whicher & D. Carpenter (Eds.), *Yoga: The Indian tradition* (pp. 70–82). New York, NY: Routledge.

Salman, S. (2009). The creative psyche: Jung's major contributions. In P. Young-Eisendrath & T. Dawson (Eds.), *The Cambridge companion to Jung* (pp. 57–75). New York, NY: Cambridge University Press. (Original work published 1997)

Shroder, T. (2001). Old souls: Compelling evidence from children who remember past lives. New York, NY: Fireside.

Sparks, J. G. (2007). At the heart of matter: Synchronicity and Jung's spiritual testament. Toronto, Canada: Inner City Books.

Taimni, I. K. (1961). The science of yoga: The yoga-sutras of Patañjali in Sanskrit with transliteration in roman, translation and commentary in English. Wheaton, IL: The Theosophical Publishing House.

Timalsina, S. (2009). Consciousness in Indian philosophy: The Advaita doctrine of "awareness only." New York, NY: Routledge.

Tucker, J. B. (2008). Ian Stevenson and cases of the reincarnation type. *Journal of Scientific Exploration*, *22*(1), 36–43.

Watts, A. (1971). *Psychotherapy east and west*. New York, NY: Ballantine.

Whicher, I. (1998a). The integrity of the yoga darśana: A reconsideration of classical yoga. Albany, NY: State University of New York Press.

Whicher, I. (1998b). Yoga and freedom: A reconsideration of Patañjali's classical yoga. *Philosophy East and West*, *48*(2), 272–322.

Whicher, I. (2001). *Patañjali's metaphysical schematic: Puruṣa and prakrti in the yogasutra*. Chennai, India: The Adyar Library and Research Center.

Chapter 4

Jung on Yoga

The bodies of work of both Jung and Patañjali provide deeper insight into human nature, psychospiritual development, and the alleviation of suffering. Nonetheless, the research in the previous chapters suggests that Jung and Patañjali perceive the world in notably different ways. Jung's assertion of an ego and an unconscious, which are ontically real, appears as their most significant disagreement. Other notable differences also exist. In their ideas around mental imprints, Patañjali focuses on *saṃskāras* and *vāsanās*, which are of an individual nature, while Jung focuses on archetypes of a collective nature. Whereas Patañjali makes a sharp distinction between two orientations of consciousness, orientation A, where consciousness abides in true nature, and orientation B, where consciousness is enmeshed with mental modifications, Jung does not make this distinction at all. Furthermore, while for Patañjali, freedom from suffering is possible, for Jung, relief from antagonistic polarities is only temporary. The present chapter inquires into Jung's analysis and understanding of yogic texts and liberatory percepts with an emphasis on uncovering where Jung met his limits in relation to Yoga's nondual and liberatory ideas.

Quite early in his professional life, Jung researched Hindu thought, using passages of the Vedas and *Upaniṣads* in *Symbols of Transformation* – his career-altering text that heralded his break with Freud. After his break with Freud and during his resultant confrontation with the unconscious, Jung's interest in Eastern ideas continued. Throughout his writings, Jung frequently made generalizations in relation to diverse bodies of Eastern thought such as Hinduism, Buddhism, and Taoism, often referring to them all as yoga. It is nevertheless possible to discern where Jung's thought aligns and diverges with Patañjali's.

Jung shared his thoughts in regards to Eastern liberatory traditions, including yoga psychology in several papers and monographs, which are easily accessible in the *Collected Works*. In 1938 to 1939, during a lecture series on the process of individuation in Patañjali Yoga, Jung shared that he found the *Yoga Sūtra* (YS) to be an exceedingly difficult text containing profound ideas (Hannah, 1939).[1] After comparing multiple translations, he recognized how philologists struggle over correct use of language.[2] Jung understood that wrestling with language in the end might not be enough if the philologist doesn't have psychological experience. He thought that talking to yogis was imperative for a correct understanding.

Despite this feeling, earlier in 1938, when Jung was in India receiving an academic honor, he had the opportunity to meet prominent modern-day yogi Sri Ramana Maharishi but declined. In his autobiography, *Memories, Dreams, Reflections*, Jung (1961/1995) recounted that his decision to avoid all so-called "holy-men" was so he could make do with his own truth and not accept from others what he could not attain on his own (p. 305). He thought it would have been a theft had he attempted to learn from Ramana. Listening to his inner being, shaping life out of himself, and accepting what nature brings to him were Jung's directives.

While his decision not to meet with Ramana is highly curious (Stein, 2010), it is evident Jung didn't want to take on the philosophy or psychology of Yoga without truly living it. He was strictly against imitating another standpoint. The experiences he had in early life caused him to question religion based purely on belief. Early on, Jung realized that his father, a pastor in the Swiss Reformed Church, had never had a meaningful religious experience even though he preached the doctrine and dogma of his denomination. Jung felt strongly that belief should be backed up by direct experience and that worship should not be based on blind faith.

Jung's conviction that direct experience is the cornerstone to religious understanding is unquestionably in alignment with one of the pillars of Patañjali's methodology – practice. The integrative process of Yoga is grounded via a practice that is continually refined over time. It is through practice as well as nonattachment that the fluctuations of the mind are mastered in Yoga psychology. Counterfeit unitive experiences are in no way Patañjali's aim. Consciousness abiding in true nature, devoid of the subject–object split, is.

Overall, Jung accurately assessed Yoga as a unity between the subject and object and the cosmic and individual. In his 1936 text *Yoga and the West,* Jung (1936/1989e) stated, "When the doing of the individual is at the same time a cosmic happening, the elation of the body (innervation) becomes one with the elation of the spirit (the universal idea), and from this there arises a living whole" (para. 866). However, even though Jung thought the vision of unity between the subject and object was beautiful, in the final analysis, Jung (1939/1980a) believed the application of yogic methods was "scarcely to be recommended anywhere north of the Tropic of Cancer" (para. 520). He thought that Westerners could not apply yoga methods correctly because of a lack of self-knowledge – and that Europeans didn't have the necessary patience for Patañjali's methods.

In Jung's (1939/1989b) mind, a conscious ego and an enriched understanding must first be produced through analysis before we can consider abolishing egohood or rationalism. Although there is similarity to Patañjali's thought here, in the sense that Patañjali noted the subject–object means of knowing as valuable, the underlying differences between how Jung and Patañjali envision the ego and consciousness give them a different approach. For Patañjali, we mobilize subject–object knowledge temporarily, so our individual bodymind is capable of embodying the power of pure consciousness. However, in the end, the relative is the absolute, so the subject–object duality, and therefore our self-representation, is falsifiable. In Patañjali's world, when the egoic "I" has taken ownership of consciousness and assumed a false appearance, the egoic "I" must be completely deconstructed in order to clear the lens of perception. All appropriation must be released. Be that as it may, Patañjali Yoga is not saying that to embody the power of pure consciousness we don't need a functional organizing principle that is able to differentiate and discern. Nor is it implying that we should abolish rationalism. Conditional reality and ultimate reality are not in opposition. Functionality in physical form demands both an organizing principle that is in working order and rationality. Metaphorically speaking, Patañjali is saying our innate organizing principle is similar to the function that allows us to learn how to stabilize the body, attain balance, and walk. When we balance up–down, right–left, and in–out, we can stand and walk without concentrated effort each time. The integrating function becomes nearly obsolete and is only used occasionally when we lose balance or meet challenging terrain. In other words, when the thinking function that bifurcates and differentiates is used to achieve psychophysical balance, it can be quieted and used with discretion.

Patañjali Yoga is not always understood this way. The *Yoga Sūtra* is also read as dualistic and viewed as world denying. A dualistic read of the text often leads to the impression that through *samādhi,* one transcends the material world. Despite Jung's accurate assessment noted in the earlier quote, Jung also assumed that Classical Yoga would lead to a complete transcendence of the material world. Through Jung's lens, any practices aimed at egoic transcendence lead to unconsciousness. For example, Jung stated, "We can only say that to the best of our European understanding there is a far-reaching dissolution of consciousness in Samādhi" (as cited in Hannah, 1939, p. 136).

Through a nondual orientation of the *Yoga Sūtra*, we understand Yoga practitioners don't deny the world or withdraw permanently from participation in it, as Jung sensed. Yogis withdraw temporarily. Through integrative Yoga methodology, *prakṛti* does not depart in shame upon being seen by *puruṣa*, as the dualistic Sāṃkhyan scholars would tell it. Ultimately, through integrative Yoga methodology, and a complete involution of all thought forms, *prakṛti* and *puruṣa* resolve as *brahman*. Consciousness is all there is whether manifest or unmanifest. As Yoga scholar Ian Whicher (2003) has emphasized: "Yoga is not simply "*puruṣa*-realization"; it equally implies "getting it right with *prakṛti*" (p. 63).

To state the previous notion from a slightly different angle, in relation to cultural and personal expression, Yoga is a process of realizing wholeness and establishing dynamic union. It is neither spiritual bypass nor diminishment of the vast richness of images and forms. As a means toward a global comprehensive interpretation of reality, images and forms are undoubtedly relativized through Yoga; however, relativization is a teaching tool used to illuminate the abiding principle of awareness underlying all transitory mental states and phenomenal appearances. This is to say that it is the unifying background on which cultural images dance that is called into the foreground through Yoga – Seeing is drawn out from behind the veils of the Seen. Therefore, Yoga transcends patterns of human thought regardless of their nativity. Hence, Patañjali Yoga is a global means for transcending blocks of a cultural, national, and personal nature – and eliminating the patterns that are not in service to our union and essential nature. Anchored in essential nature, all creative expression is honored.

Through consistent Yoga practice and the process of cleaning the lens of perception, practitioners learn how to see differently. External and internal "objects" lose their objectification. Simultaneously, a superior form of joy and contentment arises. Liberation and psychic integration go hand in hand. Whicher (1998b) has explained,

> *Kaivalya* in no way destroys or negates the personality of the yogin, but is an unconditional state in which all the obstacles or distractions preventing an immanent and purified relationship or engagement of person with nature and spirit (*puruṣa*) have been removed. The deep-rooted "knots" (*granthi*) of the mind in the form of habit patterns (*vāsanās*) of misconceived knowledge (*viparyaya-jñāna*) have been undone ("untied").
>
> (pp. 279–280)

None of this is to say that renunciate male *sādhus* are not often thought about when pondering Indian liberatory traditions. This stereotype exists, and some practitioners do indeed withdraw from the world. "But actually this is an exception rather than the rule" (Sachdeva, 1978, p. 93). Chapple (2008) has expressed his belief that the notion of world-rejecting asceticism is put forward by those who haven't carefully examined the text. He has stated, "Yoga does not reject the reality of the world, nor does it condemn the world, only the human propensity to misidentify with the more base aspects of the world" (p. 82).

It is important to understand that there are not two separate worlds for Patañjali. There isn't this world and that world, a transcendent world and immanent world – complete opposites that don't have anything between them. For Patañjali, there is Seeing that dwells in its true nature and Seeing that is obscured by the patterns of mind. Pure consciousness is thoroughly immanent but transcendent to conceptual thought. What is transcended is illusory perception. That yogis cease to exist and have no individual expression upon *kaivalya* is considered a misinterpretation of Patañjali's text when read through the lens of nonduality.

Although in the end, Jung misinterpreted Patañjali's text, it is not that he doesn't come very close to the point. This error can be perceived in a passage from *Psychological Types* when Jung (1920/1976b) summed up his insight into Indian liberation psychology:

> The Indian purpose is therefore clear: it wants to free the individual altogether from the opposites inherent in human nature, so that he can attain a new life in Brahman, which is the state of redemption and at the same time God. It is an irrational union of opposites, their final overcoming. Although Brahman, the world-ground and world-creator, created the opposites, they must nevertheless be cancelled out in it again, for otherwise it would not amount to a state of redemption.
>
> (para. 329)

In my view, this quote is a fairly accurate portrayal of Patañjali Yoga as well as the aim of the entire Upaniṣadic tradition. Clearly, Jung is speaking here of transitioning from orientation B to orientation A. However, through Patañjali's eyes, orientation A has been coexisting with orientation B all along. Eternity and temporal manifestation are not only in partnership, but they resolve to be one and the same, as are pure consciousness and the contents of consciousness. So, although it seems like new life in *brahman* is being attained, it is actually being perceived. There never is anything to attain or redeem from the perspective of pure consciousness. The only thing that shifts is perception. A keen discernment between psychological experience and ontic reality is called for. Jung does not make this distinction. With a focus on becoming, or change, Jung misses being, the eternal now, and the stable stage upon which the flux dances.

How Jung apprehended his Christian God may also provide clues to understanding his interpretation of the Upaniṣadic tradition and why he may not have completely understood it. As has been noted in the previous chapter, Jung's God is omniscient but does not consult with this omniscience. It is the human ego that brings consciousness to God. For the Upaniṣadic tradition, being is omniscient pure consciousness, and the ego, by appropriating consciousness, gets in the way of this knowing.

In *Answer to Job* Jung proclaimed (1954/1989a), "It was only quite late that we realized (or rather, are beginning to realize) that God is reality itself and therefore – last but not least – man" (para. 631). For Jung, realizing ourselves as God "is a millennial process" (para. 631). As beautiful as Jung's mythos may sound to his peers also constrained by a Judeo-Christian God image, this idea can have resonance only to those who have inherited any psychophysical implications wrought by dualistic views, like those of Abrahamic religious traditions and scientific materialism. The entire Upaniṣadic corpus is established in the realization that *ātman* is the localized expression of, and equal to, *brahman*.[3] Not in the future but here, now.

Patañjali's discernment between orientation A and B is a very lucid recognition that there is being and there is learning about being. The epistemic states and the attempts to gain knowledge are the experience of duality, the learning through empiric consciousness. However, in the end, pure consciousness cannot be embroiled with epistemic issues for realization of ontic reality to dawn.

While aiming to steer clear of metaphysics, Jung continually conferred ontological status to the unconscious and believed his ontologically real unconscious equated to yogic ideas. But when viewing Classical Yoga through a nondual orientation, there is no metaphysical splitting of opposites – the only ontic reality is pure consciousness. As a result of the above error, Jung then falsely observes a difference between his individuation process and Yoga methodology by confusing ontological questions with epistemic issues. Ironically, or perhaps allowing for a tremendously explicit example of projection, Jung views Eastern liberatory practices as having done the same – Jung believed Indian intuition had overreached itself.[4]

Patañjali's discernment between A and B, his overall vision, and his methodology are exceptionally congruent and cohesive in regards to the differentiation between ontic reality and epistemic states. Jung's confusion is his greatest blind spot in regards to, and in comparison with, Patañjalian thought. This point of Yoga philosophy cannot be overemphasized: ontological questions must not be muddled with epistemic issues.

Over and over again throughout his writings, it looks as though Jung senses duality is the beast to overcome, yet it appears he never manages to extricate himself from the perspectives of Western civilization. "If only a world-wide consciousness could arise that all division and fission are due to the splitting of opposites in the psyche, then we should know where to begin," Jung (1957/1970) noted in *The Undiscovered Self* (para. 575). Along similar lines, in *Yoga and the West,* Jung (1936/1989e) stated that the split in the Western mind makes "it impossible at the outset for the intentions of yoga to be realized in any adequate way" (para. 867). But isn't that true only to the degree that one keeps reinscribing the split? Patañjali is also teaching people who have bifurcating tendencies and who are living in duality, or subject–object consciousness. The only difference is – and I do not want to underestimate its enormous impact – Patañjali's students were already immersed in Hindu culture and cosmology. Hence, knowledge of *brahman*, spiritual monism, and pure consciousness would have been commonplace for anyone exposed to orthodox Hindu thought.

Curiously, Jung at one point almost seemed to brag about his non-acceptance of the rigors of the yoga methodology, which leads to the question of how much yoga experience he really had. Jung (1936/1989e) shared in *Yoga and The West*, "I owe my best insights (and there are some quite good ones among them) to the circumstance that I have always done just the opposite of what the rules of yoga prescribe" (para. 868). Jung preferred his work with active imagination over the techniques aimed at *nirodha*, presumably because he thought active imagination would draw forth insight that yoga techniques could not.

Jung (1936/1989e) described active imagination as a practice of switching off consciousness, which in turn allows unconscious contents a chance to develop. His adherence to a methodology of active imagination in contrast to a methodology aimed at *nirodha* exemplifies how Jung has consciousness and the contents of consciousness enmeshed. Because, for Jung, consciousness is not an abiding principle of awareness underlying all transitory mental states, he understands consciousness as mental activity – it is fundamentally linguistic and conceptual in nature. Jung cannot conceive of the egoic consciousness not existing because it is *through conception* that he is apprehending the world. Jung either avoids or misses the point altogether of Patañjali's *nirodha*. As a result, in contrast to Patañjali's path of seeing through phenomena, Jung is swapping phenomena. Jung is switching his view from external to internal contents and between gross and subtle internal contents.

Jung's reliance on conception and his enmeshment of consciousness and its contents are also evident when Jung (1939/1989b) stated, "It still remains exceedingly obscure how any enlightenment comes and of what it consists – in other words, by what or about what one is enlightened" (para. 879). Jung (1936/1989e) is confused in regards to what he could be detaching from. Having an experience of being, where there are no objects of knowledge on the horizon of one's awareness, appears to be incomprehensible to him. His incomprehension plays a part in the problem alluded to earlier in regards to his focus on becoming. A focus on becoming and knowledge construction will confound anyone trying to understand liberation through the thinking function. This can be a frustrating endeavor, especially for intellectuals. Yoga is the unbinding, emptying, and release of the mind's fluctuations – hence, Yoga is, emphatically, not "the process of grasping and appropriating the world of objects" including intellectual knowledge (Chapple, 1990, p. 62). This is why ontic reality can be differentiated from, and ultimately supersedes, epistemic states in Classical Yoga. When Jung stated of Patañjali's YS that it was "impossible to grasp it with the intellect" (as cited in Hannah, 1939, p. 13), Patañjali would have undoubtedly agreed. In contemporary terms, Patañjali may explain his philosophy to Jung in the following way: The mind that perceives the obstacle Is. The. Obstacle.

Through Patañjali's lens, it can be seen that Jung never transitioned from *saṃprajñāta* to *asaṃprajñāta samādhi*. Looking closely at these Sanskrit terms, *samādhi* is a super conscious state of absorption, *saṃprajñāta* is accompanied by reasoning and associated with forms, and *asaṃprajñāta* has no object in which attention is absorbed. So, although Jung turns from external to internal phenomena, which is a move definitely in line with Yoga, he is never able to release his internal objects. The object and objectification persist. The background of symbolic representations, which can never be represented or objectified, remained elusive to Jung.

In his autobiography, *Memories, Dreams, Reflections*, Jung (1961/1995) explained that since he was 11 years old, his life had been permeated and held together by the singular goal of penetrating the secret of the personality. In keeping with this theme, Jung questioned what kind of character and personality God has. Jung (1961/1995) thought, "Everything depends on that, for unless one knows the answer one cannot establish a relationship to Him" (p. 75). In particular, the destructive side of God preoccupied Jung. Perhaps in part because of Judeo-Christian roots and the influence of Kantian thought, Jung met with a limit Patañjali does not. For Jung, the fully divine is beyond human understanding – ontic reality, unknowable.

So far, we have uncovered the limits of Jung's understanding of Yoga psychology mostly by reviewing material from his autobiography and the papers of his *Collected Works*. A look at Jung's letters brings even further insight. Fairly late in life, in 1953, Jung (1975) shared the following in a note to Countess Elisabeth Klinckowstroemz, a woman he first met in 1927 at Count Keyserling's forums:

> Eastern philosophy fills a psychic lacuna in us but without answering the problem of Christianity. Since I am neither an Indian nor a Chinese, I shall probably have to rest content with my European presuppositions, otherwise I would be in danger of losing my roots for a second time. This is something I would rather not risk, for I know the price one has to pay to restore a continuity that has got lost.
>
> (pp. 121–122)

Which problem of Christianity Jung is referring to here is not clear. Jung (1961/1995) sought to understand and revision at least three: the confrontation of the feminine principle with the divine triad, the origin of evil, and the incomplete image of the Christian God (p. 350). Jung (1943/1989d) may also be alluding to the "*moral conflict*" he thought the *kleśas* represent for Westerners (para. 941). In Jung's view, Westerners are separated from the shadow by an ethical dilemma – implying the fierce heretical response by the Christian institution in particular and Western civilization in general that any true seeker must face if she or he claims oneness with Christ or God. Regardless of the ambiguities, what is clear in Jung's letter is his acknowledgement that his perspective rests on European presuppositions and that the ongoing tension between Eastern and Western views remained alive for him right up until the end.

Jung, arguably one of the foremost Western pioneers in shadow scholarship, knew that turning toward our fear not only contains clues to what we reject and distrust but also the potentialities of the greatest dynamism. Perhaps given the loss of footing after his break with Freud, fear of losing his roots again deterred Jung from even further confrontation with the fundamental dualities of Christianity and orthodox science – indeed, the fundamental presuppositions of Western civilization.

The break with Feud, so fraught with fear and anxiety and so significant in its own right, may also have played upon Jung's early childhood memories of the loss of his primary caregiver. Although Jung (1961/1995) recounted the temporary loss of his mother at three years old as leading him to have mistrust around the word "love" and to associate unreliability with women, we can speculate that he may have believed the world in general to be unreliable. Hence, deep down, he may have harbored a lack of trust in his path, therefore resisting total surrender into the numinous. In other words, he would trust up to a certain degree, and then he would contract. Jung scholar Murray Stein has explained that for Jung, God was "an awesome and dangerous mystery" (as cited in Henderson, 2010, p. 98). Whatever the case may be, Jung's fear, as divulged in this letter, undoubtedly played a factor in his (mis)understanding of Eastern liberatory psychology.

In any Eastern liberatory tradition, fear must be totally eradicated in order to transcend duality and egoic identification. Therefore, Jung's admission is worthy of serious consideration. Jung's disclosure, coupled with the fact that he believed Eastern intuition had overreached itself and that any practices aimed at egoic transcendence would lead one to unconsciousness, not liberation, indicates an inability to face into even deeper layers of shadow. The deeper layers of his shadow in turn prohibited Jung from forming a holistic psychology with full spiritual development of the personality.

As Sachdeva (1978) observed, depth psychologies are sciences of a "sick psyche" that do not come close to "the psychology of 'Higher Self' or '*Puruṣa*' with which yoga is primarily concerned" (p. 257). Similarly, Saraswati (2008) explained, "Most modern psychiatric systems are mainly concerned with bringing about 'normality' in an individual, whatever this term means. Patañjali Yoga also tries to achieve this normality but goes much further" (p. 22).

While contemplating Sachdeva's and Saraswati's points of view, it is interesting to simultaneously consider Jung's (2009) revelation at the beginning of the *Red Book*, when he spoke to his pursuit of inner images:

> My entire life consisted in elaborating what had burst forth from the unconscious and flooded me like an enigmatic stream and threatened to break me. That was the stuff and material for more than only one life. Everything later was merely the outer classification, the scientific

> elaboration, and the integration into life. But the numinous beginning, which contained everything, was then.
>
> (p. vii)

Note here how Jung refers to his confrontation with the unconscious as something that "threatened to break me." Couple this alongside his admission of fearing to lose his roots for a second time. From a nondual orientation, these are red flags in Jung's depth psychological model. Jung struggled with resigning the ego to the Self for reasons outlined throughout the present chapter: Jung accorded ontological status to both the ego and the unconscious. Another way to state this is that Jung struggled to release self-representation because his God was unconscious and needed a reflecting human consciousness to know itself. Could Jung (1954/1989c) have been speaking about himself when he noted how great our fear of the unconscious is and how we harbor formidable resistances? "Because of these resistances," he noted, "we doubt the very thing that seems so obvious to the East, namely, *the self-liberating power of the introverted mind*" (para. 773, emphasis in the original).

Although Jung turned his sights from external to internal phenomena, and pursued the methodology of active imagination for individuation purposes, the gulf between active imagination and *nirodha* lies in the capacity of the mind to introvert even further. For Patañjali, complete involution – a turning back into the source, *pratiprasava* – is of the utmost importance to the process of Yoga. Thought patterns must be turned back on themselves and resolve back into the cause from which they arose. Completely. Active imagination, as its name suggests, is an evolute, not *nirodha pariṇāma*, which is the transformation of the mind that is permeated by unbinding and stilling. A mind actively engaged in seeking phenomenal appearances and stability in formal structure cannot comprehend *pratiprasava* nor the totality of the text's vision. That is why the point of the text is to lead one to direct experience.

Yoga scholar R. S. Mishra's (1963/1997) definition of mind is helpful here. He explained,

> The psychological principle by which a conscious being thinks, the psychic process by which thinking is provided, is mind. . . . Individual mind is the psychological atom. It is an abbreviation of Cosmic Mind. When this psychological atom is broken, individual mind is transformed into Cosmic Mind.
>
> (p. 106)

Following Classical Yoga methodology, the involution of thought forms is central to breaking the psychological atom. To fully invest in the methodology of Classical Yoga, however, practitioners must have sufficient faith in both the metaphysics and process described by Patañjali. Faith and devotional surrender are demanded before Seeing. Over time, knowledge that the relative is the absolute becomes certain, and yogis learn to involute even their most formidable shadow aspects fearlessly. This involves a highly focused one-pointedness of mind as it returns to the origin and what really, naturally exists. It can't be stressed strongly enough that Jung, admittedly, never broke open. He never entered the temple of Eastern wisdom as an adept (Henderson, 1985).

Taking an in-depth look at how Jung understood Classical Yoga calls Jung's understanding of nonduality and liberation into question. Be that as it may, Jungian tools and techniques – and methods of self-inquiry per se – have not been fully assessed here, and therefore the present research should not, as a consequence, take anything away from Jung's work with self-inquiry. It may even be possible that for Westerners, Jung's methods of self-inquiry are a necessary prerequisite before embarking on Patañjali's methodology. Some yoga scholars believe Classical Yoga might not be safe for those with too much mental turmoil and should "only be practiced by people who have worked out most of their desires and have already purified their mind" (Saraswati, 2008, p. 15). However, it must be emphasized that Jung's method of inquiry revolves around the ego–Self axis, or the dialogue between the ego and Self, which in turn rests on epistemic and ontic contexts. By comparing Jung and Patañjali, the question arises, can the relationship between the ontic and epistemic be understood, or any valid theories about the ontological and epistemological be constructed, without an understanding of the nature of reality itself?

In the end, Jung (1954/1989c) had found the liberatory ideas of Classical Yoga to be too contradictory to Western civilization. But are they? While keeping the differences between Jung's and Patañjali's paths in mind, it is also important to continue acknowledging that both Patañjali and Jung are healers of psychic affliction. They are both pointing us towards integration and authentic being. Furthermore, and quite significantly, in both the Jungian and Patañjalian models of integration, the teleological directedness and the religious function of psychophysical phenomena are emphasized. In the next section, we will take a closer look at the teleological direction of each model.

The teleological function of the psyche

As we have discovered in the research thus far, Jung has the ontic and epistemic enmeshed in a way that Patañjali does not. This enmeshment appears to be the blind spot in regards to Jung's understanding of the process and practice of Yoga. Although Jung and Patañjali differ on their ontic and epistemic approaches, resulting in significantly different worldviews, it is noteworthy that Jung and Patañjali both express their insights into human nature and the phenomenon of human suffering through the exploration of the religious function and teleological directedness and of the psyche.

Jung's (2009) suffering and his process of confronting the unconscious are clearly displayed in his *Red Book*. Whether he ever wanted this text printed for public consumption is debatable. The book reveals, however, that Jung followed the path of dialogue and active imagination that he used with his clients and described in his theories as the path of individuation.

In Jung's view (1916/1953), all psychic process, just like life process, is more than just a causal sequence; it is leading somewhere. Hence, our psychological suffering has teleological directedness in his view. By taking on our suffering as opposed to avoiding it, we move in the direction of wholeness.

Although we move in the direction of wholeness, as discussed in the previous chapter, Jung believed suffering can never be eradicated. For Jung, a religious view of the world helps us endure suffering, not overcome it. This idea of endurance sets Jung apart from liberatory psychologies on a critical point – the perfectibility of human nature. When looking at Jung's ideas through a yogic lens, the question arises: can we be whole and suffer? Or is suffering an indication that there are still unreconciled aspects of personality or psychic process? Furthermore, was Jung so rooted in Christian culture and the stories of Christ that he could not see beyond crucifixion? Jung admittedly wanted to stay true to both his scientific and Christian Western roots, but at what cost? Did it inhibit his vision?

We know that in Jung's (1948/1976a) world, the "undeveloped, unconscious portions of the personality which strive for integration in the wholeness of the individual," is the compensatory function of unconscious process, giving the psyche its teleological character (para. 1156). His individuation process brings the conscious and unconscious into harmony so the psyche can be directed towards the goal. But what if, as intimated through the present chapter, Jung's vision might have been obscured? After all, Jung (1958/1972) pays careful attention to the unconscious and tries to find keys to understand it but never manages to come to terms with it clinically (p. 67). What if liberation is the perfectly logical next step, in contradistinction to his belief that liberatory ideas are examples of Eastern intuition overreaching itself? Where Jung's methodology can be seen as dancing on the precipice of divine incomprehensibility with no salvation to be had because the emergence of new images continually forces new splits within ego consciousness, Patañjali's soteriology is based on the insight that we can retire suffering completely.

Patañjali instructs us to take a comfortable seat, breath in and out evenly, still the mind, and See. Seeing, and thereby perfectibility, demands the removal of impurities in the process of perception. Or to state this slightly differently, eradication of suffering lies in the perfectibility of human perception. One technique Patañjali offered was meditative absorption on our natural inner luminosity, which is beyond suffering and sorrow (YS 1.36). Luminous states free from sorrow are equivalent to a clear, purified lens of perception, which is our true nature. Another way to state this is that clear perception is the experiential awareness of pure consciousness – and the experiential knowledge of nonduality.

By beginning his text with *atha*, now, Patañjali's may have subtly implied that after all our searching has failed, and our mind is finally tired of looking for solution in phenomena, and we are truly spent from all our suffering, we will be ready to fully engage the sūtras. Therefore, Jung's and Patañjali's distinctly different views on the elimination of suffering are in keeping with the distinction between their views on the dissolution of the contents of consciousness.

In Patañjali's world, we understand that psyche, or mind, and the entire realm of phenomenal consciousness – or in other words, all objects – serve the purpose of *puruṣa* (YS 2.21). Furthermore, in sūtra 4.24, Patañjali stated, *tad asaṁkhyeya vāsanābhiś citram api parārthaṁ saṁhatya kāritvāt*, "Though variegated by innumerable impressions, the Mind should be regarded as existing for another's purpose, because it operates as a composite" (Jha, 1934, p. 252). Again, phenomena existing for *puruṣa's* sake are acknowledged, but in addition, Patañjali also addresses the amalgamation that is psychological process. For Patañjali, imprints activate mental formations in a habitual way. Because the mind exists for pure consciousness, this implies that pure consciousness correlates to phenomenology as well as ontology and that orientation B has been infused with coherence all along. By extension, because the understanding of pure consciousness is beyond conception, it may be that the unveiling of *puruṣa* is instinctual. If accurate, the similarity to the instinctual aspects of Jung's archetype of the Self is striking.

Patañjali also stated in YS 2.23, *sva svāmi śaktyoḥ svarūpopalabdhi hetuḥ saṁyogaḥ*, "Having an alliance, or relationship between objects and the Self is the necessary means by which there can subsequently be realization of the true nature of those objects by the very Self" (Bharati, n.d., p. 25). Directly implied here is the teleological function of psychophysical phenomena. As noted earlier, *puruṣa* has the qualities of self-illumination, self-knowing, immutability, abiding in its own form, and singularity. Hence, coupling *puruṣa's* qualities with the teleological function of the psychophysical phenomena, it is implied that psychophysical phenomena, or empiric consciousness, is mirroring *puruṣa*. To state this another way, phenomenal consciousness is the manifestation of pure consciousness. Therefore, through the process of mirroring, our lens of perception, our individual beingness, is able to locate itself in relation to pure consciousness as the mirror becomes less distorted. In other words, when the mirror takes on *puruṣa's* qualities of purity and stillness, *puruṣa* is revealed in the mirror, the lens of perception becomes clear, and nonduality understood. Therefore, the teleological function of the mirroring capacity of phenomenal consciousness serves the purpose of focusing and stabilizing the lens of perception, so *puruṣa* can reveal itself to itself at the level of our human awareness and henceforth unfold its power – and take a comfortable seat in its human form.

I'd like to offer an exercise to elucidate this point further: Think for a moment about standing in front of a window. When you are standing in place A, you are at a certain angle, and the light is just so, whereupon no reflection of yourself comes back to distort that which you are perceiving. If you move just a hair and stand in place B, the angle changes, and your reflection comes into the frame, obstructing the clear view. When pure consciousness is known or embodied in experience, it looks directly through a lens of perception without reflection, akin to standing in place A at the window. To say this another way, when the conflation between pure consciousness and the objects of awareness is cleared and the relinquishment of all objects has been accomplished, pure consciousness is confirmed in itself and is able to rest in its pure power. No longer appearing as self and reflection, pure consciousness, its power, and its ability to see and perceive, established in itself, resolve as singular (YS 2.25, 4.34).

As Murray Stein has explained, Jung "was the agent for a symbolic process unfolding in the psyche. *The Red Book* is a symbol, in the Jungian sense of the word – i.e., it is the best possible representation of a still unconscious content" (as cited in Henderson, 2010, p. 97). Through a nondual orientation, it is possible to recognize, that Jung, his *Red Book*, and his extensive collection of writing represent, in full blazing clarity, what we experience in the throes of the bifurcating processes of mind as we grasp for the light of salvation. A former patient called the *Red Book* a "record of the passage of the universe through the soul of a man" (Dunne, 2010, p. 57). This is an interesting take on the text. Through Patañjali's lens, Jung can certainly be seen in orientation B looking for his authentic self in the reflection of the mind. As mentioned earlier, however, Jung remained within the tension of polarities or, figuratively speaking, moving between right and left, not quite managing to rest in the stable center. Although orientation A eluded Jung, he built a large portion of his career on the religious impulse and the instinctual movement from B to A. Metaphorically speaking, Jung can be observed in the birth canal of psychological process. While witnessing the unveiling of the Self, Jung often keenly perceived and named what he could while in the psychological birth canal, although he is tossed about through various contractions and expansions.

There is no birth that does not involve bloodletting. And bloodshed is right in line with early Vedāntic thought. Vedic scripture requires some form of, either externally or internally directed, sacrifice. "The *Ṛg Veda* declares that cosmic order is maintained by sacrificial order" (Whicher, 1998a, p. 11). But yet there is life on the other side of a birth canal: quite a different life. Again metaphorically speaking, when we are released from the tight canal of our birth mother and its contractions and expansions, we begin to breathe air instead of water. The difference between these two living experiences is comparable in magnitude to the difference between understanding the world through orientation A or orientation B. There is an enormous difference between understanding the world as suffering and understanding the world after the mind has completely released its grip around objects.

As much as Jung presented the teleological and religious function of the psyche in his work, he lived that function out loud for the entire world to see. We do not have such a record for Patañjali's personal process. Nevertheless, what is it that we see when looking at Jung's life and work through Patañjali's lens, and what can we learn? In keeping with the metaphor of birth, until one has exited the canal, it may be impossible to know what is on the other side and therefore how to put the previous experience in perspective. According to yogic thought, to understand ontic reality and epistemic states, one must be able to rest in the silent stillness underpinning the images and forms. Otherwise, when thoughts arise and are severed from their roots in pure consciousness, they will be misunderstood.

For both Jung and Patañjali, our desire to understand "God" is as real as any other instinct. While Jung and Patañjali both emphasize the teleological directedness and the religious function of psychophysical phenomena, their differences in orientation lie here: where Jung's psychology couples instincts and organs of the psyche with the transformation of the God image, Patañjali's psychology couples instinct with the evolution and involution of objects of awareness. Furthermore, for Patañjali, in regards to the instinct to fully transcend suffering, he couples instinct with the total dissolution of the images of re-presentation.

Jung on Yoga: conclusion

Why couldn't Jung perceive our beingness Patañjali's way? In Patañjali's world, when pure consciousness is not known because of misperception, the I-sense, *asmitā*, arises through the confusion of the Seer and the instrument of perception. Regarding the I-sense Whicher (2001) has explained,

> *Asmitā* is that process in which *mahat* or *buddhi*, being the purest and most sattvic evolute of *prakṛti*, becomes a recipient of a "reflection" of pure consciousness. This reflected state of consciousness masquerading in the garb of *asmitā*, assumes itself to be Self/*puruṣa*.
>
> (p. 31)

Another way of saying the above is that the reflection in the lens of perception takes itself to be the fullness of what it is reflecting. In the process of ownership, the reflection concretizes, mobilizes representation, and blocks out ontic reality as well as the limited nature of its function. Any kind of representation is a form of distance, a form of separation from pure consciousness. If pure consciousness could be represented, it wouldn't be pure. Neither reflection nor representation can ever portray the actuality, just as maps will never be the territory.

When looking at Jung through Patañjali's lens, it appears that Jung was immersed in reflection, or reflective consciousness, to the extent that he was unable to understand our instruments of perception in the same way that Patañjali did. This is to say that Jung, in his reliance upon tenets of empirical science, remained in the knowledge structures brought about through subject–object distinction. Although he worked hard at understanding the mind–body unity, for example, by conceptualizing the psychoid archetype and *unus mundus*, Jung remained in an epistemological paradigm of duality. Whether it is the ego–Self or conscious–unconscious dynamic, Jung's theories rest upon theories of the isolated mind, knowledge construction, and representation.

In contrast to Jung, it appears that Patañjali uses the same dualistic metaphysics of Sāṃkhya for provisional, descriptive, and practical purposes. Dualism for Patañjali is open to falsifiability (Whicher, 2001). When duality is falsified, *prakṛti* and *puruṣa* resolve as *brahman*, and only consciousness exists. For Patañjali, pure consciousness is the nondual immanent reality. Given that pure consciousness is our true nature, we know, or embody, nondual immanent reality through our ability to transcend the limitations wrought by the "apparently" isolated mind's appropriation of pure consciousness.

Although both scholars attempt to ground their work in the direct experience of life, unearth deeper insights into human nature, and guide us towards wholeness, embodying wholeness appears beyond the reach of Jungian methodology. Jung believed that God, the collective unconscious, or the Self would never be known directly; hence comprehension comes about through objects of experience. Through the nondual view, it is continued objectification that leaves us bound to indirect knowledge and unable to embody our wholeness. *Kaivalya* is direct experience of the totality of our true nature. Any kind of splitting or binding influences cease.

To emphasize what appears to be the limitations of Jung's vision when compared with Patañjali's *darśana*, I would like to state a former point one more time: there is a contradiction brought forward through Jung's revelation of "fearing to lose his roots" in his 1953 letter to Countess Klinckowstroem. Because Jung's fear is not divulged in his main body of work, there is a lack of transparency that needs heavy consideration when comparing his ideas with Patañjali's. Jung's pessimism and negativity toward Eastern liberation psychology may very well be founded on his own fear. Furthermore, if he did not submit completely to Patañjali's methodology, is he really in a position to comment on it? As Mircea Eliade (2009) has similarly noted, although not in direct reference to Jung, "Denial of the reality of yogic experience . . . is inadmissible from a man who has no direct knowledge of its practice, for yogic states go beyond the condition that circumscribes us when we criticize them" (p. 39).

Without a doubt, to fully experience anything, one has to be willing to submit to the experience in question without reservation. Jung knew this. For example, Jung (1925/1981) noted, "one understands nothing psychological unless one has experienced it oneself" (para. 343). Furthermore, Jung (1925/1981) understood that "progress may be permanently arrested," at any time "with complete unconsciousness of what might have followed at the next stage of development" (para. 344). Knowing about arrested development, and seemingly having clear sight of the bars on the cage of bondage, Jung (1925/1981) explained, "As a rule graduation to the next stage is barred by violent prejudices and superstitious fears" (para. 344) because "a complex can really be overcome only if it is lived out to the full" (Jung, 1938/1980b, para. 184).

Up to this point in the present study, significant differences can be observed in Jung's and Patañjali's notions of consciousness; the rooting out of imprints; and the stilling of the grasping, bifurcating mind. While Patañjali's model is nondual, Jung's resolves to dualism. Yet Jung's explorations aimed towards a discovery of psychosomatic unity. Along those lines, Jung's work on synchronicity, parapsychology, and the *unus mundus* was in direct alignment with the nonduality of Patañjali's text and therefore may offer the greatest area of opportunity to synthesize these two bodies of work.

Notes

1 Barbara Hannah (1939), one of Jung's best-known students and a teacher at the Jung Institute in Zurich, took lengthy notes on Jung's lectures on the process of individuation in Patañjali's *Yoga Sūtra*. Although these notes have been considered, because they are a secondary source, they are used only as supplementary material.

2 According to historian Sonu Shamdasani (1996) Jung did not know Sanskrit. The two translations of the *Yoga Sūtra* Jung studied were: *Yoga als Heilweg*, by his colleague, the German Indologist, J. W. Hauer, and *Allgemeine Geschichte der Philosophie* by Deussen (Hannah, 1939).

3 Jung's whole career appears to be an attempt to free himself from the chains of cultural ideologies and religious doctrines that did not fit the experience he was having. As Jungian analyst Lawrence Jaffe (1992) noted in the foreword to *Transformation of the God-Image: An Elucidation of Jung's Answer to Job*, "The central theme of *Answer to Job* – the transformation of God through human consciousness – is the central theme, too, of Jungian psychology" (p. 7).

4 Clarke (1994) summarized Jung's dialogue with the East in this way, "For all his good hermeneutical intentions, Jung is still vulnerable . . . to the charge of 'Orientalism' " (p. 187). Further explaining that "the East with which he claims

to be in conversation is, in the final analysis, something of his own making, a fiction conjured out of his own peculiarly Western needs" (p. 187).

References

Bharati, S. J. (n.d.). *Yoga sutras of Patañjali interpretive translation*. Retrieved from www.swamij.com/pdf/yogasutrasinterpretive.pdf

Chapple, C. K. (1990). The unseen seer and the field: Consciousness in Sāṃkhya and Yoga. In R. K. C. Forman (Ed.), *The problem of pure consciousness: Mysticism and philosophy* (pp. 53–70). New York, NY: Oxford University Press.

Chapple, C. K. (2008). *Yoga and the luminous: Patañjali's spiritual path to freedom*. Albany, NY: State University of New York Press.

Clarke, J. (1994). Jung and eastern thought: A dialogue with the orient. New York, NY: Routledge.

Coward, H. (1985). *Jung and eastern thought*. New York, NY: State University of New York Press.

Coward, H. (2002). *Yoga and psychology*. New York, NY: State University of New York Press.

Dunne, C. (2010). Carl Jung's red book. *Parabola, 35*(2), 56–61.

Eliade, M. (2009). *Yoga immortality and freedom* (2nd ed.). Princeton, NJ: Princeton University Press. (Original work published 1958)

Hannah, B. (Ed.). (1939). *The process of individuation: Notes on lectures given at the Eidgenossische Technische Hochschule, Zurich*. Retrieved from Opus archives: The Jane Hollister & Joseph Wheelwright collection

Henderson, J. (1985). Introduction. In H. Coward's *Jung and eastern thought* (pp. xi–xv). New York, NY: State University of New York Press.

Henderson, R. (2010). The search for the lost soul: An "enterview" with Murray Stein about C. G. Jung's the red book. *Jung Journal: Culture & Psyche*, *4*(4), 92–101.

Jaffe, L. W. (1992). Foreword. In E. Edinger (Ed.), *Transformation of the God-image: An elucidation of Jung's answer to Job* (pp. 7–8). Toronto, Canada: Inner City Books.

Jha, G. (1934). *Yoga-darshana: Sūtras of Patañjali's with Bhāsya of Vyāsa* (2nd ed.). Freemont, CA: Asian Humanities Press. (Original work published 1907/Revised 1934)

Jung, C. G. (1953). The relations between the ego and the unconscious. In H. Read, M. Fordham, G. Adler, & W. McGuire (Eds.), *The collected works of C. G. Jung* (R. F. C. Hull, Trans., Vol. 7, pp. 121–239). New York, NY: Pantheon. (Original work published 1916, revised 1934)

Jung, C. G. (1970). The undiscovered self. In H. Read, M. Fordham, G. Adler, & W. McGuire (Eds.), *The collected works of C. G. Jung* (R. F. C. Hull, Trans., Vol. 10, pp. 245–305). Princeton, NJ: Princeton University Press. (Original work published 1957)

Jung, C. G. (1972). The transcendent function. In H. Read, M. Fordham, G. Adler, & W. McGuire (Eds.), *The collected works of C. G. Jung* (R. F. C. Hull, Trans., 2nd ed., Vol. 8, pp. 67–91). Princeton, NJ: Princeton University Press. (Original work published 1958)

Jung, C. G. (1975). *C. G. Jung letters: Volume 2: 1951–1961* (R. F. C. Hull, Trans., G. Adler, & A. Jaffé, Eds.). Princeton, NJ: Princeton University Press.

Jung, C. G. (1976a). Depth psychology. In H. Read, M. Fordham, G. Adler, & W. McGuire (Eds.), *The collected works of C. G. Jung* (R. F. C. Hull, Trans., Vol. 18, pp. 477–486). Princeton, NJ: Princeton University Press. (Original work published 1948)

Jung, C. G. (1976b). The type problem in poetry. In H. Read, M. Fordham, G. Adler, & W. McGuire (Eds.), *The collected works of C. G. Jung* (R. F. C. Hull, Trans., Vol. 6, pp. 166–272). Princeton, NJ: Princeton University Press. (Original work published 1920, revised 1960)

Jung, C. G. (1980a). Conscious, unconscious, and individuation. In H. Read, M. Fordham, G. Adler, & W. McGuire (Eds.), *The collected works of C. G. Jung* (R. F. C. Hull, Trans., 2nd ed., Vol. 9i, pp. 275–289). Princeton, NJ: Princeton University Press. (Original work published 1939)

Jung, C. G. (1980b). Psychological aspects of the mother archetype. In H. Read, M. Fordham, G. Adler, & W. McGuire (Eds.), *The collected works of C. G. Jung* (R. F. C. Hull, Trans., 2nd ed., Vol. 9i, pp. 75–110). Princeton, NJ: Princeton University Press. (Original work published 1938, revised 1954)

Jung, C. G. (1981). Marriage as a psychological relationship. In H. Read, M. Fordham, G. Adler, & W. McGuire (Eds.), *The collected works of C. G. Jung* (R. F. C. Hull, Trans., Vol. 17, pp. 189–201). Princeton, NJ: Princeton University Press. (Original work published 1925)

Jung, C. G. (1989a). Answer to Job. In H. Read, M. Fordham, G. Adler, & W. McGuire (Eds.), *The collected works of C. G. Jung* (R. F. C. Hull, Trans., 2nd ed., Vol. 11, pp. 355–470). Princeton, NJ: Princeton University Press. (Original work published 1954)

Jung, C. G. (1989b). Foreword to "Introduction to Zen Buddhism." In H. Read, M. Fordham, G. Adler, & W. McGuire (Eds.), *The collected works of C. G. Jung* (R. F. C. Hull, Trans., 2nd ed., Vol. 11, pp. 538–557). Princeton, NJ: Princeton University Press. (Original work published 1939)

Jung, C. G. (1989c). Psychological commentary on "the Tibetan book of the great liberation." In H. Read, M. Fordham, G. Adler, & W. McGuire (Eds.), *The collected works of C. G. Jung* (R. F. C. Hull, Trans., 2nd ed., Vol. 11, pp. 475–508). Princeton, NJ: Princeton University Press. (Original work published 1954)

Jung, C. G. (1989d). The psychology of eastern meditation. In H. Read, M. Fordham, G. Adler, & W. McGuire (Eds.), *The collected works of C. G. Jung* (R. F. C. Hull, Trans., 2nd ed., Vol. 11, pp. 558–575). Princeton, NJ: Princeton University Press. (Original work published 1943)

Jung, C. G. (1989e). Yoga and the west. In H. Read, M. Fordham, G. Adler, & W. McGuire (Eds.), *The collected works of C. G. Jung* (R. F. C. Hull, Trans., 2nd ed., Vol. 11, pp. 529–537). Princeton, NJ: Princeton University Press. (Original work published 1936)

Jung, C. G. (1995). *Memories, dreams, reflections* (R. Winston & C. Winston, Trans., A. Jaffe, Ed.). London: FontanaPress. (Original work published 1961)

Jung, C. G. (2009). *The Red Book: Liber Novus* (S. Shamdasani, Ed., M. Kyburz, J. Peck, & S. Shamdasani, Trans.). New York, NY: Philemon series & W. W. Norton.

Mishra, R. S. (1997). The textbook of yoga psychology: The definitive translation and interpretation of Patañjali's yoga sutras for meaningful application in all

modern psychological disciplines (A. Adman, Ed.). Monroe, NY: Baba Bhagavandas Publication Trust. (Original work published 1963)
Sachdeva, I. P. (1978). *Yoga and depth psychology*. Delhi, India: Motilal Banarsidass.
Saraswati, S. S. (2008). Four chapters on freedom: Commentary on the yoga sutras of Patañjali. Bihar, India: Yoga Publications Trust.
Shamdasani, S. (1996). Introduction. In *The psychology of kundalini yoga: Notes of the seminar given in 1932 by C. G. Jung* (pp. xvii–xlvi). (S. Shamdasani, Ed.). Princeton, NJ: Princeton University Press.
Shamdasani, S. (2003). *Jung and the making of modern psychology: The dream of a science*. New York, NY: Cambridge University Press.
Stein, R. (2010). Snapshots from the void: Reflections on Jung's relationship to Indian yoga. *Jung Journal: Culture & Psyche*, *4*(2), 62–84.
Taimni, I. K. (1961). The science of yoga: The yoga-sutras of Patañjali in Sanskrit with transliteration in roman, translation and commentary in English. Wheaton, IL: The Theosophical Publishing House.
Whicher, I. (1998a). *The integrity of the yoga darśana: A reconsideration of classical yoga*. Albany, NY: State University of New York Press.
Whicher, I. (1998b). Yoga and freedom: A reconsideration of Patañjali's classical yoga. *Philosophy East and West*, *48*(2), 272–322.
Whicher, I. (2001). *Patañjali's metaphysical schematic: Puruṣa and prakrti in the yogasutra*. Chennai, India: The Adyar Library and Research Center.
Whicher, I. (2003). The integration of spirit (*puruṣa*) and matter (*prakṛti*) in the yoga sūtra. In I. Whicher & D. Carpenter (Eds.), *Yoga: The Indian tradition* (pp. 51–69). New York, NY: Routledge.

Chapter 5

A synthesis of Jung and Patañjali

In the chapters thus far, the similarities and differences between the works of Jung and Patañjali have been explored along with the areas where Jung met his limits in relation to yogic thought. At the end of the previous chapter, the idea was raised that because of Jung's aim at discovering a psychosomatic unity, the elements of Jung's work that grappled with notions of duality and unity may offer areas of synthesis with the nondual orientation of Classical Yoga. A brief review illuminates the central elements upon which a possible synthesis of their models may be drawn.

The main similarities explored up to this point include Jung's ideas on complexes, which map very closely to Patañjali's description of *vṛttis* and *saṃskāras*, the habit patterns of the mind that lead to the experience of constrained psychophysical states. Both scholars are also in agreement that forms of affect lie at the heart of these painful mental disturbances. The agreement between Jung and Patañjali on the teleological directedness and religious function of the psyche has also been considered as highly significant. Their ideas on ego-consciousness and what is actually transforming in the transformation of consciousness, however, are markedly different. While Jung emphasized the transformation of the God-image at the core of his individuation process, Patañjali guided his students to a critical discernment between two orientations of consciousness, which I have designated as orientations A and B. In orientation A, pure consciousness, the Seer, abides in its essential nature; and in orientation B, the Seer conforms with the fluctuations of the mind.

The difference between Jung and Patañjali in their approaches to the unconscious is one of the most striking aspects of the dialogue between them. When defining his concept of the unconscious Jung (1920/1976a) stated, "The concept of the unconscious is for me an *exclusively psychological* concept, and not a philosophical concept of a metaphysical nature" (para. 837, emphasis in the original). But, as it turns out, Jung's metaphysics are actually hidden, as encountered, for example, in his notion that the collective unconscious is an original psychic entity (Ajaya, 1983; Brooks, 2011; Coward, 1985; Watts, 1971). Hence, although Jung may have originally intended the unconscious to be an exclusively psychological concept, it is not. For Jung, the unconscious is ontically real, but for Patañjali, it is not. As the most prominent difference, bridging their ideas on the unconscious is imperative if we are to begin to facilitate a synthesis of their worldviews.

The synthesis explored in the present chapter calls for an approach that is as broad as it is deep – using work within several scientific disciplines, which are far from complete and prodigious in scope. In places, the material is quite technical, drawing on quantum physics and holography. In other places, topics such as Taoism and neurobiology are factored in, albeit briefly. My aim, however, is to locate the debate between Jung and Patañjali – and likewise the synthesis – in our own bodymind.

Chapter 5 is broken down into two sections. The first section, "The efficacy of the concept of the unconscious," takes a closer look at the all-important depth psychological notion of the unconscious and questions whether the unconscious is indeed unconscious. The mind–body unity as it relates to depth psychology and Classical Yoga is also studied. The second section, "Validating the consciousness of the unconscious," examines the intersection of affective neuroscience and Jungian depth psychology and the possible remediation of the conscious–unconscious dynamic. This section also considers mysterious phenomena and synchronicity as well as a holographic heuristic device as possible pointers towards the aforementioned validation.

The efficacy of the concept of the unconscious

In *Jung and the Making of Modern Psychology: The Dream of a Science*, historian Sonu Shamdasani (2003) noted the landmark study by Michel Henry, which revealed that "the concept of the unconscious made its appearance in Western thought "*simultaneously with and as the exact consequence of the concept of consciousness*" (p. 168, emphasis in the original). Objective knowing and representational metaphysics created the ground from which the concept, and *affirmation*, of the unconscious arose. This affirmation has not been without controversy however. Many philosophers have found the concept of the unconscious problematic and have questioned its efficacy (Henry, 1993; Thompson, 2001). Furthermore, a close read of Jung's writing reveals that Jung himself had questions around the underlying metaphysics of his theories. In "Late Thoughts," the final chapter in *Memories, Dreams, Reflections*, one of Jung's last texts, written within two years of his death, Jung (1961/1995) stated unequivocally, when unconscious contents come into consciousness, human beings make the Creator conscious of His creation (p. 371). While he makes the above claim unequivocally in *Memories, Dreams, Reflections*, a review of his letters reveals another story.

After Jung wrote drafts of "Late Thoughts and On Life After Death," another of the final chapters of his autobiography, he sent copies to Erich Neumann, his esteemed student and colleague, to review. In the

Neumann–Jung correspondences around these chapters it is apparent Jung struggled with his ideas on the ontological realism of the unconscious right up until publication, which was very near the end of his life. These letters also demonstrate how Jung's ideas on creation's self-illumination, or lack thereof, raised significant issues for Neumann. Neumann thought it necessary to communicate his disagreements to Jung, even at the risk of losing Jung's favor. On 18 February 1959, Neumann (Jung & Neumann, 2015) wrote, "If the Self contemplates you as the ego, then the Self is not unconscious" (p. 344). Furthermore, he stated, "The only thing that remains open to question is why creation, the answer, radiating in infinite variety what only radiates in itself in an unreflected way, is ancient, but satisfies me" (pp. 346–347). For Neumann, creation shines in itself and for itself.

In his responding letter to Neumann on 10 March 1959, Jung (1975) questioned:

> Why should the Creator stage-manage this whole phenomenal world since he already knows what he can reflect himself in, and why should he reflect himself at all since he is already conscious of himself? Why should he create alongside his own omniscience a second, inferior consciousness – millions of dreary little mirrors when he knows in advance just what the image they reflect will look like?
>
> (p. 495)

Where Jung thought the reflective capacities of *Homo sapiens* brought consciousness to God, Neumann believed strongly that to formulate God, or the Self, as unconscious was a mistake, no retroaction on God is necessary. Although it's hard to know exactly what concept, image, or belief of God, the Jewish-born Neumann had in mind here this point of contrast between Jung and Neumann is significant in that it highlights Jung's late thoughts. Neumann's overall body of work has not been researched and remains to be explored further regarding these matters.

In Jung's (1975) letter, he expressed gratitude to Neumann and explained how he was attempting "to pin down" his "volatile thoughts" (p. 493). Jung further explained what "an exceedingly painful experience" it was for him to question whether the Creator is conscious of Himself, and he thought whatever answer he was to arrive at had "well-nigh incalculable consequences," which he didn't find easy to argue about (p. 493). The Neumann–Jung correspondences throw light on the fact that Jung struggled with the ontological realism of the unconscious right up until the end of his life.

Another interesting point to note regarding Jung's late-in-life inquiry around the consciousness of the Creator and the meaning of creation is the language Jung used when describing our world. In letters to other associates, as well as in his autobiography, when Jung (1961/1995) described our world, he used depreciating language to do so. He spoke of "monstrous, apparently senseless biological turmoil" and a Creator who has squandered "millions of years upon the development of countless species and creatures" (p. 371). He spoke of "errors," "impasses," and "the most cruel consequences, disease, mutilation, and horrible fights" (Jung, 1975, p. 312). In these texts, Jung appears judgmental and averse to any form of natural violence. It is not just the harshness within our species but also nature's organic and routine cycles of destruction that seem to disturb Jung in such a way that it causes him to question creation. Creation must be wrong, blind, or in need of human stewardship to have come about in this violent and destructive way, he believed. By prescribing creation meaning, he believed, humans will set it right. In Jung's (1961/1995) view, "the Occidental feels the need to complete the meaning of the world" (p. 349). As far as he could discern, "the sole purpose of human existence is to kindle a light in the darkness of mere being" (p. 358).

In the same correspondence, Neumann appears to have a much less judgmental view of evolution and an unconditional acceptance of things as they are. As Neumann (Jung & Neumann, 2015) expressed to Jung, "Precisely because the psyche and the archetypes have developed with their meaning content in development of nature, this meaning is not something foreign to nature but rather belongs to it from the outset – it seems to me" (p. 346). For Neumann, meaning is inherent in life; we don't need to search for it or place it. Patañjali would undoubtedly agree with Neumann here, as the search for meaning is a mental construct, or psychological experience, associated with orientation B and oftentimes states of suffering.

Patañjali's Yoga psychology would consider Jung's metaphysical questions and dialogue with Neumann as an experience of orientation B, in which Jung was having psychological experiences without full awareness, and as a result, he classified them as unconscious. Jung then projected his concept of an unconscious, or his psychological experience, into his notion of a Creator. If Patañjali is correct, then with this in mind, as a science that lays its foundation on a concept of the unconscious, alongside of a conscious–unconscious dynamism in which ego-consciousness brings illumination to the Creator, Jungian depth psychology may be building its discipline upon very shaky ground.

Depth psychology, as defined by Jung (1948/1976b), is the "branch of psychological science which is concerned with the phenomenon of the unconscious" (para. 1142). Elsewhere Jung (1943/1989b) noted that depth psychology from its earliest days recognized "the importance of the human shadow-side and its influence on consciousness," but then, "got entangled in this problem" (para. 941). Because depth psychology until the present day still aims at formulating a clear clinical picture of unconscious contents and processes, looking backwards may assist us in moving forward.

The mind–body unity

Freud's work with Anna O, considered the first psychoanalytical case, made it clear that symptoms of illness can arise through the damming -up of affect. Freud (1925/1989) observed that affect "had got on the wrong lines" and had "become strangulated there," and when it was "directed on the normal path," it could be discharged (p. 13). In other words, our symptoms serve a purpose and point to a deeper psychophysical process. In addition to this view of symptoms, in depth psychology, dreams, fantasies, hallucinations, and delusions also serve a purpose by unveiling our deepest desires and aims. Through uncovering the hidden meaning of these psychophysical processes, depth psychology has long demonstrated the vitality of the world behind our eyes. By close observation of the secret, hidden and repressed, the discipline of depth psychology has made enormous gains in understanding not only the human mind but also human being.

In depth psychology, it is through paying attention to the "less" visible that we can direct ourselves onto the path that is normal, or innate for us, subsequently allowing for the fullest expression of our being. Indeed, people are drawn to depth psychology because they are not satisfied with themselves or the way their lives are unfolding, and thus they seek understanding or transformation. The fullest expression of their true nature has been dammed up, and as a result, the flow of their life feels off course. Often a re-orientation is sought. Allowing for nonrational processes, alongside rational reflection viewed through a depth psychological lens, assists people in getting back on course and into alignment with their authentic selves. Therefore, hasn't depth psychology right from the very beginning, with Freud and Breuer's work on the case of Anna O, proven that the unconscious is not unconscious at all, that in fact, it has a language or several languages that need new methods of interpretation? At heart, doesn't depth psychology and all its theory aim to put people into accord with their authentic being in this world?

Through depth psychology, we learn and thereby understand ourselves on a deeper level of our being. This knowledge opens the opportunity for us to experience ourselves more fully. One means of experiencing ourselves more fully comes about through understanding how finely tuned the body is with the mind. In fact, it is through depth psychological research and its healing methods that we are shown how body and mind are not separate but one whole being-in-itself. That is to say, to believe that body and mind are separate and distinct is erroneous. Many cultures already understand that there is no division between psyche and soma. Within the field of depth psychology, Freud (1925/1989) and Jung (1946/1972b) began this discovery process. The work has continued and in some cases has been radically pioneered by many others in the field (Miller, 2006; Sidoli, 2001; Woodman,

1993). As Polish psychologist Alice Miller (1998) has explained, in regards to her research on early childhood wounding,

> The truth about our childhood is stored up in our body, and although we can repress it, we can never alter it. Our intellect can be deceived, our feelings manipulated, our perceptions confused and our bodies tricked with medication. But someday the body will present its bill, for it is as incorruptible as a child who, still whole in spirit, will accept no compromises or excuses, and it will not stop tormenting us until we stop evading the truth.
>
> (p. 315)

Through its symptoms, the body shows us where we are psychophysically out of alignment with our true nature. For instance, through neuroses, we are shown where there is a damming up of affect and where we have psychologically split off to compensate for what has been unexpressed. What is made clear through the depth psychological explorations of the mind–body unity is that the realities of the flesh have to be known to experience health. Holding onto bifurcating thought patterns, which psychologically split the body and mind, is prohibitive.

The mind–body unity is another area of similarity between depth psychology and Classical Yoga. For Patañjali, distractions of the mind, or distorted thoughts, have corresponding physical features. In several sūtras, he is explicit on this point (*Yoga Sūtra* [YS] 1.30, 1.31, 2.40, 2.43). Distress, despair, trembling in the body, and disturbed breathing accompany, and therefore point to, our distracted and distorted thoughts. The process of Classical Yoga works directly with the distracted and distorted thoughts that lead us away from embodying our true nature. Through the right application of effort in the practice of Patañjali Yoga, psychological experience can be steadied, leading beyond the tension of seemingly opposing forces and the affect which accompanies them, whereupon we are able to take a comfortable seat in the body (YS 2.46, 2.47, 2.48).

Through comparing the mind–body connection as it is approached in depth psychology and Classical Yoga, it appears quite strongly that individually learning to interpret the deeper levels of thought and bodily process shows us, through direct experience, that "unconscious" is a psychological concept. In other words, regardless of Jung's conflation of psychology and ontology, the psychosomatic work within the depth psychological tradition points in a direction that shows signs of confirming that the term "unconscious," as a "representation," is psychological – not ontic.

Given all the problems that Jung's, as well as Freud's, concept of the unconscious has generated, questioning the predominant conception of consciousness that it presupposes has become unavoidable. Psychoanalyst Michael Guy Thompson (2001) has addressed this critical question:

> Whereas Freud depicted psychoanalysis as essentially a science of the *unconscious*, it is impossible to escape the observation that it is also a science – if we can call it that – preoccupied with *consciousness* itself, if only implicitly. Terms like *truth*, *epistemology*, *knowledge*, *understanding*, and *comprehension* pervade virtually every psychoanalytic paper that is devoted to the unconscious as a concept. But isn't our fascination about the unconscious and our failure to resolve questions about its nature a consequence of our obsession with consciousness and the epistemological bias it engenders?
>
> (p. 577)

Hence, if the term "unconscious" and its representation is psychological – not ontic – a "conceptual problem" lies at the core of Jungian depth psychology. Therefore, this line of inquiry is applicable to all depth psychological sciences that postulate the existence of an "unconscious" and remain entangled within its conception.

If the unconscious is indeed a psychological concept only, then, although much groundwork has been laid via the interpretation of dreams, fantasies, symptoms, and the mind–body unity, depth psychology has long been, and still remains, rooted in epistemology in contradistinction to ontology. If depth psychology must, for the most part, remain rooted in epistemology to satisfy the demands of modern-day science, what Jung revealed in his final years demands a more critical look by those who subscribe to his hypothesis of an unconscious agent that we can never know directly, alongside his theory that liberation is beyond our reach. In a paper originally written in 1916, Jung (1958/1972) developed the core part of his theory of psychological growth, "The Transcendent Function," the mediating force of the psyche. The paper remained unpublished until it was reworked some 42 years later, in which Jung stated,

> After forty-two years, the problem has lost nothing of its topicality. . . . The essay may therefore stand, with all its imperfections, as an historical document. It may give the reader some idea of the efforts of understanding which were needed for the first attempts at a synthetic view of the psychic process in analytical treatment. As its basic argument is still valid today, it may stimulate the reader to a broader and deeper understanding of the problem. This problem is identical with the universal question: How does one come to terms in practice with the unconscious? This is the question posed by the philosophy of India, and particularly by Buddhism and Zen. Indirectly, it is the fundamental

> question, in practice, of all religions and philosophies. For the unconscious is not this thing or that; it is the Unknown as it immediately affects us.
>
> (pp. 67–68)

As has been noted, for Patañjali, knowledge is structured in consciousness. Hence, when Seeing is unveiled, when the omniscience of pure consciousness and the infinity of knowledge are understood, nothing remains to be known ontically through the epistemic splits of the mind. To state this slightly differently, pure consciousness can be known in Patañjali's world because it is our very being. Far from Unknown, pure consciousness is knowledge itself. To the extent that we reflect or embody that knowing, we are yoked. The mind comes to rest in the silent stillness underpinning the images and forms. Hence, what is Unknown for Jung is pure consciousness for Patañjali.

Despite significant difference between Jung's and Patañjali's approaches to the unconscious, the mediating force of Jung's transcendent function is undoubtedly similar to the integration that takes place through Classical Yoga methodology; however, "How does one come to terms in practice with the unconscious?" is not a question posed by Patañjali. In Patañjali's world, the contents of consciousness that distort the lens of perception are addressed – in particular, our egoic "I" sense and all its related attachments and aversions.

As already mentioned in the previous chapter, through Patañjali's lens, Jung has pure consciousness and the contents of consciousness enmeshed. The enmeshment of the Seer and the Seen appears to be Jung's blind spot in an embodied understanding of pure consciousness. Because Jung's ontological arguments are not explicit, his theories and methods confuse ontological questions with epistemic issues. This is a critical problem and one that has become more pressing in our time. A "conceptual problem" at the core of depth psychology may, as a result, be impacting the empirical research and the clinical setting (Corbett & Whitney, 2016).

On account of Jung's conflation of the ontic and epistemic, it is understandable why he never came to terms clinically with the unconscious. Consequently and furthermore, he did not accomplish his desire to reconcile science and religious experience. Jung's body of work remained incomplete upon his death and still remains incomplete today. Moreover, although Jung (1936/1989c) believed that the West would produce its own yoga, one based on Christianity, that has yet to come to pass. As a discriminatory science of knowledge, Classical Yoga guides practitioners to direct experience of *puruṣa*, the localized expression of pure consciousness. Classical Yoga methodology, through the total involution of thought forms, mobilizes a radically empirical scientific methodology, which succeeds in reconciling science and religious experience. If those working in the field of depth psychology are open to reconsidering Jung's ontological unconscious as self-illuminating, the Jung–Patañjali dialogue may be able to assist forward movement to these open areas of depth psychology. Agreement on a self-illuminating nature to ontic reality allows for a solid foundation on which to forge a synthesis between depth psychology and Classical Yoga. With self-illuminating consciousness as the ground, then, perhaps, a depth psychology–Classical Yoga fusion can yield a contemporary, and more lucid, understanding of the multiplicity of forms on the foreground.

Validating the consciousness of the unconscious

Although Jung did not view ontic reality as self-illuminating pure consciousness, his archetype as an image of instinct draws upon the idea that our epistemologies and epistemic states are driving us to understand the Self, whether we are aware of it or not. If we subscribe to the orientation that ontic reality is self-illuminating – or, stated slightly differently, self-revealing – then what phenomena might offer empirical science an opportunity to validate the consciousness of the unconscious? Given that life does not stand outside itself, it must be phenomena that cannot be controlled by the so-called conscious mind.

For depth psychology, the understanding of the conscious–unconscious dynamic in the human psyche places affect in center stage. In effect, depth psychology found evidence of phenomena that cannot be controlled. Couple the evidence with Patañjali's certainty of ontic reality as pure consciousness, which is a single unique power that always knows what it is doing, and our affective states then may offer empirical evidence of life's power realizing itself over and above our knowledge construction and re-presentation. Contemporary research in neuropsychoanalysis may support this idea. Neuropsychologist Marks Solms (2013) has stated,

> The brainstem mechanisms derived from the autonomic body are associated with affective consciousness, and the cortical mechanisms derived from the sensorimotor body are associated with cognitive consciousness . . . the upper brainstem is intrinsically conscious whereas the cortex is not; it derives its consciousness from the brainstem.
>
> (Solms, 2013, p. 5)

A clearer understanding of consciousness, therefore, may have less to do with reflective cognition than with instinct – and perhaps, in particular, with the drive towards (or away from) religious experience.

While affective neuroscience may offer depth psychology empirical evidence of a collective measure that will allow for a deeper understanding of the religious instinct, still, the essential nature of Patañjali's methodology resolves to personal experience. So even if, for example, neuroscience correlates anxiety to bifurcating mental processes, which inhibit direct experience of whole being and pure consciousness, the map will never be the territory. Whole being will not arise by reading research results: each of us individually must root out the bifurcating habit patterns of the mind. Furthermore, as healing as the transference may be within the clinical, or any supportive setting – and I do not want to underestimate the enormity of its nurturing impact – the interpretive moment, the re-collection of projection, and the integration of traumatic experiences are accomplished in our interiority.[1]

Patañjali guides us to sit comfortably, even out the breath, quiet the mind, See, and integrate any and all fragmented aspects of psychic process. While the instructions may sound simple, they are more often than not found to be quite challenging. The practice of Patañjali Yoga demands the correct application of effort to fix the concentration of the mind. Furthermore, through a process of involution, all objects must be removed from the horizon of awareness, including, especially, the objects that carry our transference. The methodology is rigorous. There is no alternative. The involution of thought forms radically empirical. Because Patañjali Yoga is rigorous, it demands an investment of time, energy, and focus. Classical Yoga therefore requires unwavering faith in the text and the teachings in order to commit to the focus of the methodology. For those not immersed in orthodox Hindu cosmology and culture, how would this faith arise? Perhaps further empirical parallels, in addition to affect, can be drawn between Classical Yoga and depth psychology? Given that ethics, morality, and authenticity all, quite significantly, factor into both the individuation and Yoga process, then perhaps experiments that link authenticity and morality may be instructive (Gino, Kouchaki, & Galinsky, 2015). One means of moving forward may also be to visualize new models, which draw from both scientific discovery and numinous experience. New models and ways of viewing the world could perhaps then draw us closer to remediating the conscious–unconscious demarcation.

Remediating the conscious–unconscious demarcation

Although Patañjali does not use the term *unconscious* in his text, he does refer to *kleśas*, spiritual hindrances or afflicted thought patterns, which lead to the obscuration of our true nature and result in suffering. The main *kleśa* in Classical Yoga is *avidyā*. As discussed in Chapter 1, although most often translated into English as "ignorance," *avidyā* etymologically means "not wisdom" or "not pure vision" and therefore a fundamental misunderstanding of the nature of reality or absence of vision.

Developing the notion of *avidyā*, in sūtra 2.5, Patañjali defined four types of misunderstanding: "1) regarding that which is transient as eternal, 2) mistaking the impure for the pure, 3) thinking that which brings misery to bring happiness, and 4) taking that which is not-self to be self" (Bharati, n.d., p. 20). *Avidyā*, therefore, has to do with confusing something for something else.

Despite the elusive nature of *avidyā*, finding a way to explain, or represent, our everyday experience of the mind can be seen as an all-important task if we are to formulate new models that may facilitate a synthesis of depth psychology and Classical Yoga with an aim towards validating the consciousness of the unconscious. Contemporary minds in general, and orthodox scientific minds in particular, demand this. The most fundamental question that arises is, why is there is *avidyā* in the first place? How can *brahman* be *sat* (being) and *cit* (consciousness) and yet appear as *avidyā*? If we are indeed pure consciousness, self-illuminating, eternal, and absolute, nearly all of us don't know it. *Avidyā* is indisputably experienced psychologically by most. Patañjali's text makes it clear that metaphysical speculation on *avidyā* will not remove it. To remove the cause of suffering, there must be a fundamental shift in the way we perceive and experience reality. We need new optics.

Thankfully, an optical shift has been taking place in several disciplines over the past few decades, notably, in neuropsychology, a discipline pioneered by neurosurgeon Dr. Karl Pribram. Challenging the established paradigm Pribram has contended,

> It isn't that the world of appearances is wrong; it isn't that there aren't objects out there, at one level of reality. It's that if you penetrate through and look at the universe with a holographic system, you arrive at a different view, a different reality. And that other reality can explain things that have hitherto remained inexplicable scientifically: paranormal phenomena, synchronicities, the apparently meaningful coincidence of events.
>
> (as cited in Talbot, 1991, p. 11)

Because Patañjali's YS exposes the synchronous nature of past, present and future, and because Patañjali spent a good portion of his writing, in fact most of Chapter 3, on paranormal, or – more preferably termed – mysterious phenomena, Pribram's suggestion of looking at the universe with a holographic system is applicable to frame Patañjali's vision in contemporary terms. As synchronicity and mysterious phenomena were highly significant underlying drivers to Jung's sizeable body of work as well, a holographic heuristic that illuminates the possibility of synchronicity and mysterious phenomena might allow further construction of a bridge between depth psychology and Classical Yoga. Additionally, a holographic heuristic may provide further assistance on validating the consciousness of the unconscious.

Mysterious phenomena and synchronicity

Jung was drawn to mysterious psychic phenomena throughout his life (Main, 1997). For example, in his early 20s, around 1899 while he was still in school, Jung studied and experimented with his 15-year-old medium cousin, Hélène Preiswerk. Subsequently, it was Jung's (1961/1995) conversations with the dead in the early years of his career that formed a kind of prelude to what he had to communicate to the world about the kind of pattern or order that he detected in the unconscious. For Jung, unconscious phenomena appear chaotic and unsystematic, but below that appearance lays an often-imperceptible order. In other words, because the unconscious never seemed to be at variance with itself, Jung thought it may very well possess a unity and self-consistency. Jung's (1951/1985) work with ESP in particular led him to view the unconscious, in its most important and overpowering manifestations, as a collective phenomenon that is identical everywhere. Jungian scholar Roderick Main (1997) has noted that it was Jung's lifelong interest in mysterious phenomena that eventually resulted in his theory of synchronicity.

Jung developed his theory on synchronicity through his clinical research into the collective unconscious and through his intimate collaboration with several scholars in various disciplines. One of his primary collaborators in this endeavor was German sinologist Richard Wilhelm. Wilhelm had spent decades living in China and researching Eastern thought. In Wilhelm's (1931/1962) translation of the classic Taoist alchemical text, *The Secret of the Golden Flower*, Jung found parallels to his research on the collective unconscious. Jung wrote the introduction to this Wilhelm translation as well as Wilhelm's translation of the *I Ching, or Book of* Changes (1950/1989a). The *I Ching's* divination system greatly impacted Jung. To formulate direct experience of the Taoist system, Jung experimented with the hexagrams and prophetic nature of the text. Jung noted (1950/1989a) that to the Taoists, "the hexagram was understood to be an indicator of the essential situation prevailing at the moment of its origin" (para. 971). In reference to his direct experience with the hexagrams of the *I Ching*, Jung (1930/1966) explained,

> Anyone who, like myself, has had the rare good fortune to experience in association with Wilhelm the divinatory power of the *I Ching* cannot remain ignorant of the fact that we have here an Archimedean point from which our Western attitude of mind could be lifted off its foundations.
>
> (para. 78)

The Archimedean point is the principle of synchronicity (Stein, 2005).

While Jung rejected certain aspects of Upaniṣadic–Patañjalian thought, he fully accepted Taoist thinking. So, although Patañjali directly addressed synchronicity, the Eastern ideas of Taoism on the correlation between the inner psyche and outer world impacted Jung the most when formulating his theories around synchronicity. The depths of the Taoist liberatory philosophy, Jung's understanding of it, and its comparison to Classical Yoga, are, however, beyond the scope of the present project. In brief, the Tao manifests in creation as *yin* and *yang*, a fundamental pair of opposites. The interplay of *yang* and *yin* is the foundation for the constantly changing and transitory nature of all phenomena. In regards to a correct understanding of the underlying nondualism of *yin* and *yang*, Wilhelm (1931/1962) explained,

> Since both yin and yang have their common origin in an undivided One and are active only in the realm of phenomena, where yang appears as the active principle and conditions, and yin as the passive principle is derived and conditioned, it is quite clear that a metaphysical dualism is not the basis of these ideas.
>
> (p. 12)

The underlying nondualism is the natural reality in Taoism and can be known when we are in the *tao*, which means in line with our true nature. True nature signifies a union of opposites and is symbolized through the principle of *wu wei*, action through inaction, in which nature is effortlessly flowing (Wu Wei, 2004).

Similar to Jung's connection with Wilhelm, Jung's relationship with theoretical physicist Wolfgang Pauli also nourished his long percolating ideas on synchronicity, and in 1932, when Jung was 55 years old, he and Pauli began working closely together on mind–matter relations. The Jung–Pauli collaboration was, in essence, an attempt to link depth psychological processes with the quantum processes of theoretical physics. Swiss psychiatrist and Jungian psychologist C.A. Meier explained,

> Both sciences have, in the course of many years of independent work, amassed observations and systems of thought to match them. Both sciences have come up against certain barriers which . . . display similar basic characteristics. The object to be investigated, and the human investigator with his organs of sense and knowledge and their extensions (measuring instruments and procedures), are indissolubly bound together.
>
> (as cited in Jung, 1946/1972b, para. 440)

Thus, the recognition that the observer plays a fundamental role in experience was highly significant to the work of both Jung and Patañjali.

In Jung's (1952/1972c) world, synchronicity is a formal factor in nature, which is "the meaningful coincidence of an absolutely natural product with a human idea apparently independent of it" (para. 946). In addition to "meaningful coincidence," Jung also described synchronicity as "an acausal connecting principle." For Jung, synchronistic phenomena appear meaningfully related but not causally so.

While formulating his theories on an acausal connecting principle, Jung came to speculate on the nonpsychic aspects of archetypes. He called this the psychoid aspect. "It is the primal form of the contents of the human psyche when they have not yet become specifically psychological, or when they have dropped down from the psychological level to touch the undifferentiated state of nature" (Progoff, 2008, p. 157). It is in the psychoid, where the psychic and the physical are no longer differentiated, that synchronistic events appear to take place in Jung's world.

In describing the foundational elements of the synchronicity hypothesis, Jung explained (1963/1977), "The common background of microphysics and depth-psychology is as much physical as psychic and therefore neither, but rather a third thing, a neutral nature which can at most be grasped in hints since in essence it is transcendental" (para. 768). In Jung and Pauli's model, the mental and material arise as complementary aspects, neither of which can be reduced to the psychophysically neutral third thing, which Jung termed the *unus mundus*.

Jung and Pauli's approach is referred to as a dual-aspect monism – a dual-aspect quantum framework that aims to understand the correlations between the mental and material domain. There are at-least three main points to understand in the Pauli Jung framework. First, the aspects of mind and matter are neither reducible to one another nor to the neutral third. Second, the underlying domain is holistic and does not consist of separate elements. Third, rather than being compositional, the mental and physical aspects emerge by a decomposition of the whole: The holistic symmetry is broken, and distinctions are made. Notably, ontic states designate the underlying domain, which is independent of its observation and any knowledge construction, while epistemic states are available for observation and measurement. Where "the cut" lies, between the observer and observed, conscious and unconscious, or subject and object, in the epistemic states, is a question of measurement (Pauli as cited in Jung, 1946/1972b, para. 439fn]).

Just as *avidyā* is a problem for Advaita when it comes to its description, as noted in Chapter 1, and the unconscious a clinical problem for Jung right up until the end; the measurement problem has pervaded quantum theory since its inception. In brief, at the heart of the quantum measurement problem lies the intriguing effect whereby quantum objects appear to behave differently when observed than when unobserved. In essence, quantum theory points toward the possibility that the material world is not independent of observation, as Jung and Patañjali both indicate. How the observer and observed are quantumly entangled still remains a mystery, however. The process of observation is an open question. For instance, is there one observer or many? Does the observer create the observed, or does the observer unfold its enfolded nature for experiential purposes?

Because quantum physicists cannot directly observe the process whereby the wave function collapses, the measurement problem has given rise to many interpretations. "From a conceptual point of view, measurement can be viewed as an intervention decomposing a system constituting an inseparable whole into locally separate parts" (Atmanspacher, 2012, p. 106). This is to say that, from the local point of view, objects look separate, but their measurement has suppressed the holistic reality that constitutes their connectedness (Atmanspacher, 2012).

The holistic reality is exemplified in quantum physics through research on subatomic particles. In quantum theory, when an atom is split, no matter the extent of the distance between the subatomic particles, the particles remain in correspondence. The split objects continue to directly influence each other even if their distance is thousands of miles away. This implies an instantaneous signal, which is faster than the speed of light. In contradistinction to the quantum model, from the perspective of classical physics, instantaneous signals violate the time barrier, thus rendering influence impossible. The quantum model therefore suggests that nonlocality, or correspondence between subatomic particles at great distances, is independent of space-time. It may also very well indicate that the particles were never measurable distinct and separate entities to begin with. In the quantum worldview, "things" appear to be singular and eternal. As Pribram (2007) explained, "the dualism of mental versus material holds only for the ordinary world of appearances – the world described in Euclidean geometry and Newtonian mechanics" (p. 11).

Jung and Pauli used synchronicity as an interpretive principle of universal process, just as physicists use causality and relativity (Progoff, 2008, p. 164). Denoting meaningful coincidence as acausal, Jung and Pauli suggested non-locality and independence of space-time as fundamental to their synchronicity hypothesis. Jung (1951/1972a) explained,

> Synchronistic phenomena prove the simultaneous occurrence of meaningful equivalences in heterogeneous, causally unrelated processes; in other words, they prove that a content perceived by an observer can, at the same time, be represented by an outside event, without any causal connection. From this it follows either that the psyche cannot be localized in space, or that space is relative to the psyche. The same applies to the temporal determination of the psyche and the psychic relativity of time.
>
> (para. 996)

Jung (1951/1972a) went on to state that the verification of these findings would have far-reaching consequences. Through acausalism, synchronicity moves beyond causation and transcends the usual limits of space-time. If accurate, then behind the world of five-sensory perception of discrete and independent objects is hidden a world view of a completely different "order."

Notably, the measurement problem in quantum physics subsequently gives rise to the ability, or inability, to establish a correlation between the quantum and classical worlds. From a nondual orientation, we lack rigorous links because we are attempting to relate things that are actually singular and indivisible on their deepest level. Hence, how the microscopic level translates to the macroscopic – or how probability relates to determinism – remains an open question. As one attempt to establish correspondence between quantum and classical reality, theoretical physicist Juan Malcedona's 1997 holographic model "solved apparent inconsistencies between quantum physics and Einstein's theory of gravity" (Cowen, 2013, p. 1). Considering synchronicity and its historic relationship to quantum physics, alongside Pribram's holographic model of the brain, holography becomes a particularly potent contemporary heuristic device given recent work by physicists that back up Maldacena's model that the universe is a hologram (Cowen, 2013).

The universe as a hologram

Just as Malcedona's holographic model solved apparent inconsistencies between quantum physics and Einstein's theory of gravity, religious studies scholar Dr. Stephen Kaplan (2007) has used a holographic model to address the problem of *avidyā*. Earlier, one of the persistent questions in orthodox Hinduism was noted – if *brahman* is both *sat* (being) and *cit* (consciousness), why is there *avidyā*? Kaplan (2007) has used a holographic model to illuminate how *vidyā* (pure vision, wisdom) and *avidyā* (absence of vision, misunderstanding) can be simultaneous and coterminous in Advaita Vedānta. Kaplan's (2007) analogy is not intended to be an actual replica or scale model of the Advaita worldview but is used as a heuristic device capable of providing insight into nonduality.[2] This heuristic device also provides insight into the nondual orientation of Classical Yoga and further assists in forging a synthesis of the works of Jung and Patañjali.

Holography means to write the whole and is a process whereby a three-dimensional image is recorded on high-resolution film via interference patterns produced with a laser and beam splitter. Kaplan (2007) elucidated,

> In order to produce a hologram, the laser is aimed at a device that splits the beam into two separate light waves. One of the waves is directed toward the film; the other is directed toward the object and then, reflecting off the object, toward the film. The former is called the reference

> beam and the latter is the scene or object beam. At the film, the two beams of light converge. Their convergence creates the interference patterns, which spread across the film. These interference patterns are like waves created in a pool of water into which two stones are thrown.
> (p. 188)

As we embark on this heuristic, there are four immediately noteworthy points about holography relevant to the present study. The first is that only interference patterns exist on the film, in contradistinction to the two-dimensional replicas of objects that appear on ordinary photographic film. This means that we cannot see images encoded on holographic film with our eyes. The film doesn't contain the subject–object dichotomies found in our everyday world of time and space. Therefore, these "interference patterns do not resemble in any way, shape, or form the object that is being filmed" (Kaplan, 2007, p. 188). The second interesting point to note about holography is that the interference patterns have information enfolded throughout them. Third, the film has enormous storage potential. Multiple objects or scenes can be recorded on the film simply by switching the angle or frequency of the laser. And fourth, each part of a hologram "can reproduce the whole yet the sum total of all the parts of the hologram also only produce one whole" (Kaplan, 2007, p. 187). No matter how many times you shred a piece of holographic film, the whole will appear in each part.

Kaplan's (1983) body of work draws on the holographic psychology of Karl Pribram (2007). Author of *The Holographic Universe* Michael Talbot (1991) has noted that the holographic model was first developed by Pribram as well as by renowned University of London physicist and former protégée of Einstein, David Bohm. In their own research, independently, Bohm and Pribram found that the brain and the subatomic properties of our world demonstrate evidence of operating holographically. Both Bohm and Pribram proposed that a hologram was a good metaphor for understanding the universe, albeit not necessarily a literal one.

In addition to drawing upon Pibram's work, Kaplan (2007) has also used Bohm's (2002) implicate and explicate domains as descriptive devices for his holographic model, which seeks to illuminate how *vidyā* (pure vision, wisdom) and *avidyā* (absence of vision, misunderstanding) can be simultaneous and coterminous. Similar to the Hindu notion of *brahman*, Bohm's implicate order has the totality of existence enfolded within each region of space-time. The indication being that "whatever part, element, or aspect we may abstract in thought, this still enfolds the whole and is therefore intrinsically related to the totality from which it has been abstracted" (Kaplan, 2007, p. 190). Bohm (2002) used an ink–glycerine analogy to illuminate his implicate order. Bohm & Hiley (1987) explained:

> In this device, a droplet of insoluble ink was inserted into a viscous fluid such as glycerine, which was then subject to a shearing rotation in

> a controlled way. The ink droplet gradually became invisible as it was drawn out into a fine thread. When the rotation was reversed, this time the thread was gradually drawn together, until the ink droplet suddenly emerged again into visibility. When it was drawn out and invisible, the distribution of ink particles appeared to be "at random" with no order. Yet it had a hidden order, which was revealed when the droplet came together again. This order was described as implicate or enfolded, while the ink droplet itself was explicate or unfolded.
>
> (p. 335)

Extrapolating the same visual to Classical Yoga methodology, the implicate order may be why Patañjali guided students to find one object to focus on. Discriminatory discernment of the gross and subtle aspects of only one *apparent* object is needed to pull our perception back, so to speak, into the whole.

Because all information resides undivided and whole in the implicate domain, there is no subject standing in relation to an object. It is not a domain where duality appears. Furthermore, the implicate domain is unchanging even as images are unfolded from it. In other words, enfolded nature is not altered by the unfoldment of "objects" or holographic images. The explicate (unfolded) mode and the implicate (enfolded) mode are different ways of being. Here, there is similarity with Classical Yoga also. For Patañjali, the fluctuating forms of *prakṛti* do not alter the immutable *puruṣa* (YS 4.18).

In Kaplan's (2007) analogy, the being that is consciousness, or the implicate domain, exists unchanged, and it is simultaneous and coterminous with the appearance of explicate artifacts, including subjects, objects, and *avidyā* (p. 192). Hence, if we imagine that we live in a holographic universe, it is possible to infer that *avidyā* appears at the level of human awareness, in part, because although it appears that we are looking at distinct phenomena only, we may actually be perceiving patterns of energy, or in keeping with our holographic heuristic device, information encoded into interference patterns.

A closer look at Patañjali may help us out here. Patañjali makes it plainly evident that pure consciousness knows exactly what the mind is doing as it moves and grasps (YS 4.18). So even though *avidyā* appears at the level of our human awareness, orientation A always knows what orientation B is up to. Therefore, pure consciousness never loses sight of its, relatively speaking, "blind spots." Nothing in the world then becomes conscious in an ontic sense because it is conscious all along. As the implicate unfolds into the explicate, the immutability of consciousness remains. The implicate always knows the explicate because the explicate was unfolded from it. From this perspective, it can be understood that absence of knowledge is, in some sense, a means of knowledge. When we want to know why shadows are created, we have no choice but to discover the stable self-illuminating source of the sun and its relationship to moving phenomena. By extension, and very significantly regarding our reliance on orthodox science and its worldview, certain types of consciousness may be correlated to brain processes, but consciousness in and of itself does not arise there.

The point just mentioned is so important that I will attempt it another way. If ontic reality is pure consciousness, then there is an implied equation between the explicate and implicate, *prakṛti* and *puruṣa*, and orientation B and orientation A. In Patañjali's world, *puruṣa* and *prakṛti*, although distinct, are somehow equivalent because they are, in some manner, nondual. As Chapple (2008) has expressed, "Both are necessary; neither is sufficient unto itself" (p. 107). In direct regards to this necessity, Patañjali explained in sūtra 2.23, *sva svāmi śaktyoḥ svarūpopalabdhi hetuḥ saṁyogaḥ*, the union of Owner (*puruṣa*, very loosely speaking absolute subject, pure consciousness) and owned (*prakṛti*, objects of knowledge, the contents of consciousness) causes the recognition of the nature and powers of them both. Right on the heels of 2.23, in sūtra 2.24, Patañjali very clearly stated that *avidyā* causes the union, or enmeshment, of *puruṣa* with *prakṛti*. Suffering therefore is a red flag, a marker so potent – that when recognized – leads to the realization that a fundamental misunderstanding of nature has been at the root of the dis-ease. This recognition in turn leads to the recognition of the nature and power of pure consciousness.

Returning to our holographic heuristic, the two separated light beams, the reference beam and the object beam, originate from one source. Because light is so often used metaphorically in Upaniṣadic thought, it is useful to elicit it further in this holographic analogy. In this heuristic device, the light of the holographic laser beam can be used as an analogy for pure consciousness. Kaplan (2007) explained, "A laser is a single-frequency light source that is in phase – in other words, the light waves are in step with each other" (p. 188). Furthermore, "in order to reconstruct an image of the original object, a laser beam of the same frequency as that which was used to construct the hologram" must be used (p. 188). Then, in analogy to the two earlier paragraphs, just as a specific light source, a laser, is needed to unfold what is encoded on holographic film, an understanding of pure consciousness is needed to have a holistic picture of our world because pure consciousness knows and understands – indeed, is – the totality of manifestation and the awareness in which it arises (YS 4.18, 4.23, 4.34). Hence, according to Classical Yoga, knowing the Seer, or pure consciousness, is crucial if we want to understand reality, just like the correct laser beam, one that is of the right frequency, is crucial, if we want to unfold the holograph it is in reference to. Similarly, if we want to understand natural light on earth, we must learn the difference between the self-illuminating nature of the sun and the reflected light of the moon. Both lights originate from the same source but manifest in completely distinct ways.

In orientation B, when the mind is moving and grasping, we see the world through subject–object distinction, and we psychologically solidify "something" that in essence cannot be solidified ontically. To claim subjects and objects are literally distinct, and not just apparently distinct, is to confuse the epistemic with the ontic.

The confusion of the ontic and epistemic is elucidated in part by Patañjali in sūtra 3.17 in which he noted how words and names are associated to objects. These words, alongside the object they point to, and the concepts formed around such an object, all "interpenetrate or commingle with one another" (Bharati, n.d., p. 41). However, just because we name something and even classify it as an object does not make it such. Jha (1934) has translated sūtra 3.17 as, "Among (1) the *Word*, (2) the *Denotation* and (3) the *Conception* – there is mutual 'imposition,' and hence commingling; when 'Discipline' is converged upon the distinction among them, there follows comprehension of the cries of all living beings" (p. 177). Through yogic discipline, we are able to move beyond, beneath, within, and through, mental constructs and objectification, which allows us to hear, or perceive, how our subject–object constructs can box us in. If objectification is ultimately ontically false, then the process of conceptualization can fuel psychological confusion, and thereby, suffering.

In translating sūtra 3.17, Carrera (2006) used superimposition as a means of describing the confusion between "a word, its meaning, and the idea behind it" (p. 180). In addition to the superimposition of words, meanings, and ideas of our everyday experience leading to distorted perception of reality, superimposition of images is another way of attempting to envision *avidyā* through the holographic heuristic device. As noted earlier, much information can be encoded in one hologram. Because of the density of information, as the holographic images are projected, potentially, many images are superimposed upon each other. Some are more visible than others, with very few visible to the naked eye. Looking at reality through the lens of Patañjali, this means that when we perceive through orientation B where *avidyā* "resides," it is possible we are currently, unknowingly, perceiving many aspects of unreconciled psychic process. Furthermore, given Patañjali's emphasis on past and future lives, these other lives may be superimposed on each other. Because reincarnation and rebirth are never fully approached by Jung, we only have Patañjali's body of work to draw on here. However, it is important to briefly note that Jung does makes much use of projection, transference, and re-collection throughout his vast body of work.

In the YS, Patañjali never out rightly says time is an illusion, but he attempts to clarify the nature of time. In several threads, Patañjali explained that past, present, and future already exist (YS 2.39, 3.54, 4.12). For

Patañjali, different characteristics cause different forms to be manifest at what appears to be different times. Again using our holographic model, the hologram can contain an endless amount of information. Each lifetime, or even each phase of a lifetime is, potentially, a different snapshot, a different pattern, on the holographic film. Likewise, what appears as multiple lives over the course of time, are known by Bohm's implicate domain because the implicate domain is imagined to be everywhere and everything, implicating all, because it is the enfoldment of all spatiotemporal entities (Kaplan, 2007). With serious consideration of the implicate domain, the concept of time in the explicate begins to take on new meaning, just as it did for Jung with his synchronicity hypothesis.

In Patañjali's world, all times, past, present, and future, don't just exist; they exist simultaneously. They are simultaneous because we can access them in the present (YS 3.54). Inasmuch as what is described by Patañjali in sūtras such as 2.23, 2.24, and 3.54 can feel esoteric and ungrounded, I think it is important to insert here that Patañjali mobilized other sūtras to give yogis sensory analogues. For Patañjali, the big picture, the more cosmic picture, isn't "enough." Bridging abstract ideas to a direct experience of the mind in the body was important to him. In Chapter 2, Patañjali gave several sensory and grounding analogues. For example, in sūtra 2.35, he explained that when we are grounded in non-violence, hostility ceases. Another example is sūtra 2.42, in which Patañjali stated that a superior form of joy is realized within us as a result of contentment. Therefore, although Classical Yoga can feel esoteric when contemplating synchronicity, because Yoga practice is linked to a calm mind and steady breath, being in tune with our nervous system is a key component to stabilizing our psychophysical being. Classical Yoga is concerned with integration. Patañjali's threads interweave the local and nonlocal, or the individual with the cosmic. Grounding is vital.

To reiterate: as integration takes place, and upon attaining the highest levels of discriminatory discernment, Patañjali explained that all objects in all conditions are able to be comprehended simultaneously. The individual and the cosmic have been realized as one. Looking at this from a slightly different perspective, when all the superimposed images align in a way that we are able to discriminate them, in contradistinction to having them interfere with each other, we are able to see without distortion. While our everyday five-sensory perception cannot perceive behind ordinary space-time objects, the enfolded becomes visible via *prajñā*.

Using Bohm's ink–glycerin analogy again, Patañjali's seemingly abstract and more cosmic vision becomes strengthened in contemporary terms. Because synchronicity is quite esoteric, approaching the topic from yet another angle might be helpful. In sutra 3.12, Patañjali stated, "Then, again, the condition of the mind in which the 'object' (in the mind) which subsides is always exactly similar to the 'object' which rises (in the next moment) is called *Ekāgratā Pariṇāma*" (Taimni, 1961, p. 299). *Ekāgratā Pariṇāma* is one-pointedness, an all-important experience in Patañjali's world if we are to remove distortions from our lens, embody yogic union, and understand both nonduality and pure consciousness. If we meditate on an object that is unfolded as clearly as Bohm's unfolded ink and if we watch that one object – constantly – over the transformation to the enfolded order, our optics change and we can see reality with a different lens – one akin to the holographic heuristic. This is to say that misunderstanding of the nature of reality, or absence of vision, in Patañjali's world, is removed when one object is focused on, and all thought forms associated to that object eventually involute until no object remains on the horizon of awareness.

Yogis follow Patañjali's Classical Yoga methodology to discern the meeting point of unity and multiplicity. On account of the fact that the unconditioned and undivided intelligence encompasses all conditions and all times simultaneously, which means that all apparent space-time objects are present in the eternal now, then it follows that just because a discrete observation is made, which reduces our worldview to the classical Newtonian model, and the appearance of differences between a subject and an object in Cartesian space-time, that does not mean that information of the whole isn't there. It is merely blocked from view. Notably, the accumulation of the research points to the fact that information is not blocked from view completely. Our nervous system and the affect it produces offers demanding evidence that the knowledge of the whole is "running" throughout our bodymind.

Patañjali's choice of the word *avidyā* becomes very rich from the perspective of a holographic–Cartesian space-time comparison. Like *avidyā*, viewing reality through discrete observation only is both absence of vision and a misunderstanding of the fundamental nature of reality. In relation to classical Newtonian and quantum physics, at the level of our human awareness, discrete observation creates absence of vision in respect to both gross and subtle aspects of the manifest world. In relation to our psychological understanding, discrete observation perpetuates misunderstanding of the interface between the visible and invisible world, as well as the interface between epistemic states and ontic reality. Confusing ontological questions with epistemic issues is a critical problem in our time. The resolution, however, poses a serious challenge to the dualistic worldview underpinning both the Abrahamic religious traditions and Western scientific orthodoxy.

As Patañjali explained in sūtra 4.14, *pariṇāmaikatvād vastu tattvam*, "From the unity of modification, follows the unity of the thing" (Jha, 1934, p. 238). There is a coordinated mutation of the three *guṇas* at the deepest level of manifestation. *Puruṣa*, pure consciousness, is absolute and singular. Whether we speak of absolute subject or absolute object, we are talking about a whole that ultimately cannot be diminished. The subject can never become objectified and be seen accurately. Ever. Holographically speaking, the implicate flows into the explicate seamlessly, as one whole mechanism of manifestation. As Talbot (1991) has expressed, "This is an astounding notion. Virtually all of our commonsense prejudices about the world are based on the premise that subjective and objective reality are very much separate" (p. 80). Hence, difference is in the cognition. Cognitive impairment is why Patañjali emphasized seeing and the removal of the failure to see at the level of our human awareness. A science of knowledge, or a science of how the mind works, is imperative in order to live comfortably, and authentically, in physical form.

As has been noted repeatedly throughout the present study, whether we view the past, present, or future or whether we are differentiating mind from matter or subject from object, in Classical Yoga, "The modifications of the mind are always known due to the immutability of their master, *puruṣa*" (Whicher, 2001, p. 334 fn 190). This is to emphasize, again, that no matter how we shred the holograph through discrete observation, it is still one indivisible all-knowing whole. When the indivisible all-knowing whole is really understood, from the perspective of Patañjali's world, any form of objectifying phenomena becomes unsatisfactory because it is known to be inhibitory. Then the mind is inclined towards discrimination and gravitates towards *kaivalya* (YS 4.26). Epistemology, or knowing our world through subject–object distinction, is given up in favor of ontic reality, or Seeing being-in-Itself. Mental modifications and obstructions, and therefore *avidyā*, vanish.

For those, like Jung, working from a duality in search of a unity, synchronicity appears as a special circumstance when phenomena align and are perceived conjointly. However, Jung (1952/1972c) speculated that if the relation between body and soul proves to be synchronistic, his view that synchronicity is a relatively rare phenomenon would have to be corrected (para. 938 fn70). With the revision of Jungian synchronicity from a relatively rare phenomenon to a pervasive quality of manifestation, Jungian ideas come further into alignment with Patañjali Yoga (YS 4.09, 4.18).

In summary: through the lens of nonduality, which holds *brahman* to be being (*sat*) and consciousness (*cit*) and through a synthesis of the visions of Jung and Patañjali, it is feasible to speculate that if the universe is in any way holographic as contemporary physicists are theorizing, it is possible that ontic nonduality and alignment become obscured at the level of our human awareness due, at least in part, to interference and superimposition. Interference patterns are triggering the absence of vision at the level of our human awareness, not an absence of pure consciousness. In other words, our blocks are psychological, not ontic. This obscuration can trigger misidentification and misunderstanding and lead to such depth psychological concepts as an unconscious and an egoic "I" that are ontically real.

Jung (1952/1972c) stated that his work on synchronicity, aimed "to open a very obscure field," which he believed to be philosophically of the "greatest importance" (para. 816). However, Jung's work with an acausal connecting principle was never completed. As his one time student Ira Progoff (2008) has expressed, Jung's synchronicity vision "was so rich and essentially valid, but he could not reduce it to a form that he could communicate, and he could not say the things that needed to be said in order to reflect his vision" (p. 158). Furthermore, contemporary Jungian analyst David Tresan (2013) has noted that Jung's synchronicity hypothesis "signaled an incomplete picture of reality and serves as the goad to discovering a fuller one" (p. 252). A hypothesis that has remained open to contemporary research,[3] von Franz (1964) insightfully envisioned synchronicity to be a Jungian hypothesis "pregnant with future possibilities of investigation and application" (p. 227).

As depth psychology continues to evolve and develop, it will be imperative to clearly discern between ontological and epistemological arguments. For dual-aspect monists such as Jung, epistemic splits generate the distinction of aspects from the distinction-free, unseparated underlying domain, where the underlying domain is not capable of being directly perceived. In contrast, by eliminating epistemic splits and falsifying dualism, yogis are able to perceive wholly the meeting place of unity and multiplicity, and the Seer resting in true essential nature. Discerning between the ontic and epistemic was Patañjali's strong suit and an area of weakness for Jung. As the broad strokes of this body of research reveal, epistemic appearances may not apply to ontic reality.

Notes

1 While Jung undoubtedly agreed that we must have direct experience of the numinous for it to be known and indisputable, his theories rest on the notion of an isolated mind – hence, as mentioned in Chapter 3, his process and vision result in a different path with different goals, from that of Classical Yoga. Therefore, a depth psychology–Classical Yoga fusion can perhaps yield an understanding of affective states and affective neuroscientific results in the area of religious instinct, only if they share a mutual ground as implied at the end of the previous section.

2 Although an in-depth comparison of Advaita Vedānta and Classical Yoga is beyond the scope of this project, the orientation in this study is the nondual lens of Classical Yoga. Furthermore, it is possible to align Advaita Vedānta's and Classical Yoga's visions of consciousness as singular, eternal, and absolute. Duality is false in both systems. Therefore, even though Advaita Vedānta and Classical Yoga are not the same schools and may even have some fundamental disagreements, through the lens of both Patañjali and Advaita, Jung's subject–object, conscious–unconscious, or ego–Self are all incorrect ways of describing and therefore experiencing ontic reality and therefore causing obstruction to the reconciliation of science and religious experience. Hence, using Western scholarship of the Advaita tradition in general, and Kaplan's heuristic device in

particular, might assist in uncovering potential insights into new worldviews and ways in which we can forge a bridge between Patañjali and Jung.

3 Atmanspacher & Fach, 2013; Atmanspacher, 2014; Connolly, 2015; Cambray, 2004; Martin, Carminati, & Carminati, 2014

References

Ajaya, S. (1983). *Psychotherapy east and west: A unifying paradigm*. Honesdale, PA: The Himalayan Institute.

Atmanspacher, H. (2012). Dual-aspect monism à la Pauli and Jung. *Journal of Consciousness Studies, 19*(9–10), 96–120.

Atmanspacher, H. (2014). Psychophysical correlations, synchronicity and meaning. *Journal of Analytical Psychology, 59*, 181–188.

Atmanspacher, H., & Fach, W. (2013). A structural-phenomenological typology of mind-matter correlations. *Journal of Analytical Psychology, 58*, 219–244.

Bharati, S. J. (n.d.). *Yoga sutras of Patañjali interpretive translation*. Retrieved from www.swamij.com/pdf/yogasutrasinterpretive.pdf

Bohm, D. (2002). *Wholeness and the implicate order*. New York, NY: Routledge Classics.

Bohm, D., & Hiley, B. J. (1987). An ontological basis for the quantum theory. *Physics Reports, 144*(6), 321–375.

Brooks, R. M. (2011). Un-thought out metaphysics in analytical psychology: A critique of Jung's epistemological basis for psychic reality. *Journal of Analytical Psychology, 56*(1), 492–513.

Bryant, E. (2009). *The yoga sutras of Patañjali*. New York, NY: North Point Press.

Cambray, J. (2004). Synchronicity as emergence. In J. Cambray & L. Carter (Eds.), *Analytical psychology: Contemporary perspectives in Jungian analysis* (pp. 223–248). New York, NY: Routledge.

Carrera, J. (2006). Inside the yoga sutras: A comprehensive sourcebook for the study and practice of Patañjali's yoga sutras. Buckingham, VA: Integral Yoga.

Chapple, C. K. (2008). *Yoga and the luminous: Patañjali's spiritual path to freedom*. Albany, NY: State University of New York Press.

Connolly, A. (2015). Bridging the reductive and the synthetic: Some reflections on the clinical implications of synchronicity. *Journal of Analytical Psychology, 60*(2), 159–178.

Corbett, L., & Whitney, L. (2016). Jung and non-duality: some clinical and theoretical implications of the self as the totality of the psyche. *International Journal of Jungian Studies, 8*(1), 15–27.

Coward, H. (1985). *Jung and eastern thought*. New York, NY: State University of New York Press.

Cowen, R. (2013). Simulations back up theory that universe is a hologram. *Nature: International Weekly Journal of Science*. Retrieved from http://www.nature.com/news/simulations-back-up-theory-that-universe-is-a-hologram-1.14328

Freud, S. (1989). An autobiographical study. In P. Gay (Trans.), *The Freud reader* (pp. 3–41). New York, NY: W. W. Norton. (Original work published 1925)

Gino, F., Kouchaki, M., & Galinsky, A. D. (2015). The moral virtue of authenticity: How inauthenticity produces feelings of immorality and impurity. *Psychological Science, 26*(7), 983–996.

Henry, M. (1993). *The genealogy of psychoanalysis*. Stanford, CA: Stanford University Press.

Jha, G. (1934). *Yoga-darshana: Sūtras of Patañjali's with Bhāsya of Vyāsa* (2nd ed.). Freemont, CA: Asian Humanities Press. (Original work published 1907/Revised 1934)

Jung, C. G. (1966). Richard Wilhelm: In memoriam. In H. Read, M. Fordham, G. Adler, & W. McGuire (Eds.), *The collected works of C. G. Jung* (R. F. C. Hull, Trans., Vol. 15, pp. 53–62). Princeton, NJ: Princeton University Press. (Original work published 1930)

Jung, C. G. (1972a). On synchronicity. In H. Read, M. Fordham, G. Adler, & W. McGuire (Eds.), *The collected works of C. G. Jung* (R. F. C. Hull, Trans., 2nd ed., Vol. 8, pp. 520–531). Princeton, NJ: Princeton University Press. (Original work published 1951, revised 1957)

Jung, C. G. (1972b). On the nature of the psyche. In H. Read, M. Fordham, G. Adler, & W. McGuire (Eds.), *The collected works of C. G. Jung* (R. F. C. Hull, Trans., 2nd ed., Vol. 8, pp. 159–234). Princeton, NJ: Princeton University Press. (Original work published 1946, revised 1954)

Jung, C. G. (1972c). Synchronicity: An acausal connecting principle. In H. Read, M. Fordham, G. Adler, & W. McGuire (Eds.), *The collected works of C. G. Jung* (R. F. C. Hull, Trans., 2nd ed., Vol. 8, pp. 417–519). Princeton, NJ: Princeton University Press. (Original work published 1952, revised 1955)

Jung, C. G. (1972d). The transcendent function. In H. Read, M. Fordham, G. Adler, & W. McGuire (Eds.), *The collected works of C. G. Jung* (R. F. C. Hull, Trans., 2nd ed., Vol. 8, pp. 67–91). Princeton, NJ: Princeton University Press. (Original work published 1958)

Jung, C. G. (1975). *C. G. Jung letters: Volume 2: 1951–1961* (R. F. C. Hull, Trans., G. Adler & A. Jaffé, Eds.). Princeton, NJ: Princeton University Press.

Jung, C. G. (1976a). Definitions. In H. Read, M. Fordham, G. Adler, & W. McGuire (Eds.), *The collected works of C. G. Jung* (R. F. C. Hull, Trans., Vol. 6, pp. 408–486). Princeton, NJ: Princeton University Press. (Original work published 1920, revised 1960)

Jung, C. G. (1976b). Depth psychology. In H. Read, M. Fordham, G. Adler, & W. McGuire (Eds.), *The collected works of C. G. Jung* (R. F. C. Hull, Trans., Vol. 18, pp. 477–486). Princeton, NJ: Princeton University Press. (Original work published 1948)

Jung, C. G. (1977). *Mysterium coniunctionis*. In H. Read, M. Fordham, G. Adler, & W. McGuire (Eds.), *The collected works of C. G. Jung* (R. F. C. Hull, Trans., 2nd ed., Vol. 14). Princeton, NJ: Princeton University Press. (Original work published 1963)

Jung, C. G. (1985). Fundamental questions of psychotherapy. In H. Read, M. Fordham, G. Adler, & W. McGuire (Eds.), *The collected works of C. G. Jung* (R. F. C. Hull, Trans., Vol. 16, pp. 111–125). Princeton, NJ: Princeton University Press. (Original work published 1951)

Jung, C. G. (1989a). Forward to the "I ching." In H. Read, M. Fordham, G. Adler, & W. McGuire (Eds.), *The collected works of C. G. Jung* (R. F. C. Hull, Trans., 2nd ed., Vol. 11, pp. 589–608). Princeton, NJ: Princeton University Press. (Original work published 1950)

Jung, C. G. (1989b). The psychology of eastern meditation. In H. Read, M. Fordham, G. Adler, & W. McGuire (Eds.), *The collected works of C. G. Jung* (R. F. C. Hull, Trans., 2nd ed., Vol. 11, pp. 558–575). Princeton, NJ: Princeton University Press. (Original work published 1943)

Jung, C. G. (1989c). Yoga and the west. In H. Read, M. Fordham, G. Adler, & W. McGuire (Eds.), *The collected works of C. G. Jung* (R. F. C. Hull, Trans.) (2nd ed., Vol. 11, pp. 529–537). Princeton, NJ: Princeton University Press. (Original work published 1936)

Jung, C. G. (1995). *Memories, dreams, reflections* (R. Winston & C. Winston, Trans., A. Jaffe, Ed.). London: FontanaPress. (Original work published 1961)

Jung, C. G. & Neumann, E. (2015). *Analytical psychology in exile: The correspondence of C. G. Jung and Erich Neumann* (M. Liebscher, Ed., H. McCartney, Trans.). Princeton, NJ: Princeton University Press.

Kaplan, S. (1983). Mind, māyā, and holography: A phenomenology of projection. *Philosophy East & West*, *33*(4), 367–378.

Kaplan, S. (2007). Vidyā and avidyā: Simultaneous and coterminous? A holographic model to illuminate the advaita debate. *Philosophy East & West*, *57*(2), 178–203.

Main, R. (1997). *Jung on synchronicity and the paranormal*. Princeton, NJ: Princeton University Press.

Martin, F., Carminati, F., & Carminati, G. G. (2014). Synchronicity, entanglement, quantum information, and the psyche. In M. C. Kafatos & D. Chopra (Eds.), *The time machine of consciousness: Quantum physics of mind: Time travel, cosmology, relativity, neuroscience* (pp. 236–244). Cambridge, MA: Cosmology Science Publishers.

Miller, A. (1998). *Thou shalt not be aware: Society's betrayal of the child*. New York, NY: Farrar, Straus and Giroux.

Miller, A. (2006). The body never lies: The lingering effects of hurtful parenting. New York, NY: W.W. Norton.

Pribram, K. H. (2007). Quantum information processing in brain systems and the spiritual nature of mankind. *Frontier Perspectives*, *16*(1), 4–12.

Progoff, I. (2008). Jung, synchronicity, and human destiny: Noncausal dimensions of human experience. New York, NY: Dell.

Shamdasani, S. (2003). *Jung and the making of modern psychology: The dream of a science*. New York, NY: Cambridge University Press.

Sidoli, M. (2001). *When the body speaks: The archetypes in the body* (P. Blakemore, Ed.). New York, NY: Brunner-Routledge.

Solms, M. (2013). The conscious id. *Neuropsychoanalysis*, *15*(1), 5–19.

Stein, M. (2005). Some reflections on the influence of Chinese thought on Jung and his psychological theory. *Journal of Analytical Psychology*, *50*(2), 209–223.

Taimni, I. K. (1961). The science of yoga: The yoga-sutras of Patañjali in Sanskrit with transliteration in roman, translation and commentary in English. Wheaton, IL: The Theosophical Publishing House.

Talbot, M. (1991). *The holographic universe*. New York, NY: Harper Perennial.

Thompson, M. G. (2001). Is the unconscious really all that unconscious? The role of being and experience in the psychoanalytic encounter. *Contemporary Psychoanalysis*, *37*(4), 571–613.

Tresan, D. (2013). A commentary on "A structural-phenomenological typology of mind-matter correlations" by H. Atmanspacher and W. Fach. *Journal of Analytical Psychology*, *58*, 245–253.
von Franz, M. L. (1964). The process of individuation. In C. G. Jung & M. L. von Franz (Eds.), *Man and his symbols* (pp. 157–254). New York, NY: Dell.
Watts, A. (1971). *Psychotherapy east and west.* New York, NY: Ballantine.
Whicher, I. (2001). *Patañjali's metaphysical schematic: Puruṣa and prakrti in the yogasutra.* Chennai, India: The Adyar Library and Research Center.
Wilhelm, R. (1962). *The secret of the golden flower: A Chinese book of life.* Orlando, FL: Harcourt Brace. (Original work published 1931)
Woodman, M. (1993). Leaving my father's house: A journey to conscious femininity. Boston, MA: Shambala.
Wu Wei, W. (2004). *All else is bondage: Non-volitional living.* Boulder, CO: Sentient.

Chapter 6

Conclusion

The present study has explored how consciousness is accounted for in the work of Jung and Patañjali. Additionally, this project has discussed numinous experience, dualistic and nondualistic worldviews, and the nature of the egoic "I." As a result, the research has revealed not only decisive areas of divergence between the works of Jung and Patañjali but also many intriguing places where their visions intersect despite significant differences in the cultures and time periods in which they lived.

Through the research, we have found that in Jungian depth psychology, the clinical focus, most succinctly, is on the conscious–unconscious dynamic, the spiritual development of the personality, and the advancement towards wholeness. These moves, infused with Jung's belief in the religious function of the psyche, are, for Jung, highly significant for evolution, in that they make the Creator conscious of His creation. Without this movement, the world is dark and meaningless for the Creator. Through suffering, the tension of the opposites and maintaining the consciousness of the egoic self, humans provide a service for the Divine by shining a light on the darkness of mere being. Jung's ideas on an unconscious, non–self-illuminating Creator, which is ontically inaccessible, set the foundations of his depth psychology on distinctly different ground than that of Patañjali's Classical Yoga.

This distinctly different ground begins to surface within the first four lines of the *Yoga Sūtra*, when Patañjali points to two distinct orientations of consciousness: orientation A, in which ontic reality is accessible, and pure consciousness abides in its own essential nature, and orientation B, in which epistemic states are overriding and pure consciousness assumes the forms of mental modifications. In stark contrast to Jung's model, which sees humans as world redeemers, Patañjali's perspective of pure consciousness sees no need to redeem anything because the only thing that shifts is perception. However, notably, Patañjali stated that shifting perception from orientation B to orientation A is highly significant because it is a realization of the power of pure consciousness. In Classical Yoga, when there is appropriation, or enmeshment of consciousness and the "I-sense," there is a lack of discernment between ontic reality and psychological experience or between the unchanging reality and the changing world. Without this discernment, our innate embodied knowing of the power of pure consciousness cannot be realized.

Interestingly, Jung's thoughts head in a direction that would encourage depth psychology to change the name of the unconscious to something more akin to Patañjali's *puruṣa*, although Jung never fully takes a stand there. For example, Jung (1939/1997) wrote, "in what we call the unconscious – the sum of autonomous contents – each of those contents has a consciousness in itself . . . therefore what we call the unconscious would be another form of consciousness" (p. 154). In another context, he stated, "The unconscious is not limited only to the instinctual and the reflex processes of the cortical centres; it also extends beyond consciousness and, with its symbols, anticipates future conscious processes. It is therefore quite as much a 'supraconsciousness' " (Jung, 1942/1983, para. 229).

If Patañjali is correct in his vision of an unconditioned, unoriginated, self-illuminating pure consciousness that is absolute and fundamental to the structure of the universe, then the whole foundation of the discipline of depth psychology lies on a profound misunderstanding of our true nature. Although it may be true that human consciousness transforms as it reflects and moves with the mind, it is also true that pure consciousness is singular, stable, and fully aware of, or synonymous to, its being. The blind dynamism of Jung's unconscious Creator would then be a false impression. Jung would have been picking up on his own absence of vision due to the appropriation of consciousness, and binding effects of the "I-sense," and transferring the imperceptions onto an "Unknown" Creator.

Perhaps tellingly, right up until the end of his life, Jung never felt as if "the time for an all-inclusive theory, taking in and describing all the contents, processes, and phenomena of the psyche from one central viewpoint" had arrived (Jacobi, 1973, p. ix). As Jung (1961/1995) himself explained, he had not found the right language. In contrast, Patañjali authored 195 lines of text, with his methodology summed up in the second line. Still the mind, Patañjali taught, thereby cleaning the lens of perception of all distortions, and pure consciousness will have no alternative but to be reflected in the clarity of the instrument. In other words, when the mind is still, multiplicity and any resultant confusion and suffering, resolve to Seeing, being-in-Itself, otherwise stated as pure consciousness resting in true nature. While the amelioration of human suffering is also of great concern to Jung, Jung never spoke of stilling the mind – while Patañjali's opus hinges on it. The fluctuating mind of Jung never came to rest in the silent stillness that underpins all images and forms. By this one nuance alone, the significant difference in what these two psychologists envisioned through their work shines through. Yet, knowingly, or perhaps presciently, Jung (1946/1972) emphasized that psyche is the world's pivot – and therefore the smallest alteration in the psychic factor, if it is an alteration of principle, might be of supreme significance in regard to our knowledge of the world and the picture we make of it (para. 423).

Grounded in a well-defined metaphysical schematic, Classical Yoga is a process of realizing wholeness and establishing dynamic union. While Jung's clinical work and spiritual development of the personality also aimed at realizing wholeness, an underpinning unifying model eluded him. This shortfall is most likely due, in part, to the lack of a strong, grounding metaphysical foundation in Jung's work. For Jung, an ontic and epistemic subject–object distinction remained. Whether scientists are aware of it or not, their theories always rely on metaphysical ideas. Both the ontic and the epistemic must be theoretically acknowledged. Given that Jung did not pronounce metaphysical acknowledgements outright, his body of work does not present a clear distinction between epistemological and ontological arguments.

Notably, at the core of their healing methodologies, Jung and Patañjali are both working with integration and psychospiritual alignment. However, if we look through the lens of Patañjali, Jung's work, for example, his search for the psychoid, or the unity of psyche and matter in the *unus mundus*, can be seen to reside in Patañjali's orientation B. In Patañjali's world, when we are within orientation B, focused on the plane of intellectuality (*vijñãnamaya*), engrossed in the mundane mind stuff (*citta vritti*), we search for our true reflection in various ways. Therefore, Jung's body of work maps into Patañjali's very clearly. In contrast, Patañjali cannot be incontrovertibly mapped into Jung's body of work on account of the fact that, in the end, Jung deemed Patañjali's exposition as Eastern intuition overreaching itself. To state this another way, Patañjali acknowledged that consciousness has both a conceptual and a linguistic nature as well as a non-conceptual and non-linguistic nature. In fact, the decisive point of Classical Yoga is that resting in the true nature of pure consciousness (*kaivalya*) is beyond conception. For Jung, non-conceptual consciousness falls into the schema of the unconscious.

Significantly, even though Jung's search never resolved to Patañjali's orientation A, Jung's search did reveal the phenomenon of synchronicity. As the results of this research demonstrate, it is through Jung's synchronicity hypothesis whereby the empirical consciousness of Jung is closely aligned to – not only Patañjali's empirical consciousness but also Patañjali's overall vision. Therefore, finding models, or heuristics, that support the viability of synchronicity – such as the holographic ideas of Pribram, Bohm, and Malcedona – might aid us in furthering the Jung–Patañjali dialogue in particular and the East–West dialogue overall.

In our current global and contemporary scientific search for reality, it is perhaps imperative that psychologists the world over come to agree on psychic and psychophysical structure – and approaches to consciousness – if we are to flourish into the next level of our potentiality. In the end, wherever we may reside on this beautiful, rotating, round rock, our body parts all function the same, and we all bleed red blood. Jung (1936/1976) himself advised, "Some day psychologists will have to agree upon certain basic principles secure from arbitrary interpretation if psychology is not to remain an unscientific and fortuitous conglomeration of individual opinions" (para. 987). If depth psychologists are open to considering Patañjali's ontic reality of self-illuminating pure consciousness as the grounding metaphysic of the discipline, then, with the vision of synchronicity as bridge, Jungian depth psychology and Classical Yoga have the potential to form a powerful alliance.

The results of the present study also show that Jung, Patañjali, and Freud all found affect to be an empirical means of entering the psyche. Both Freudian- and Jungian-oriented depth psychologies utilize the findings in neuroscience (Schore, 2012; Tresan, 1996; Wilkinson, 2003, 2005). In these neuropsychoanalytic frameworks, the right brain is understood as the neurobiological core of the human unconscious. Notably, much research has already been done in terms of affect regulation and the developing right hemisphere of the brain – where the right hemisphere is understood to contain the ability to grasp reality as a whole. Furthermore, the research shows that the cortex derives its consciousness from the brainstem and that brainstem mechanisms are associated with affective consciousness (Solms, 2013). Therefore, if depth psychology must remain within the empirical sciences and if we must persist on the road of reductionism in our efforts to understand consciousness, then the phenomena of affect, signaling a more primal, instinctual and non-conceptual form of consciousness, may also offer empirical means of more closely aligning the work of Jung and Patañjali. Despite epochal and cultural differences, both Jung and Patañjali note affect and suffering states as symptoms with split-off aspects of psychic process. If Jung and Patañjali are correct, then following the trail of affect leads us not only to the roots of our psychic splits but also, as Patañjali further indicates, to the eradication of suffering in general and sorrow in particular. Through the eradication of the symptoms of suffering and the affect that accompanies them, we should then be at rest in true nature, which is at the same time the experiential knowledge of pure consciousness. The radical empiricism entailed – for the eradication of the symptoms of suffering and the affect that accompanies them – may then, because of shared brain structure, offer cross-cultural similarities in regard to religious experience and the religious function of the psyche as it relates to pure consciousness. These empirical results could perhaps in turn – because of depth psychology's acceptance of pure consciousness as ontic reality – offer an opportunity to reconcile science and religious experience in the West. To look at this from another angle, a science of affect, which is linked with the eradication of suffering, may also assist in paving the way for a global science of consciousness.

Many neurobiological studies focusing on the clinical application of various yoga and meditative techniques provide preliminary support for their effectiveness in the reduction of suffering (Siegel, 2009; Chung, Brooks, Rai, Balk & Rai, 2012). Also worth considering is that many of these researched techniques have been recontextualized and secularized. However, because Patañjali used meditation not only to reduce stress and ameliorate suffering but also to reveal the true nature of pure consciousness – and because Buddhism understands mindfulness as a means to experience *nirvāṇa* and Buddha nature – the spiritual components of the traditions should not be dismissed (Bergemann, Siegel, Belzer, Siegel, & Feuille, 2013). From Patañjali's point of view, they cannot be. Only orientation A allows for the removal of suffering. The dismissal of the spiritual components of orthodox and non-orthodox Hindu traditions and the appropriation of yoga and meditation methodology to suit Western frameworks must not be overlooked.

As much as Jung acknowledged the primacy of empirical science in his time and culture, he was certain that no matter how comprehensive and precise orthodox science was, it would not "satisfy the human imagination when it comes to understanding our purpose here, why we suffer, or how we can keep faith in our everyday lives" (Young-Eisendrath & Dawson, 1997/2008, p. xi). Patañjali would undoubtedly agree. Both scholars are in complete alignment when it comes to the necessity of direct experience. Along these same lines. Zen Buddhist scholar D.T. Suzuki (1970) once stated,

> Scientists can never expect to reach the Self, however much they desire to. They can no doubt talk a great deal *about* it, and that is all they can do. . . . Self-knowledge is possible only when the identification of subject and object takes place; that is, when scientific studies come to an end, and lay down all their gadgets of experimentation, and confess that they cannot continue their researches any further unless they transcend themselves by performing a miraculous leap over into a realm of absolute subjectivity.
>
> (p. 25)

Corbett (2004) has expressed a similar sentiment regarding the widespread disenchantment that exists within traditional Abrahamic notions of God and the doctrinal systems to which these ideas belong: "No concept of divinity that is not the result of personal experience will ultimately hold sway" (p. 2). While Jung and Patañjali were in disagreement in the fundamentals of their worldviews, they both aimed at deconstructing systems of thought that constrain numinous experience.

Through studying the work of Jung and Patañjali, in particular their approaches to consciousness and their approaches to numinous experience, this project has raised questions and uncertainties about the subject–object split as well as the ontic reality of the unconscious. As a result of these uncertainties, various questions arise. Above all, what did Jung (1961/1995) mean when he expressed that his life was a story of the self-realization of the unconscious? And how can depth psychology realistically formulate a science of the unconscious, when the unconscious, by definition, is beyond experience and, according to Jung, not only "Unknown" but also eternally unknowable? Jung's search of the depths was an objectification of what might very loosely be termed the absolute subject. Using the representational schema of the unconscious, through phenomenology in general and affect in particular, Jungian depth psychology has long been trying to understand an inexpressible "something," or what Jung termed an "Unknown x." As the main means of research, depth psychology has used derivative consciousness to re-present intrinsic consciousness, which the discipline has done by formulating *the unconscious*. But a representation is a symbol for something else, an *other*. Any kind of representation is therefore a form of distance, a form of separation from pure being. Patañjali does not make this move, which is why when we look through Patañjali's lens, what is "Unknown" to Jung, is already together and not in need of being pieced together: unable to be ontically known through any kind of splitting. *The actuality can only be lived*, never re-presented.

As a consequence of adhering to a philosophy of the unconscious, Jung's work remained within the confines of the predicament of egoic knowing, whose Western roots can be traced at least as far back as Descartes' meditations (Henry, 1993). Yet Jung (1946/1972) was clear that psychology would cancel itself out as a science when it reached its scientific goal. As soon as the psychic process itself is brought to reflected consciousness, psychology actualizes the psychic process, and the discipline attains completion. In direct alignment with this idea, the present study, through looking closely at the work of Jung and Patañjali, essentially argues for the pure consciousness that subsists through all the epistemic states of consciousness and yet remains strikingly absent in Western thought.

In summary, although the present study can stand on its own, it formulates introductory material to the confluence of two significant and open areas, in the continuing dialogue between Jung's depth psychology and Patañjali's Classical Yoga: the reconciliation of the differences in the underlying metaphysics and the reconciliation in the approach to consciousness. The reconciliation of the aforementioned dyad may in turn lead to the reconciliation of science and religious experience in the West. Whether reconciliation can happen within the bounds of orthodox science remains a mystery. Therefore, this conclusion might best be understood as a potential crossroad for the underlying theory of depth psychology, and possibly, a crossroad for humanity.

I hope the reader understands that this research project has not, *in any way*, discounted the value of Jung's work in the realm of self-inquiry or what he experienced or endured in order to create his depth psychology. Jung's life and work were chosen precisely because of their value; however, he left us with an incomplete model. We do his legacy the greatest justice by facing head on where he met his limits and by attempting to unveil the blocks that prevented him from completing his aims.

In the West, so much effort and so many resources have been expended towards the ways and means of knowledge construction. While a dialogue between the worldviews of Jung and Patañjali is here on these pages, the heart of this discussion also exists in each and every human being who struggles with notions of separation and feelings of alienation, whether it is from Mother Nature, each other, or ourselves. The natural state of the non-dual mind, which is heart centered and in tune with Cosmic Mind, has been marginalized in Western society, and, perhaps more significantly, more or less abandoned by the academic powers that be. For psychology to flourish, in the ways in which Jung and Patañjali both envisioned – where numinous experience is tended and the psychospiritual realized – it is imperative that we have the right framework. Hence, in times like ours, when wars rage on and anger, anxiety, and stress are all too common; when psychotropic medicines are being prescribed at an ever-increasing pace; when women and the feminine the world over still oftentimes find second-class status; and when our children are often born into families, governments, and political regimes that are power hungry, bloated, and tense, a dialogue that points us in the direction of a common psychological language and psychospiritual framework – with an aim towards the amelioration of human suffering and perceiving beyond the bondage of the subject–object duality – is a wholeheartedly worthwhile endeavor.

References

Bergemann, E., Siegel, M., Belzer, M., Siegel, D., & Feuille, M. (2013). Mindful awareness, spirituality, and psychotherapy. In K. I. Pargament (Ed.), *APA handbook of psychology, religion, and spirituality: Vol. 2 an applied psychology of religion and spirituality* (pp. 207–222). Washington, DC: American Psychological Association.

Chung, S-C., Brooks, M., Rai, M., Balk, J., & Rai, S. (2012). Effects of Sahaja yoga meditation on quality of life, anxiety, and blood pressure control. *The Journal of Alternative and Complementary Medicine*, *18*(6), 589–596.

Corbett, L. (2004). *The religious function of the psyche*. New York, NY: Brunner-Routledge.

Henry, M. (1993). *The genealogy of psychoanalysis*. Stanford, CA: Stanford University Press.

Jacobi, J. (1973). *The psychology of C. G. Jung*. New Haven, CT: Yale University Press.

Jung, C. G. (1972). On the nature of the psyche. In H. Read, M. Fordham, G. Adler, & W. McGuire (Eds.), *The collected works of C. G. Jung* (R. F. C. Hull, Trans., 2nd ed., Vol. 8, pp. 159–234). Princeton, NJ: Princeton University Press. (Original work published 1946, revised 1954)

Jung, C. G. (1976). Psychological typology. In H. Read, M. Fordham, G. Adler, & W. McGuire (Eds.), *The collected works of C. G. Jung* (R. F. C. Hull, Trans., Vol. 6, pp. 542–555). Princeton, NJ: Princeton University Press. (Original work published 1936)

Jung, C. G. (1983). Paracelsus as a spiritual phenomenon. In H. Read, M. Fordham, G. Adler, & W. McGuire (Eds.), *The collected works of C. G. Jung* (R. F. C. Hull, Trans., Vol. 13, pp. 109–189). Princeton, NJ: Princeton University Press. (Original work published 1942)

Jung, C. G. (1995). *Memories, dreams, reflections* (R. Winston & C. Winston, Trans., A. Jaffe, Ed.). London: FontanaPress. (Original work published 1961)

Jung, C. G. (1997). *Visions: Notes of the seminar given in 1930–1934* (Vol. 1, C. Douglas, Ed.). Princeton, NJ: Princeton University Press. (Original work published 1939)

Schore, A. N. (2012). *The science of the art of psychotherapy*. New York, NY: W.W. Norton & Company.

Siegel, D. (2009). Mindful awareness, mindsight, and neural integration. *The Humanist Psychologist*, *37*, 137–158.

Solms, M. (2013). The conscious id. *Neuropsychoanalysis*, *15*(1), 5–19.

Suzuki, D. T. (1970). Lectures on Zen Buddhism. In *Zen Buddhism and psychoanalysis* (pp. 1–76). New York, NY: Harper Colophon.

Tresan, D. (1996). Jungian metapsychology and neurobiological theory. *Journal of Analytical Psychology*, *41*, 399–436.

Wilkinson, M. (2003). Undoing trauma: Contemporary neuroscience. *Journal of Analytical Psychology*, *48*, 235–253.

Wilkinson, M. (2005). Undoing dissociation. Affective neuroscience: A contemporary Jungian clinical perspective. *Journal of Analytical Psychology*, *50*, 483–501.

Young-Eisendrath, P., & Dawson, T. (2008). Preface. In P. Young-Eisendrath & T. Dawson (Eds.), *The Cambridge companion to Jung* (2nd ed, pp. xi–xx). Cambridge, UK: University Press. (Original work published 1997)

Afterword

Over that past decade and a half, while making this unceasing exploration of the world in front of our eyes, and behind it – in an effort to viscerally experience the interface of duality and nonduality – a tremendous amount of grief was suffered through and released from my system. There are no words that could ever do that experience justice. The present study now stands in its place.

Index

Lightning Source UK Ltd.
Milton Keynes UK
UKHW022324200121
377421UK00004B/54

9 780367 198725